CHOOSING YOUR HOMEBUILT
the one you'll finish and fly!

"This book covers all the bases. The prospective homebuilder who decides on a project after reading *Choosing Your Homebuilt* will have made a well-educated decision in a highly technical arena, not an emotional excursion into an obscure niche of aviation."
— Dave Martin, Editor, *Kitplanes* magazine

"Building your own plane is a journey of a thousand miles, so you want to be sure about your first steps. *Choosing Your Homebuilt* is the resource with all the answers to get you started on the right foot and eliminate the surprises down the road."
— Steve Werner, Editor/Publisher, *Plane & Pilot* magazine

"*Choosing Your Homebuilt* by Kenneth Armstrong is a most comprehensive reference manual that is packed full of the kind of information sought after by most ambitious sport aviation enthusiasts. This book fills a void in the amateur-built aircraft community. It should become a cherished addition to the aviation library shelves of lightplane pilots around the world. Congratulations to the author for a job well done."
— Bill Peppler, General Manager, Canadian Owners & Pilots Assn

CHOOSING YOUR HOMEBUILT
the one you'll finish and fly!

Kenneth Armstrong

Butterfield Press

Queries regarding rights and permissions should be addressed to the publisher, Butterfield Press, 990 Winery Canyon Road, Templeton, CA 93465. Phone 805-434-1093, FAX 805-434-3185.

Printed in the USA by McNaughton & Gunn, Saline, Michigan.

Typography consultation by Fred Felder of Cragmont Publications, Oakland, California.

Editing and index by Anne Leach.

Cover design by Quentin Eckman.

Cover photo by James Lawrence. Photo on page xi by Jim Larsen. Other photos provided by the manufacturers and the author.

First edition.

ISBN 0-932579-25-6

ACKNOWLEDGMENT

The author would like to thank his constant companion, photographer, walking notebook, and wife, Linda, for her dedication and support in this endeavour to promote and support recreational aviation in North America.

Appreciation is also expressed for Stoddard-Hamilton's president, Ted Setzer, and his entire staff. The company's level of support, quality assurance, and high ideals are goals we can all strive towards.

Chris Heintz, designer extraordinaire, not only provides fine, safe designs suitable for almost all pilots, he is also a tremendous source of philosophical information and forecasts of recreational aircraft market direction. Thank you, Chris and sons, Sebastien and Matthew.

I am very grateful to the numerous aircraft designers and promotional staff who took the time to provide accurate information, serviceable aircraft for evaluation, and proofreading of all data to ensure that there were no errors or omissions.

Lastly, I would like to thank the many individuals in the sport flying movement who have dedicated themselves to the betterment of safety and performance of modern day designs. Their tireless efforts have made my decade of research, flying, and writing a very pleasurable and fulfilling time.

—Kenneth Armstrong

Contents

Section Four
Regulations, Paperwork, and Insurance

Foreword

For many of us who love flight, there is nothing so satisfying as fashioning, with one's own hands, an airplane — and then launching it successfully into the sky.

The homebuilding movement took root many years ago, and today is flourishing everywhere. Designs for amateurbuilt aircraft run from the simple to the sophisticated. Materials range from wood, fabric, and metal to the latest in composites. Many kits are available to reduce the builder's workload.

In short, there is a broad spectrum of choices for the person who is prepared to commit his or her time and efforts to the supremely satisfying project of building an airplane.

A significant milestone in homebuilding came with the founding of the Experimental Aircraft Association in 1953, in Milwaukee, Wisconsin. One of the primary missions for the organization was to foster the ability to build your own airplane. From a local club, EAA has grown in size and purpose, but homebuilding is still a cornerstone of our activities.

Through the years, the amateur-built aircraft program has expanded and has gained credibility because of the excellent designs that were developed along with a fine safety record. Over 12,000 airplanes have been completed and are flying. It has provided thousands of enjoyable flight hours for pilots around the world. In addition, this activity has provided the opportunity for people to use their hands and minds to construct an airplane that meets their aviation needs and desires.

With the changing aviation picture, the homebuilt aircraft movement has taken on a new meaning. It has become a focal point for much needed development in the aviation community. New designs, improvements, innovation...they all have become an important part of homebuilding activities, along with the ability to explore the use of new materials.

If you want to build an airplane, making the proper choice is the most important decision you must face. You must consider what materials you are best suited to work with. What are your needs? Do you want to go fast or slow? How many people do you want to carry? Is range important to you? There are so many questions to be answered.

Fortunately, a wealth of experience has been developed over the past forty years. Thousands of people have built airplanes. This book gives you an opportunity to learn from what they have accomplished. Many projects are started and are never finished. The reasons are many, from underestimating the time needed, to lack of commitment, to choosing the wrong airplane. Financial considerations are also important.

Choosing Your Homebuilt provides information that will be invaluable in making "the right choice" for you. It provides background on what you should be aware of and the types of questions you should ask. Flight evaluations are provided, featuring a representative group of homebuilts. Even if the design you are interested in is not listed, there is sure to be one that is comparable.

Welcome to the exciting world of sport aviation. Good building and good flying!

Tom Poberezny
President
EXPERIMENTAL AIRCRAFT ASSOCIATION

Introduction

The Exciting World of Homebuilt Aircraft

Why are homebuilt plans and kits vastly outselling factory light aircraft production? Higher performance is one reason. (What production airplane will cruise at more than 230 mph on 200 hp?) Lower initial cost, lower maintenance cost, and a huge selection of designs are other motivations for the build-it-yourself pilot. With approximately 400 designs available from half as many companies, the homebuilt selection is vast compared to the factory certified aircraft offerings.

However, experimental aircraft have their share of pitfalls for the unwary builder or buyer. The construction trail is strewn with dejected homebuilders who failed to reach the goal of flying a plane they built themselves.

In fact, the unhappy truth is that a large majority of homebuilt projects are not completed by the original builder — the figures we've heard run as high as *90 percent* — and many are never finished at all!

But for the builder who takes the time to make the right choice — selecting a project that fits his capabilities as well as his desires, and realistically estimating the time and effort involved — the likelihood of becoming the proud owner of a beautiful and capable airplane is great. Many have done it, as a visit to Oshkosh, Sun 'n Fun, or any of the other experimental fly-ins will prove.

And for some, the ultimate thrill is flying their aircraft in competitions, proving the quality of their construction and flying skills. The speed and efficiency challenges held at Oshkosh and a number of regional events attract the best of the homebuilts, where they once again conquer the production-line Spam Cans.

Whether you're embarking on a first-time project, or are seeking a second or third project more suited to your current needs, this book will lead you through the bewildering maze of homebuilt aircraft designs, helping you to select one that is suitable for your skills and desires. We will guide you around the government obstacles, over the monetary hurdles, and past the family barriers.

Kits Can Make Life Easier

Realizing that most would-be builders have failed to accomplish their goal, you will be aware of the challenge ahead. Nonetheless, those who have succeeded generally claim it wasn't all that difficult, but it required a stick-to-it attitude. And the advent of partially completed kits, with most of the difficult work completed by the factory, has greatly increased the project completion rate.

The Choice is Wide

For example, with over 400 kits sold, the Lancair series of retractables is perhaps the hottest seller in the two-place market. Capable of cruising 1000 miles at 190 to 225 mph with useful loads in the 700-lb range on engines of 100 to 160 hp, these models use high technology composites to provide light-weight/high-strength structures.

At the other end of the spectrum, the Canadian Zenair STOL CH-701 kit is powered by a liquid-cooled 64 hp Rotax 582 engine. With takeoff and landing distances of 120 feet, the STOL is a true Short Take Off and Landing aircraft, well suited for pilots with a large back yard — and understanding neighbors. Cruising near 75 mph, the 701 weighs 440 lbs empty and grosses at 900. You won't find many other kits that can carry more than their own weight!

The aircraft that started the composite kit revolution — and there are 400 of them now flying — is the 230 mph fixed-gear Glasair from Stoddard-Hamilton. The kit requires approximately 1200 hours to complete. The ultimate performer in the series, the 300 mph Glasair III has set numerous world speed and climb records. It is a delight to fly as it has controls that feel similar to the Snowbirds' Tutor jets. The wing loading of approximately 29 lbs/sq ft really tames turbulence.

Amphibian aficionados have a large selection of sleek and speedy steeds that cruise in the 150 mph to 200 mph range with two to four souls on board. Try to find a factory-built amphibian or even a monoplane on fixed gear that can top this on 150 hp! The three most popular "airboat" companies recently reported the sale of more than 200 kits with large backorders ensuing. The prices for these airframe kits vary from $20,000 to $30,000, not including engines or instruments for these high steppers.

And there are excellent aircraft for float flyers, including the Avid Flyer and Macair Merlin. (At least 200 Avid Flyer kits were shipped in 1990.) I will evaluate these aircraft and more in the Flight Evaluations section.

When it comes to rotary wing aircraft, the RotorWay Exec and the older model Scorpion II are the only helicopters that can be found in numbers. As of May 1990, the company has marketed an improved version of the helicopter known as the Exec 90. The kit sells for less than half the price of a new factory-built helicopter.

Alternative Powerplants

With numerous two-stroke and automotive engines undergoing conversion to aircraft use, significant advances are expected over the old horizontally opposed powerplants of the 1940s. Car conversions not only run well on the inexpensive auto fuel they were designed for, but they also burn far less, with their efficient combustion chamber designs and superior liquid cooling. To give you an idea of the diversity of auto engine use, two Mustang replicas are powered by Honda Prelude and Chevy V-8 engines of 115 to 300 hp. I'll give you a comprehensive listing of automotive, aviation, two-stroke and turbine engines — along with operating and selection tips.

Good News in the Regs

Recent regulation changes, current and pending, have made building and flying homebuilt aircraft extremely attractive. The new recreational pilot's license with its lowered flying training requirements almost seems intended to stimulate the homebuilt aircraft market. Similarly, the high quality planes that will ensue from the proposed Primary Aircraft category will provide all pilot classes with a tremendous selection of aircraft that are custom made but to government controlled standards. I'll tell you about these developments, too.

Join the Fun

Combined with advances in composites and aerodynamic refinements that have been perfected with homebuilders' experimentation, custom-made aircraft have become immensely popular with the public.

Contrast that with the poor sales of new production aircraft. Due to high certification costs and because liability suits can reach back for decades to punish factory-built aircraft manufacturers, these designs have remained overly conservative with few performance improvements. While the high cost of labor has driven factory aircraft beyond the means of most pilots, low-cost engines and high quality, fast-build kits have made homebuilts a reasonable alternative for many. To see if you should join the growing throngs of happy builders, and what project, if any, you should consider, "let your fingers do the walking" through the following chapters.

Section One

Choosing the Airframe

– 1 –

Can You Build It?

Why Do So Many Fail?

Ninety percent of first time would-be builders fail to complete their aircraft projects! There are numerous and varied reasons for these flops. Marital, financial, and time problems are major stumbling blocks, as we will see. However, there are other obstacles that few builders consider. For example, frustration with suppliers, difficulty of construction, and personal changes in direction all take their toll.

In this chapter, I will help you assess your skills, dedication, and resources, as well as outside factors that could affect the success of your project. We'll examine the considerations you should make before committing to a project or purchasing a used homebuilt plane. And we'll help you appraise your assets and marital situation to determine whether homebuilding is really for you.

Let's assume that you are attracted by the challenge and pleasure of building, as well as by the anticipated excitement of flying your own custom aircraft. Before you commit to the lengthy, arduous, but rewarding process of constructing a homebuilt aircraft, it is wise to sit down and ask yourself a number of questions. And be honest with your answers! To objectively evaluate yourself might be the most difficult part of the aircraft building process. To fail at honestly appraising yourself is to doom your project in advance.

Here is another caution: Don't plan to build an airplane just to save money. Few projects succeed when economy is a major motivation. Instead, it is imperative that homebuilders have a strong desire to work with their hands to produce a work of art. To do otherwise foreordains failure when the true immensity of the workload assails the helpless money saver. If you really want a homebuilt, and cost is the major factor, land a second job that you could work during the time you would have been building, and buy a completed homebuilt with the proceeds.

Thousands of successful homebuilders testify that the most important driving force in the completion of the project was their sense of

pride and accomplishment. They had perseverance, strong motivation, ability, confidence, and a desire to learn, and these are the personality traits most needed by the homebuilder. Many builders have
put together more than one aircraft, and some don't even have a pilot
certificate! That's dedication to the pleasure of building.

How Long Will it <u>Really</u> Take?

Many "fast-build" kit manufacturers claim completion times ranging from 200 to 1200 hours. While this may seem initially to be very fast
and require only a small commitment of building time, a look at the
truth is quite surprising. Depending on the manufacturer involved, the
actual building time may be double the claimed amount. Hundreds of
first-time builders have told me of construction times of 200 to 400
percent of the totals claimed in sales information. While factory tech-
nicians who are used to the plans and fabrication details on a given
aircraft are able to assemble the aircraft in the published time, finishing and detailing add considerably to the project's duration.

Moreover, most builders are not able to work full time on their
dream machine, with the result that much effort is wasted with shop
cleanup and re-familiarization with the plans. Therefore, the astute
builder should double the anticipated assembly/finishing estimate to
reach a more accurate conclusion on his time investment. For example, a 600-hour kit becomes a 1200-hour project, and so on.

Next, we must ask how long will it really take to invest, say, 1200
hours of planning, constructing, finishing and licensing your creation?
The retired individual working an average of eight hours per day could
be flying in five months. The average family man who is entirely dedicated to working as often as possible on his project can expect to
average two hours nightly during the week and — without experiencing
the wrath of the family — perhaps eight hours over the weekend. At this
rate, a committed builder could expect to fly in 16 months.

But historically, many begin with this level of devotion, only to find
that they taper off to a mere few hours per week of activity, due to
increased demands of a growing family, diminished motivation, etc.
Sound familiar? For this hapless builder, it may take five to ten years
to finish the plane — if, indeed, it is ever finished. Will you be able to
keep up the pace?

How Strong is Your Marriage?

Ask yourself this question: how long will your marriage last with your project cluttering up everything—the garage, your togetherness time, your life? Building is a team effort. Be sure to consult with your flock. Who knows? With a little sales pitch, there may even be a lineup of helpers and well-wishers. The fortunate among us have wives who enjoy rib-stitching fabric and who even take upholstery courses that enable them to produce award-winning interiors. For a father-and-son (or daughter) team, the process can be very worthwhile in the building of a good relationship.

On the other hand, be selective on whom you bestow the honor of "helper." Don't enlist helpers who will be detrimental to the construction quality or individuals who will simply get in the way. Many builders are plagued by visitors who slow down progress with questions and requests for tours. Try a sign on the workshop door that says "No Admittance."

Face the facts. Partially completed projects adorn the classified advertisements—a mute, sad testimony to the effects of family or financial failures. Before the problems can develop, discuss your plans with your spouse and children in an effort to enlist their support. If they aren't with you, perhaps you should abandon the idea of homebuilding—or them?

With the aid of a set of riveting and aluminum working tools, the Lindsays completed the first Renegade Spirit prototype in only 288 hours.

Life as a Prisoner

Due to family or other demands, the less blessed homebuilders often become sluggish after the initial surge of enthusiasm. This despondency is sometimes attributable to the "I'll never be able to finish this" syndrome.

Don't kid yourself. There is going to be a tremendous amount of hard labor involved. You'll be chained to the project. Essentially, upon financial commitment to the plane, you will be a prisoner to its completion, to your pride, and to your monetary investment. Consider whether you are prepared to finish your "sentence" *before* the gates of commitment lock you into your workshop.

Another financial consideration is the "me too" complex. In this situation, the family bemoans the cash flow going into the motley mess in the garage and starts demanding its share of time and money. New cars, washers, dryers, bicycles, and toys are just a few of the possibilities to add to the mid-project malaise.

A Question of Skill

To determine your suitability as a custom builder, try answering this question: "Do I have at least average shop skills?" There is no sense in starting a project that you will be incapable of completing. Will your workmanship be first class or second rate — or worse? Perhaps the best way to find out is to ask yourself, "Would I want to fly in an aircraft that I built?"

If you doubt your capability to achieve, or your desire to strive for, excellent craftsmanship, forget building. Without skill and pride in your work, you will run out of steam and your partially completed derelict will gather dust. Essentially, you will have created a very expensive pile of artistic scrap.

Be honest with yourself when you evaluate these factors. If your skills are mediocre, your workmanship will become an object of scorn and your project will become totally worthless. A poorly crafted plane will not only fail the government inspections because it is unsafe to fly, it will also leave you with a partially completed project that you can't sell at any price. On the other hand, a diligent builder will earn praise from observers, foster admiration of his workmanship, and produce an aircraft that will pass inspections and fly well. Additionally, the machine could win awards and be valued well above its construction costs.

So be truthful: Are you the type of individual who completes what he begins, or is your garage littered with ventures you will get around to later? If you are a non-finisher, don't saddle yourself with an undertaking that has very little chance of success.

Let's Talk Money

Do you have — and can you afford to spend — the money to see the project to completion? The average building price for a basic single-place aircraft is in the $5,000-$15,000 range. Multi-place projects cost $7,000-$70,000. And the sky is the limit when comprehensive avionics, electronics and exotic paint schemes are added. A decade ago, the nav/comm was the sole occupant in the radio stack of most homebuilts. Nowadays, it seems that a higher percentage of instrument panels are filled with more and more valuable devices, such as audio panels, dual comms and navs, DMEs, lorans, transponders, encoders, etc. There is a lot to spend your money on.

For the budget-minded individual who is prepared to spend time in lieu of money, judicious shopping can locate bargains, thus greatly reducing expenditures. Some of us have been collecting "bargains" for years in anticipation of a new project, and could be convinced to part with one. For those willing to spend money instead of time, some very complete kits price out at over $50,000, and while it's not really legal to do so, there are builders out there who will assemble the aircraft of your choice for approximately twice the kit price.

The reason it's not really legal is that the regulations are set up essentially to allow us to build experimentals for our own education and skill development, not as a method of avoiding the high cost of factory-produced aircraft. (See the chapter entitled "Regulations" for more information on this.)

By the way, in the US, if someone else builds your custom aircraft, you will not be authorized to sign off the annual inspection — unless you have been issued a repairman's certificate by the FAA. While you may be able to do the inspection work, an AI (an aircraft mechanic with an Inspection Authorization rating) will have to be paid to check your efforts and provide the signature in the logbook.

Give Some People Enough Rope...

To be quite candid, certain types of people should think twice about building. Loners or those who like to fight bureaucracy and regulations will have an uphill battle. You'll require outside help in your struggle with the complexity of the rules, with interpretation of instructions, and with some difficult construction techniques. You'll find it helpful to join groups, work with federal aviation officials, and subscribe to various "how to" magazines (and subsequent chapters will stress this). While it is not impossible for skilled individuals to walk the trail alone, there are many hazards and pitfalls that can trap the unwary.

Here are some examples:

A recent phone call had a builder crying in my ear because he failed to register his project with the local federal inspector. Normally, this is not a major oversight. Unfortunately, he had built a $75,000 kit that exceeded the Canadian maximum wing loading limit and therefore could not be flown. His airplane makes a gorgeous conversation starter, but an awfully expensive lawn ornament.

A Sea Hawk builder had 19 major building flaws on his "completed" project. During his initial takeoff, the rudder fell off on the runway just before the "peel ply" composite on his right wing peeled off. He did not survive the crash. Bypassing the normal inspection process and ignoring a knowledgeable builder's warnings that the aircraft was unsafe compounded his building errors. Unfortunately, this individual's personality was such that he chose to disregard the experts who were trying to help him. His attitude cost him dearly.

In conclusion, be honest in your self-assessment. Your family situation, finances, skills and attitudes are all critical components to factor into your decision. Don't consider homebuilding unless the deck is stacked in your favor.

What's Next?

Even if you decide not to build, but still want the performance and benefits offered by experimentals, you'll find plenty of information and recommendations in the pages to come, including the selection of a plane that meets your needs and flying skills, as well as chapters on the costs and necessary procedures that relate to aircraft ownership.

– 2 –

Can You Fly It?

Take an Honest Look

Basically, the question is, are you qualified to fly the aircraft you have chosen to build or buy?

Perhaps the Glasair III and Questair Venture are great designs, but are you skilled enough to safely fly them? Is it possible that they or similar aircraft will make you late for supper some sad day?

Don't get caught up, as many do, in the "extension of your manhood" syndrome. While some individuals will be envious of you, few will really care about your project. If you end up with too much airplane for your skill level, more folks will be recounting the number of landings that ensued from your last approach instead of the sleek sexiness of your plane.

Consider your aviation background and experience. If you tend to make embarrassing mistakes in one of the simpler planes, do not plan to jump right into a high performance aircraft with a wing loading over, say, 15 lb/sq/ft.

Also, shy away from complex aircraft with constant speed propellers and retractable landing gear. They will cost you far more money than you anticipated for operational expenses — especially after your first gear-up landing. You will find that there is little sex appeal in having your aircraft wreckage sitting on the airport ramp for all to ridicule.

Quality Time

Pilot skill level is not measured by hours alone. We've all flown with excellent pilots who have only a couple of hundred hours and with terrible pilots who have thousands. It's the quality that counts.

That's not to say that low-time aviators shouldn't fly the high performance homebuilts. But they should do so only after some related experience. For example, aircraft such as Mooneys and Bonanzas are good trainers for some of the super steeds. Pay particular attention to the difficulty of slowing these sleek aircraft down without shock-cooling the engine. Note that you must plan your descents and pattern procedures well in advance in order to effectively manage the high kinetic and potential energy these hot and heavy planes possess. Their high wing loadings will certainly tame the turbulence; however, they will also produce extravagant sink rates on final approach that could culminate in the gear protruding above the wing rather than below.

For those of you who will be flying retractables and constant speed or variable pitch propellers, get into the habit of completing a final landing check *on short final*. Ensure that the gear is down and locked and that the pitch is full fine in case a go-around is necessary. Those who rely on checking the gear and prop on the downwind leg will eventually pay a king's ransom for their oversight. Too many pilots join the pattern on base leg or final, only to forget the landing checks. You will always fly short final as a portion of landing, so get in the habit of doing a landing check then.

Jet Jockeys: Caution!

If you're an ex-high-performance jet jockey, I have a word for you before you climb aboard a speedy homebuilt, perhaps for an initial flight test: *Caution!* While considerable skill and flight planning are required to fly airliners and military jets, it doesn't prepare you for the light and sensitive controls of today's homebuilts. I know. I was a military jet pilot who subsequently checked out numerous airline and military pilots on rental aircraft as sales manager and chief pilot at a Cessna dealership. Military and airline pilots were always the most difficult to convert to general aviation aircraft because their customary aircraft are so entirely different. A 20,000-hour Hercules pilot/friend currently holds the world's record for the most consecutive bounces in a Cessna 150 from his light plane checkout at the San Carlos Airport — and that was with an instructor aboard!

Here's another reason. Pilots, especially those with lots of flying hours, are used to standard operating systems and standard procedures. When dealing with unusual controls, however, your automatic reflexes could be catastrophic. For example, because not all homebuilt designs follow the guidelines of FAR 23, some experimentals have unusual control systems and unique powerplant management — maybe a throttle that *decreases* power when nudged forward, or landing gear levers that must be selected in the correct order to avoid crushing the doors and jamming the gear.

With average-size occupants, the Sparrow Hawk has such a forward CG and relatively impotent elevator power that the nose tends to drop through during the round-out, thumping the nose wheel down. Other experimentals exhibit characteristics such as unrecoverable spins, control reversal, and various quirks in engine operation that make them downright dangerous to venture forth in without an adequate type check.

This goes doubly for the pilot/builder who has poured every spare penny into his creation and has no money left over to keep his piloting skills current. After spending two or three times longer to build the aircraft than originally anticipated, he is really keen to get airborne. Then, because he has the right to, he decides to test fly his creation. I have examined the wreckage from a number of these fiascoes. You may say it will never happen to you because you're conservative. However, when the glow of seeing your creation completed is overwhelming, beware of the temptation to be the test pilot "because I built her and know her better than anyone else." That expression is in quotes because that's exactly what a lot of the survivors say at the accident site.

Be Sure You're Ready

A couple of touch-and-goes in a Cessna 150 is not an adequate preparation to allow you to climb into your new Glasair III and fly it with much chance of success of returning it to the hangar undamaged. Sure, you might get away with a simple circuit. But what happens if that newly installed engine has fuel starvation (for any of a dozen reasons) and you have to deadstick your prized possession onto the busy freeway? Are you ready for that? Be honest!

Also, consider the type of flying you will be doing. If almost all of your operations have been out of a small airport, and you now plan to take your Venture on lengthy cross-country flights, you are in for major surprises. Penetrating radar environments with ARSAs, TCAs, etc., will more than double your piloting workload. Looking out for other traffic, switching frequencies, copying clearances, and following air traffic control instructions (accurately) can load you down so much that your judgment may suffer drastically. Recent collisions in densely populated radar environments easily prove that pilots and controllers are overworked.

And if you have been attracted by the aerobatic capability of a certain design and plan to cavort with the clouds, it is absolutely mandatory to qualify yourself with recent aerobatic training and the regulations that apply.

The High Cost of "Pilot Error"

Pilots who are not accustomed to high performance operations typically damage their projects with heavy landings, gear-up landings, shock cooling and detuning of large counter-balanced engines, as well as overboosting with constant speed propellers and turbochargers. These errors are very costly and will result in considerable down time. A half-dozen hours of instruction, coupled with some book time, will prepare the wise owner for life in the fast lane.

In conclusion, don't try to fly more aircraft than you can handle. Your selection process must include an honest appraisal of your capabilities as well as aircraft designs. Do whatever is necessary to match your capabilities to the demands of the airplane. Otherwise, your beloved homebuilt may end up in a smoldering pile of rubble. Worse, you could be in the rubble, too — and worst of all, you might take some innocent people with you.

This pilot's skills are being taxed severely after a drive system failure on his BD-5. The hot landing, well downfield, nearly ended up in the weeds!

3

Can You Afford It?

Calculating the True Cost of Owning Your Plane

Few starry-eyed aircraft owners have any real idea of what they are getting into when they buy their first aircraft. For that matter, even after a dozen, this owner is still amazed at the time and money that is drained from his resources by love affairs with fabric, composite, and aluminum birds. The following information will allow would-be owners an opportunity to appreciate the real expenses and demands involved during a relationship with an airplane.

Two Types of Cost

To properly evaluate the costs of ownership, you should calculate two types of outlay: *fixed* and *operating*. Fixed costs are expenditures that accumulate regardless of whether the aircraft is flying or sitting on the ground. Operating costs are the expenses incurred during a flight, and are usually calculated on an hourly basis. Let's take a detailed look at each type of expense .

Fixed Costs

To protect your aircraft from accidental damage, theft, or vandalism, you will probably want hull insurance. To protect everything you own, you should have liability coverage. The tab will most likely run into four figures a year, depending on your plane and your qualifications to fly it. Check before you build or buy. You may have to switch to a cheaper aircraft, or reduce the coverage while increasing your exposure to financial risk.

Will you tie your aircraft down on a public field or hangar your prize? Typical monthly tiedown rentals vary from $15 to $50 or more.

For $40 to $250 or more per month, depending on location and availability, you may be able to obtain a rental hangar, or share one with someone else. At some airports, you can buy a hangar, at prices ranging from about $8,000 to $12,000 for a small-plane structure; then you pay monthly ground rent equivalent to the prevailing tiedown charge. Many owners feel that a hangar is a cost-effective expense when it comes to protection of their investment from vandalism, theft and the rigors of weather. (If you can fold or remove the wings and store your plane at home, you'll save this expense.)

Don't forget the annual inspection. Even though you may be qualified to do some or all of the work, annuals can cost hundreds of dollars for supplies and parts, depending on the deficiencies that surface.

Once all of these hurdles are cleared, remember that your steed requires exercise occasionally, in order to avoid certain illnesses it is subject to. The curse of rust on my cylinder walls cost me more than $2,600 for a top overhaul when I was away and unable to fly for three wet winter months. So trot it out for a good run now and then. After all, you're buying or building to fly, aren't you?

While you're at it, don't forget to include the costs of your aviation medical, charts and other publications, and unscheduled repairs. Some state and local governments levy an annual license fee and/or property tax on an airplane. Another expense might include that "something special" your wife feels she should have, since you bought an airplane for yourself.

Losing Interest?

Another price seldom considered is the loss of return on investment. In other words, when you "invest" $50,000 in an aircraft and sell it for $40,000 seven years later, you don't just lose $10,000. If you had put that half a hundred thousand into a term deposit at, say, 10 percent interest, you would now have over $100,000. In effect, the fixed cost of your ownership will have totaled $60,000 in terms of loss of investment! (This simple scenario overlooks possible tax considerations.) Of course, if you buy the "right" aircraft, at the "right" time, and sell it for the "right" price, you might do "all right" and actually make money — but don't count on it.

As far as all those other fixed costs are concerned, you would be wise to make realistic estimates of each item, total them up, and divide by the number of hours you expect to fly yearly. This will convert your fixed costs into an hourly rate, which, when combined with the hourly operating expense, will tell you what the aircraft will really cost you for an hour of freedom.

Remember, the more hours you fly each year, the lower your fixed costs will be on an hourly basis. For instance, assuming yearly fixed costs of $5,000 and flying times of 50 hours versus 150 hours, the former would result in a fixed cost of $100 per hour and the latter would amount to only $33.33 hourly.

Operating Costs

Let's start with fuel. Compared to your car sipping gas at the rate of 1 to 5 gallons an hour, you can count on your bird "chug-a-lugging" 4 to 14 gph at normal cruise — per engine! With aviation fuel costing more than $2 per gallon, this amounts to a considerable cash flow each flying hour. Based on an average of 100 hours of flying each year and an hourly consumption of 10 gph, the tally will exceed $2,000 annually — for fuel alone! Owners who are able to burn super unleaded auto gas would be able to reduce this to approximately $1,500 yearly. (See the chapter entitled "Should You Use Auto Gas?")

Then there's the cost of engine oil. While the recommended drain-and-replace interval is generally 50 hours, I suggest that 25 hours is a better idea — especially if your aircraft engine has no oil filter. This will reduce wear associated with the sandpaper effect of dirt and other contaminants in suspension. For the average single engine light aircraft, with a consumption of one quart every five hours, and a change every 25 hours, the hourly cost of the oil alone would be approximately 88¢. That doesn't seem like much, but at 100 hours of flying per year, it adds up to $88. This assumes that the owner changes his own oil and does not have a filter to replace.

Remember the TBO

Another expense seldom considered by first-time buyers is the reserve towards overhaul for components that have a TBO (Time Between Overhauls). In the case of most fixed wing aircraft, this includes engines and propellers. While overhaul is not mandatory for non-commercial operations on the expiration of the TBO, many owners have the work done in order to feel more secure about the condition of the components.

A major overhaul for a four-cylinder Lycoming, for example, typically costs $8,000 to $10,000 every 2000 hours (if you are lucky enough to have the engine reach its TBO). Even if an operator is able to optimize propeller and engine usage, his/her minimum cost for a reserve towards overhaul would exceed $5 per hour. For helicopters, we must add gearboxes, shafts, and bearings, to name a few.

The above figures relate to certified aircraft engines. Some homebuilts are flown with other types of engines, and costs could be considerably lower.

Then there's the bugaboo of scheduled and unscheduled maintenance. For a broad spectrum of homebuilt aircraft, an average of $200 per 100-hour inspection would be in the ballpark. This translates to $2 per hour for scheduled maintenance. Of course, if major problems are discovered during an inspection, or between inspections, this rate could be higher.

Conclusions

While it may appear otherwise, I am not trying to deter you from buying an aircraft. If you're really set on having your own plane, you will likely go ahead with the purchase, almost regardless of the expenditures. However, to avoid the pain of having to give up your dream machine, or keep it by eating Kraft dinners five times a week, you need to be aware of the facts.

Lower expenditures associated with homebuilt aircraft can make them more attractive financially. Not only is initial acquisition cheaper, but so is the maintenance and overhaul expense, since the owner is allowed to perform these tasks himself. (However, the FAA requires that non-builders have the annual inspection signed off by a properly qualified aircraft inspector.)

The following chart will help you to calculate the true costs of ownership. (I've included for comparison's sake production fixed-wing and helicopter models versus homebuilts in the same horsepower range.) You can adjust the financial variables to suit your situation, since the chart is laid out in a manner that will allow you to predict your expenses. This type of planning will help keep your dream machine from turning into a financial can of worms.

Chart of Comparative Ownership Costs

Type of Aircraft:	Cessna Skyhawk	Glasair II-S FT	Robinson R22 Beta	RotorWay Exec 90
	Factory-built Fixed wing 160 hp $30,000 (Used)	Homebuilt Fixed wing 160 hp $30,000 (New)	Factory-built Helicopter 160 hp $100,000 (New)	Homebuilt Helicopter 152-160 hp $40,000 (New)

Annual Fixed Costs

Loss of interest on investment at 8% per year:	2,400.00	2,400.00	8,000.00	3,200.00
Full insurance at 6.5%:	1,950.00	1,950.00	6,500.00	2,600.00
Maps, medical, annual inspection, misc. costs:	480.00	220.00	1,600.00	380.00
Storage	600.00	600.00	400.00	400.00
Total:	5,430.00	5,170.00	16,500.00	6,580.00

Hourly Fixed Costs

(At 100 hours per year):	54.30	51.70	165.00	65.80
(At 200 hours per year):	27.15	25.85	82.50	32.90

Hourly Operating Costs

Avgas:	20.00	20.00	22.00	18.00
Oil, grease, lubricants:	2.50	2.50	2.50	2.50
Reserve toward overhaul:	8.00	5.00	30.00	20.00
Maintenance:	5.00	2.00	9.00	3.00
Total:	35.50	29.50	63.50	43.50

Total Cost per Flight Hour

(At 100 hours per year):	89.80	81.20	228.50	109.30
(At 200 hours per year):	62.65	55.35	146.00	76.40

4

Selecting the Bird You'll Build

Take Your time!

So you've decided you want to build an airplane. Which one? Will it be a speed demon like the 300-mph Questair Venture, or a go-anywhere fence hopper like the 75-mph Zenair CH 701, or perhaps something in between?

Whatever you select, your project should endow you with a great deal of satisfaction and pleasure during construction, and countless hours of safe, trouble-free flying adventures afterwards. To select the wrong type of aircraft could cost you a lot more than your time. The following tips will help you determine the best homebuilt for your purposes and skills.

The Criteria

The two areas that we will consider are: 1) Which aircraft meet your flying requirements? And 2) Which are good designs from respectable and stable companies?

Sounds simple doesn't it?

However, we've all seen that macho 50-hour pilot take off in his sleek dream machine, only to come back ashen-faced declaring, "I'll never fly her again. She tried to kill me!" Then there's the fellow who spends his weekends ground-bound, working on the technical snags on his complex airplane.

To avoid these errors in judgment, be prepared to be honest with yourself, and read on.

The Compromises

Many aspects of aircraft design are tradeoffs that lead to compromises. Perhaps the ultimate compliment one could pay an aircraft would be to say that it is a perfect compromise — one that does every-thing very well but perhaps excels at nothing. A good example of a metal plane that does this is Dick Van Grunsven's RV-6. While it isn't the best at anything, it performs so well in all performance testing that it could be rated as an excellent buy for all-around flying.

When it comes to plastic planes, the buyers are lining up to buy Glasair and Lancair kits for the same reason — maximum bang for the buck.

On the other hand, individuals looking for very specific, one-of-a-kind use such as all-out aerobatics or racing will want a design that is optimized for that one purpose. Pity the poor pilot ferrying an un-stable unlimited aerobatic aircraft on a long cross-country flight, harassed by turbulence.

It is therefore necessary for you to decide what performance you require and what you are capable of flying safely. Here are some of the topics you may wish to consider.

Runway Requirements

If your flights will be less than 100 miles to local airport coffee shops, does it really pay to have a 300-mph speedster that requires 4000 feet of runway for safe operation? Sure, it will get you there slightly faster, but you won't be able to use hundreds of airports be-cause of your plane's runway requirements.

When you consider a plane and its reported takeoff and landing distances, I suggest you double the claims to allow for a number of variables. They are: pilot skill, condition or possible failure of brakes, crosswind and wind shear effects, company exaggerations, wet or slushy runway surfaces, and the true distance required to clear a 50-foot obstacle (many airports have them). If you choose to build the Questair Venture, for example, with its published landing distance of 1600 feet, don't plan to land on runways less than 3200 feet long. If you want speed and short field capabilities for runways less than 2000 feet, consider aircraft like the Glasair II series or Van's RV series.

Let's Look at Legs

Should you consider a taildragger for rough field operations and optimum flight performance, or a tricycle gear for its controllability?

Truly rough fields are best tamed with a taildragger, because propeller clearance is greater and turning capability is increased due to the fully castering geometry of most tailwheels. Additionally, this configuration offers less weight and drag, and thus somewhat better performance. If you are wary of the crosswind and general runway handling of taildraggers, you should note that only a few hours of training are necessary for a checkout.

The tricycle gear offers the advantage of better over-the-nose visibility, and it's less likely to turn on you during crosswind takeoffs and landings. Of course, one can never fully relax whenever the aircraft is moving on the ground — but then, that's the way it should be.

Both types of fixed gear are mechanically simple and easy to maintain.

If you like the sex appeal of a retractable, there are a few more thoughts that should occupy your mind. Retracts are not only more complex and expensive to build, but they are also more expensive to maintain. Motor, hydraulics, and other paraphernalia will also add more weight, thus reducing payload. (This is less true of the mechanically operated gear.)

Pilots who cut their teeth on tri-gear planes will need some training to tame the taildragger's tricks.

How Many Seats?

Will you fly alone for the solitude, or do you like to take company along?

If almost all of your flying is solo, or with one passenger, don't get trapped into building a four-place. Not only will construction costs be higher, but so will the operating costs of flying those empty seats around. If your needs for a four-place are rare, consider renting for those occasions.

But most people err in the other direction. They build aircraft with insufficient seats to accomplish their goals. If you plan to carry two people, lots of baggage, and full fuel, you may find that most two-place aircraft are incapable of hauling the load. To accommodate heavy occupants and large baggage loads, you may have to consider a three- or four-place project.

Stability and Load Limits

Normal, utility or aerobatic? In other words, how many Gs do you want your airborne chariot to be capable of handling? Aircraft with high G tolerance tend to be more ruggedly constructed in order to withstand the stresses. Unfortunately, this also results in a heavier machine that won't carry as much payload. If you plan to indulge in aerobatics, ensure that the designer approves the plane for this type of use. In Canada, check to see if the plane is legally approved for aerobatics.

If your main form of aviating is IFR and cross-country flying, avoid all-out aerobatic aircraft with their neutral stability. There are a few designs, such as the Glasair, Lancair and RV series, that are very acceptable at both ends of the stability spectrum for cross-country and acrobatics.

Open or Closed Cockpit?

You say you love to feel the rushing summer slipstream on your face? Remember the cold wintry blasts that January brings. The open cockpit is exhilarating, as it allows you to commune with the surroundings, but it is also very noisy. On the other hand, when you pull the power back, you will be able to hear the soaring hawk challenge you for the airspace. Perhaps the best of both worlds would feature a removable canopy, or one that could be opened in flight.

Speed, Sweet Speed

Speed...ah, how intoxicating. "How fast will she go?" questions the spectator. The maximum level speed or diving V_{ne} (Velocity Never Exceed) are seldom experienced by most pilots. But so many builders select their project based on looks and top speed.

Because top speed is rarely encountered, I suggest it should not be your criterion for selecting an experimental design. More important are the airplane's stall, cruise, and maneuvering speeds. You may have to give up some top end or cruise performance in order to have a low enough stall speed for short field operations. Regardless of the size of the airstrip you call home, remember to account for the fields you would like to visit. That speed demon may get you there quickly—but will you be able to land?

How Far Can You Go?

Will you fly locally or will cross-country cruising be your desire? If distant destinations lure you, how much useful load do you require for pilot, passengers, tools, fuel, and baggage? Remember that most prototypes quote empty weights that are likely to be considerably lower than you will be able to achieve. Adding options and beefing up parts of the structure have the effect of reducing the payload. If you want to be able to carry a large load, you will require a large engine and large fuel tanks for a given range. The secret is to build the minimum aircraft that will do most of the job, most of the time.

Knowing When to Fold

Folding or easily detachable wings give owners the option of home storage or parking under another aircraft's wing at the hangar. The folding mechanism typically adds 15 to 30 pounds to the empty weight but could save storage costs and security problems. Being able to take your prized possession home for repairs or winter storage can save a lot of hassle—not to mention corrosion, rot, and wear and tear.

This Avid Flyer is at home on the road and in the garage.

Visible Means of Support

How many wings does it take to make you happy? The monoplane will likely be faster, have better visibility, and be easier to build, since there are only two wings. The biplane, on the other hand, will have smaller dimensions for parking, may be more maneuverable both on the ground and in the air, and will be aesthetically pleasing to many pilots. The choice here will simply be a matter of personal taste.

High-wing, low-wing, or mid-wing? Many would select the wing planform and location based on appearance. However, before buying, consider the following factors: visibility, ground and obstacle clearance, gear mounting complexity, and possible interference where the wing spar crosses inside the fuselage in the case of a low- or mid-wing plane.

Also, if the fuel tanks are in the wings, will the engine require a pressure fuel system or will the engine pump suffice? High-winged aircraft generally allow gravity to do the work, whereas low- and mid-wing aircraft often need an auxiliary pump to ensure positive fuel pressure to the engine.

What It's Made Of

The choice of construction materials is also a matter of preference. Essentially, you must decide which is best to use, considering your skills. Your choices are metal, composites, wood, or a combination of materials. Which do you like best, and which do you have the most success with? Let's examine your options.

Composites. While composite aircraft tend to be lighter and have gorgeous, smooth, curvaceous lines, many say the work of sanding and filling is very frustrating and boring. Voids or production flaws in kit portions are also difficult to locate, making load testing of the finished aircraft a wise move. Depending on the type of fiberglass used and the curing process, you may be restricted to a white or similar color to avoid overheating the glass structure and causing it to flow, resulting in deformation of the structure.

The more advanced technologies are starting to show up in designs such as the Lancair 320, with its red-all-over paint scheme and heat-resistant epoxy composite construction that has been cured under high temperature and high pressure in ovens. The result is a finish that resists moisture and corrosion found in ocean spray and in the acid rains concentrated in industrial environments.

No construction material has been more capable of shaping than the current crop of composites. The voluptuous, smooth, graceful lines have lured more than smooth airflow to their contours. Few would argue that the most attractive aircraft available on the market are the fiberglass kits. The Lancair and Glasair series are two very popular examples.

Aluminum. Until composite structures establish fully acceptable track records, many builders will continue with the proven aluminum designs. The strength and building techniques are well known for this material, as are the repair methods. (Try to find an A&P with repair experience on composites.)

Other than their susceptibility to the corrosive effects of acid rain and other electrolytic action, aluminum—especially in its coated variations—is very durable. Most designs require only simple aluminum-working hand tools, and kits generally avoid the use of a bending brake by supplying pre-bent parts. Very successful aircraft include the Prowler, Van's RV series, and the Questair Venture.

Wood. Most builders surveyed feel that wood is easiest to work with because wood construction uses simple tools found around the house. Many call it the "ultimate composite" because wood is indeed a composite material, and some types possess very high strength-to-weight ratios.

Years ago, plans-built wooden aircraft were more challenging to build because all you received from the designer was a materials list. You then had to shop around to secure every piece that was necessary.

Now, companies can provide materials packages that simplify this task immensely. The combination of a phone call and a payment will cause the complete materials package to arrive at your door. Other attractions of wood structures include their tendency to absorb vibration and insulate the cabin from engine noise better than metal, fabric, and most composites.

The major drawback to wood is its susceptibility to rot. This occurs when moisture is allowed to contact wooden members over a prolonged period. The subsequent breakdown of the cellulose produces a weakened structure that could fail during the next flight. The other drawbacks to wood construction are the increasing cost and decreasing availability of high quality stock that is able to meet FAA specifications.

These difficulties suggest that it would be wise to purchase a materials package from one of the major suppliers. (For further information, see Appendix A, "Directory of Manufacturers and Suppliers" and Appendix B, "Collecting Information.") Check for the availability of stock before you commit to this type of construction.

Be sure you employ the correct adhesives, nails, and screws for the woods you will be using. The government inspector, EAA and RAAC chapters can help you here.

Some of the successful wood designs are the Emeraude, 5151 Mustang, Rand's KR series, VP Volksplane series, GP-4, and Barracuda.

Tube and Fabric. This type of construction has been with us a long time, and for good reason. It's strong, easy to build and repair, and best of all, it's lightweight and inexpensive.

Of course, it helps if you can weld. For those who aren't handy with a torch, many factories will provide completely welded structures that were built in shop jigs. This service typically adds a couple of thousand dollars to the project. As with wood construction, the builder will have to construct jigs to line up and tack weld the structure together.

The better fabrics, such as Stits products, tend to be relatively sun-proof. However, time and ultraviolet rays will take their toll on aircraft tied down outside. Similarly, moisture in the chromoly steel tubing will wreak havoc with the strength of the structure. For longevity, this type of construction should live in a dry climate, preferably out of the sun or in a hangar.

Successful aircraft using the tube-and-fabric method include the Avid Flyer series, the Christavia series, the Marquart Charger, and the Macair Merlin.

Potpourri. Some aircraft use a combination of materials in the design in order to optimize the strengths of each. A few of these are the Rotorway helicopters, Renegade, Celerity, Mini Master, Laughing Gull series, Kestrel, and Air Command Gyro Planes.

Another consideration would be the availability and cost of products in your area. Some builders may be located near an inexpensive source of quality lumber and others near a fiberglass production facility. Suffice it to say, work with the medium you prefer.

One Yoke or Two?

Dual controls will give you the capability of checking out other pilots and controlling the aircraft from two cockpit positions. So what's the tradeoff? Extra weight and construction complexity. Is your preference a control wheel, a center stick, a side stick, or perhaps a T-shaped pole as found on the Zenair CH 701? You may not get much choice here, as kits or plans generally stick, so to speak, to one type. If you have the skills, you could always design your own controls for individuality.

Start from Scratch, or Get a Head Start?

How much of the work are you prepared to do? While kit planes cost more, they save a great deal of time, frustration, and parts chasing. Those who work from plans will tell you that half of their time is spent reading catalogs, ordering parts or chasing them down all over town. First-time builders may also want to go the kit route; it generally requires less skill, since many of the difficult-to-form portions may already be shaped and joined. However, starting from scratch with the plans-only option will perhaps give the greatest thrill and sense of satisfaction on completion.

Consider whether you will perhaps be able to buy the components cheaper locally, or if you prefer to have all of it shipped to you with the plans. For instance, builders in the Seattle area are often able to buy aircraft-quality materials for pennies on the dollar due to the proximity of the Boeing Aircraft Company Surplus Store. The Aircraft Salvage Company at Omak, Washington supplies aircraft parts for approximately 30 cents on the dollar from their selection of 600 aircraft.

With these storehouses close by, locals are often able to produce a high performance aircraft for less than half the price of a builder in a remote area such as Hawaii or the Yukon. (See Appendix B for a more detailed look at this part of the selection process.)

The Quest for Power

Half of your aircraft is the powerplant. Will you use an aviation engine, or a converted automotive engine?

If you are prepared to do some modifying of systems and perhaps produce a gear reduction system, then consider the automotive engine. It is cheaper to purchase and much easier to obtain parts for. Auto engines use far more modern technology than most of the relics of the 1940s that power the production aircraft. As a result, they are more fuel efficient and in many senses more reliable. For instance, I have been told that Noah's Ark used those maintenance hogs we call magnetos. The modern day automotive ignition systems are much cheaper, lighter, produce a hotter spark with more reliability, and are able to be "excited" on only a few volts of battery power. The one benefit of the magneto is its ability to operate with absolutely no aircraft electrical system.

On the other hand, the proven aircraft engine will require less experimentation or builder effort. Which suits your skills and budget?

Will you choose an air-cooled or liquid-cooled engine? Lower fuel consumption, greater engine reliability, and cheaper operating costs are benefits normally associated with liquid-cooling. Air-cooled (read fuel-cooled) engines, on the other hand, tend to be slightly lighter and easier to install. Also, with an air-cooled design one never worries about freezing or leaking coolant.

Don't forget that you will have to build good baffles or a radiator system regardless of the engine type you chose. In the case of air cooling, the details for baffle construction are well documented. With radiator installations, you may have to be a little more experimental — unless you copy some existing system that works well.

Here's the Pitch on Props

While the prop may be the third most important portion of the project, few builders give it any consideration 'til they happen to notice they need one.

Will you choose a constant speed, variable pitch, or fixed pitch propeller? The first two are more efficient because the pilot can change the pitch. Fine pitch for takeoff and climb allows the engine to develop full power for short takeoffs and steep climb gradients, while coarser pitch provides higher speeds and lower fuel consumption during cruise.

Along with higher acquisition costs, the price you pay for this added efficiency is approximately 30 pounds or so of extra weight and the need for additional maintenance.

For the most part, variable pitch props will be considerably cheaper to buy and maintain than constant speed units because they have no governor. Instead of setting an rpm with the pitch control, as a pilot does with a constant speed unit, the variable pitch prop simply has its pitch angle held by the amount of engine oil pressure the operator allows to the hub through the use of the pitch lever or vernier control. (Counterweights work in opposition to the engine oil in both systems to bring the blades back in the other direction.)

The benefits of the simple fixed pitch propeller are lower weight, less maintenance, and much lower costs.

To help you make the decision, consider this. If your engine is less than 150 hp, you should stay with fixed pitch, as there is little performance to be gained with the more complex propellers.

When it comes to propeller materials, wood is lighter, cheaper, reduces vibration better, is more flexible, and will sacrifice itself on ground contact rather than damage an expensive crankshaft. Metal, on the other hand, provides a better flywheel effect and will handle rain erosion and outside storage with little harm compared to wood.

Who Sits Where?

If you're opting for a two-placer, you'll want to consider the pros and cons of tandem vs side-by-side seating. The slimmer profile of the tandem aircraft should result in higher cruise speeds and perhaps wider seats. Another benefit, especially for aerobatics, is that the pilot sits on the aircraft's natural centerline to aid lining up with references.

On the other hand, side-by-side seating is a friendlier setup for traveling and for instructing, and better for center of gravity considerations. Since both occupants sit on or near the center of gravity in two-place side-by-side aircraft, there is little or no moment arm. This arrangement avoids the problem, common with tandem seating. of people being too heavy or too light to sit in a given location.

How About the Baggage?

Will you need a baggage compartment or not? A storage area will likely be necessary for cross-country flights. If you need one, ensure that the stowage area will be large enough to meet your needs. Some of the goodies you might like to have in that area include survival gear, emergency locator transmitter, first aid kit, tool kit, spare oil, and, oh yes, even baggage.

Also consider the effect on the CG. With most storage areas well aft of the aircraft's balance point, all items added there will move the CG towards the aft limit. In a nutshell, pilots learn with experience to travel as lightly as possible.

The Modern Electronic Cockpit

What radios and antennae will you need? With TCAs and ARSAs sprouting virtually everywhere, many owners consider a nav/comm, transponder, and altitude encoder to be minimum avionics equipment. Others feel a second Nav/Comm, plus DME, loran, and possibly ADF are mandatory for their needs.

Unless you are planning Instrument Flight Rules (IFR) operations, skip the weight and install the minimum possible. Avionics can always be added later. However, it might be wise to install the lightweight antennae during construction for future radio additions. Consider hiding/burying the antennae in composite materials to reduce drag thus increasing cruise speed. This can also be done behind fabric/wood structures. Ensure that the cockpit and panel have enough room for instruments and avionics you might wish to add.

And for the Real Do-It-Yourselfer...

If your needs are very special or perhaps novel, would you want to design your own aircraft? It's been done, but unless you really know design engineering, plan to stick with the plans.

Or you might like to consider modifying an existing project for your needs. Again, this is not a job for the novice. Depending on the amount of modification, you may or may not have to make numerous stress calculations. If you are capable of design and modification, you will know what I mean. If you have the training to design your own flying flivver, you will also know that hundreds of hours will be required researching and drafting the creation. Also, beefing up a structure can actually result in its being weakened and possibly failing! This occurs when your additions end up transferring stresses to a section not designed for the loads. If any doubt exists, check with the designer. Who knows, he may even have a better idea, resulting in a project that will be lighter and stronger for your individual needs.

Let's Inspect Your Factory

While your garage may not have entered your design selection considerations, perhaps it should. Wherever your building location will be, you must consider the overall size of the project and whether wings and tail surfaces can be joined to the fuselage inside the building.

Will you be able to heat the enclosed area to high enough temperatures for fiberglass layups or wood glues to cure correctly?

Is there adequate room to store completed wings or other flying surfaces while the fuselage is worked on? (Perhaps overhead in the loft?) Some aircraft require a very large working area because the entire wing is fabricated in one piece. Others have a very high vertical fin. Some types of construction will require you to build jigs and/or work benches that will consume valuable space.

Check with prospective kit/plans suppliers to find out how much room is needed, and then add 50 percent for comfort. You may also have to find a temporary dwelling for garden tools, bicycles and other paraphernalia — like cars — that seem to clutter up the work area.

Tools of Your Trade

Does the plane of your dreams need special skills or tools? You may have to farm out some portions of the aircraft construction such as welding or machining. Paying craftsmen can add greatly to your costs. Also, are the services available locally? Do you have the tools necessary for the type of construction you have chosen? Some of the possibilities are drill press, lathe, milling machine, spray gun for painting, riveting equipment, bending brake, saws, planer, bandsaw, sanding machine, plexiglass forming oven, welding equipment, etc.

How about safety and protective gear such as goggles, gloves, respiratory masks, solvents, and barrier creams? If you have allergies or other medical problems, think about possible reactions and perhaps a different building medium.

Conclusions

Finding an aircraft that suits all of your personal requirements is no easy task — especially if you haven't really researched what you truly want or need.

Many prospective builders choose their project based on what their peers are fabricating or because a certain aircraft looks good. Unfortunately, this method of selection will likely result in an abandoned project or an aircraft that doesn't suit your true needs. Take your time selecting the machine that's best for you.

Armed with the preceding considerations, you should be able to select a design that will be suitable in every way for your needs.

In the chapter titled "Plans, Kit, or Materials Package," you will find questions you might want to ask other builders, to generate tips and warnings concerning the design of your choice.

– 5 –

Plans, Kit, or Materials Package?

Which is for You?

This Glasair kit gets you flying a lot faster than if you started building from scratch.

For a number of years, the market rage has been the 49-percent-complete kit. That's a kit that comes with all of the parts necessary to complete the airframe (minus the engine and instruments), with approximately half of the fabrication completed by the factory, leaving 51 percent of the construction for the builder to complete. The packaged kit has become very popular to the time-sensitive buying public and has resulted in more projects reaching completion.

There is a downside in the form of higher costs. Compared to a plans-built plane, where the builder shops around for surplus parts, etc., a kit plane will likely cost 50 to 100 percent more.

Buying Time with a Kit

The advantages of building from a kit are numerous. Firstly, in many instances the entire package can be ordered — albeit with a large cash outlay — and the builder will be able to work on any portion of the aircraft he chooses, at any time. Many builders are depressed by the fact that half their "building" time with plans projects is spent chasing down bargains and parts. With a kit, hundreds of hours spent as a gofer (going for parts you need next) will be eliminated, as all necessary parts normally arrive at the same time.

Some manufacturers will even ship partial kits to help solve the cash flow or storage problems their customers might otherwise encounter.

A huge blessing of most kits is the factory completion of chores that many builders would be uncomfortable with or incapable of performing. These tasks include welding, metal bending and lay-ups of composite forms in molds. Fabrication of machined parts such as a retractable gear, shaping of bell cranks, and forming and laminating composite box spars are a some of the responsibilities few builders wish to tackle.

Then there's the question of quality. Could you build a female mold and turn out composite fuselage halves as well as the Glasair or Lancair factories? (The Glasair team makes parts for Boeing.) Would you happen to have a garage-sized oven for curing the completed sections? Enough said. The caliber of materials produced by many of the suppliers is second to none.

Bird Makers Can Fly the Coop

Possibly you are aware of the vanishing acts pulled by the manufacturers of the Sparrow Hawk, Prescott Pusher, BD-5, and Swearingen SX-300. These kit producers folded their tents and in some cases left their customers holding the bag. Before buying a kit, get as much information as you can about the company's stability and profitability, and then think twice.

This worry is really for the builder who buys the kit in sections. If you buy the first three of four portions, only to have the company declare bankruptcy, you have a major problem. (It has happened.) For those who have made deposits on a kit, it would be wise to ensure that your money is held in a trust account, earning interest, until the company fulfills its delivery obligation to you.

Just Plain Plans

Some folks will say that this is the only way to build in order to get full challenge and satisfaction. Well, this may be so, if you have all the skills necessary to complete a given project. However, others pursue this route because they have more time than money.

This should certainly be the least expensive way to get an airplane in the air. For instance, the super slick, plans-built GP-4 could be built for $15,000, while the kit-built Glasair RG, of similar performance, would require twice as much money—but half the construction time. You pays your money and takes your choice.

If you live near an area where materials or parts are available at greatly discounted prices, further coin of the realm can be saved. Still other builders have collected mountains of materials that can be used on any project—thus increasing their savings.

The downside to plans-built projects is the reading of catalogs and the chasing of parts. This also puts the onus of determining quality of materials, and substitution of same, on the builder. Frequently, these individuals are more experienced and more skilled, as they will have to complete some of the advanced procedures such as welding and machining on their own. Alternatively, they can chase down someone to perform these operations.

The Middle Route: A Materials Package

Using plans and a materials package will be a balance of saving money and time. A number of the major suppliers, such as Wicks and Aircraft Spruce, provide complete or partial packages of such basic materials as wood or composites to complete a given aircraft type.

For individuals in remote areas, both time and money will be saved. For those who shop around, you will do better financially putting together your own package; however, you may wear out a set of tires rounding up your bargains. To compound the decision-making, some aircraft are better materials package bargains than others.

Once again, my advice is: Shop around and get suggestions from the knowledgeable members in your local experimental aircraft club.

(See Appendix E for a listing of various aircraft models in the following categories: Kits Only, Kits or Plans, and Plans Only.)

– 6 –

What to Ask the Manufacturers

Better Now than Later

Only 50 percent of the kit factories listed five years ago are still in business. While some companies that looked like they would disappear at the first sign of recession are now expanding their businesses to keep up with customer demand, conversely, other companies that looked really good have gone the way of the Dodo bird. You can bet numerous builders are sitting with nothing more than tail kits and promises.

This type of fiasco and heartbreak can easily be avoided by determining the reliability of the company, using the following questions as a guideline. While positive responses to all these queries do not guarantee a manufacturer's stability, honesty, and dependability, they go a long way toward ensuring good products and sustained customer support.

Getting answers in writing will help to avoid shifty answers, and effectively document the company's responses. If they don't bother to answer your letter, perhaps this is an indication of the quality of their support and you should deal elsewhere.

How long has the company been selling aircraft? Obviously, the longer a company has been marketing its product, the more likely it is that they'll be around tomorrow. Another positive indication is a company run by someone who has successfully operated other businesses.

Will You Be Building a Lemon Design?

How many aircraft kits have been sold to date? How many are flying? Answers to these questions will give an indication of the popularity of the kit, the ease of kit completion, and the likelihood the company will be able to remain active due to profitability. Of course, a very new offering won't have many "flyers" until builders have had enough time to complete their projects. Consider these factors in assessing the reply.

Is there a list of builders available and will the company provide a copy for you? If there is no list, how will the kit manufacturer notify builders about errors in the plans or mandatory structural modifications? (There are almost always some of both.) Also, if the company won't let you contact builders, are they perhaps afraid of bad reports on their products?

Some Design Considerations

What type of flying was the aircraft expressly designed for? This will help determine the suitability of the plane for your specific needs.

Was the aircraft designed by an individual or a team? This one is complex. Generally, good designs are produced by a team in consultation with each other. However, this is often not the case. There are numerous brilliant designers who individually produce excellent designs, so a few more questions should be asked to probe the expertise involved. For instance, what are the qualifications of the designer? An aeronautical engineering degree would be a desirable answer.

Nonetheless, some exceptional designs are produced by individuals with no official qualifications. (Many come to mind.) Previous successful designs are adequate to qualify his skill in most cases. But beware of the new aircraft by a first-time designer who lacks formal training or experience. While almost anything will fly, it may fly very poorly or have very unforgiving characteristics.

Another great fear concerns the integrity of the structure. Designing the intricacies of load paths and stress analysis are not arts found among neophytes. Has the aircraft been load-tested statically? Would you want to fly an aircraft that has not been tested to its claimed limits? I wouldn't.

Also, ask if the entire aircraft was proof-loaded, or just the wings. That is, was it loaded with weights, such as sandbags, to simulate the ultimate loads the aircraft designer claims the structure is rated for? Strong wings aren't much good when you attempt to pull out of a dive without tail feathers!

Ensure that the empennage has also been tested. Similarly, find out if the landing gear and engine mount have been load-tested for hard landings. The latter structure should be able to withstand the equivalent drop that would produce approximately the same impact as a 500-700 fpm descent.

Did the stress analysis examine wing torsional loads that could occur due to gusts and control deflections? Remember that movement of the ailerons changes the lift pattern differentially on the two (or more) wings, causing a twisting force that tries to rip the airfoils from the fuselage — unsuccessfully, one hopes. Be prepared for a shock when you learn that few designers perform these tests. Better *they* execute these analyses than you.

If composites or other materials that are relatively new to aviation were used in load-bearing areas, have special margins of safety been added? Some designers add an extra 100 percent for structural security.

Unfortunately, this can add excessive weight, overcoming one of the major benefits of composite construction. This topic is a constant source of argument between designers. You pays your money and takes your chances on this one.

Talk with the Designer

This topic is complex enough to require a book on its own. Suffice it to say, if a given composite design has an excellent and lengthy track record of no structural failures, it is suitable for builders. Talk with the

This Glasair wing is being subjected to a static load test.

designer of a prospective project and judge his views. Ultimately, it is you who must be satisfied with the designer's opinions.

What are the positive and negative load limits? Confirm that these are *limit* loads, not *ultimate* loads. A limit load of six Gs with a normal safety margin of 50 percent would give an ultimate load of 9 Gs. Be careful that the advertising isn't referring to ultimate (yield or failure) loads while implying limit loads.

Also, determine if the limits are based on gross weight. Some manufacturers give the G limits for a lower *operating* weight, thereby effectively quoting a higher limit than the structure can actually tolerate when loaded to gross. Ask if the prototype been flown to these limits at gross weight. Many have not been so tested.

What's the airplane's useful load? (Useful load is the prototype's empty weight subtracted from its published gross.) Many prototypes are lighter than builders will be able to accomplish once design modification, avionics, and accessories are added. Allow a little extra margin in the design's useful load to ensure an adequate payload capability for your needs. Be sure to check the baggage compartment limits insofar as weight and volume are concerned. Many homebuilts have skimpy baggage capabilities.

Has the prototype flown to its Velocity Never Exceed (red line) and beyond? During flight testing of the factory prototype, the test pilot should fly the aircraft 10 percent beyond the published V_{ne} to ensure a flutter-free safety margin for builders. Don't buy an aircraft type that the company is not prepared to fully flight test—unless you fancy yourself as an experimental test pilot. You just might have to pay the ultimate price for your selection.

A Yardstick for Design Standards

Does the aircraft design comply with FAR 23? This is the set of regulations, similar to the JAR series in Europe, that detail the standards that factory production aircraft must comply with. While homebuilt planes are not legally required to follow the requirements, many of the better designs do use FAR 23 as a guideline to ensure a reasonable safety margin in the completed project.

Also, the use of aircraft-quality materials and accepted building practices will result in a relatively maintenance-free and easier-to-fly experimental.

Are any special tools or skills required to build? If you possess neither skills nor tools for difficult projects, avoid the hassle. Choose another project.

Other Criteria

When was the prototype first flown, and how much later was the first home-built project first flown? Homebuilt planes that get built and flown quickly are an indicator that the kit is relatively easy to construct and that the company comes through on its promises of components.

Is there a company newsletter and how often is it published? This type of communication is a very effective method of keeping builders motivated and up on product refinements and builder tips. Many companies don't bother with this non-profitable service to readers. Judge accordingly. Also, who writes it? If it's authored by a first-timer or temporarily interested builder, he/she may lose interest in the project, terminating the newsletter.

What percentage of the aircraft is factory complete in the kit? Remember that the maximum legal limit is a kit that is delivered with at least 51 percent of the construction remaining for the builder. The less complete kits will cost less, but require more effort on the builder's part.

Are various components available from third party companies? Look for the availability of difficult-to-build parts such as landing gear oleos, fairings, and engine cowlings from various sources – if not the kit company.

Modifying the Design

Will the designer consider builder modifications if you submit drawings? Some companies will not take the time or effort to approve any changes to the plans. A few excellent designers, with proven products, are totally obstinate about wanting you to build exactly to plans. For those of you with special purposes in mind, an uncooperative engineer may force you to consider a different aircraft. Because the aircraft is a homebuilt, you can modify the plans yourself without approval. However, be sure you are qualified to make the changes, and be prepared to defend or prove the airworthiness of your changes to the feds when they inspect your plane. Significant changes may also affect the saleability of your project in the future.

The Safety Factor

If you are planning off-airport operations, ascertain if the aircraft can realistically be flown off rough or unimproved fields. You would want to look for adequate oleo travel for shock absorption, and (if a tri-gear) propeller clearance with a flat nose oleo.

Have there been any accidents with the type and if so, what were the causal factors? Pilot error accidents may not be a fault of the design. However, repeated crashes could indicate an unfriendly design that pilots find difficult to fly. Have there been any in-flight structural failures of the type? If so, what corrective action has been taken to eliminate the risk?

Are there any restrictions on the type? If so what are they and why are they there? Consider whether the limitations might make the plane unsuitable for your needs. Have there been any suggested modifications to the aircraft since it was released to the public, and how easy are the changes to incorporate? Are there any mandatory modifications and how are builders informed? (See how handy those newsletters can be?)

Shipping Kits and Bits

Is a complete kit available in one shipment and what is the total cost including shipping charges? Numerous builders are frothing at the bit waiting for the pony express to deliver the next section of their kit so they can proceed with construction. You may want to specify that the manufacturer not ship your kit until the complete package is assembled. This avoids backordered parts and may save money as well.

If you think it would be easier to purchase the kit in sections, find out if you're paying a penalty; what is the total cost compared to the kit portion prices? Don't forget to consider the extra shipping charges in this instance.

Is the package complete or must other components be purchased? Some kits include engine, instruments, fabric and paint. But these are few and far between. Most companies simply supply the airframe kit and leave the rest to the purchaser's option. While the complete packages tend to have a better overall price, the basic kits allow builders to experiment with different powerplants and other items of their choice.

Don't forget to ask if clients' deposits and payments are held in trust (escrow) until the items are shipped. You don't want a fly-by-night outfit to take off with your money.

What is the current waiting period for orders to be shipped? Some of the more desirable kits are backlogged a half year or so. Remember that your intentions and availability to launch a project could significantly change in that time.

What is the current monthly rate of production and how many have been shipped to date? This will give you an idea of the popularity and possible lag time involved in a current order.

Can You Follow the Instructions?

Are the plans excellent? Do they include a building manual? Are there sections that teach building skills?

A good manual with building tips is the best asset a kit can offer. Years ago, for less than $100, builders typically received rather vague plans, often not to the same scale from section to section, with frequent statements such as "as required" and "to suit the builder's option." These were fine for experts. However, with more and more first-time builders entering the exciting do-it-yourself airplane field, very complete, comprehensive building manuals are almost mandatory to ensure that the project will reach completion.

While you're at it, ask if the plans and manual have been updated due to builder input. To provide near-perfect manuals and plans, the folks who produce the Glasair III kit had the first kit builder construct the plane in their hangar, so any questions or problems he encountered could be addressed in the published version of the manual. If you are visiting the factory, ask to see a set of plans and the builder manual. The company should be more than happy to display their high quality work, unless...

Request a list of pilot reports and product reviews that have been published in various magazines. Most salesmen will only tell you of the glowing reports on the product, if there are any.

Be prepared to sign a waiver when you order a kit or plans, that "holds harmless" the kit manufacturer of any liability, since he has no control over your workmanship. While this may seem somewhat of a shocker, it has become standard practice in the industry to ship no parts until the waiver is signed and returned.

In Conclusion

As the customer, you have the right to expect reasonable answers to your questions. If the company seems reticent about giving straightforward, honest responses — shop elsewhere! Many folks have gotten so carried away with the attraction of a given aircraft, they threw caution — and their money — to the wind. The failure of companies we've mentioned previously left thousands of would-be builders aloft without any means of support. (Of course, even Cessna packed it in for single engine aircraft in the mid-80s, but at least they didn't leave their customers with half-finished airplanes.)

Remember, completely research the company and its product *before* you lay down your deposit. This will be one of the best investments you will make on your project.

Buying a Completed Homebuilt

Tips and Cautions for Those Who Would Rather Buy Than Build

So you've decided to skip building and start flying immediately with a purchased homebuilt plane. In this chapter, we'll assume you don't want the challenges — or perhaps you see them as hassles — of the construction process.

Why Not Buy a Used Production Aircraft?

Don't panic, it was a rhetorical question.

Nonetheless, let's reinforce the possible reasons you've chosen to go amateur-built/experimental class. Perhaps you want a custom aircraft with unique capabilities and looks that go far beyond the conservative factory creations. Another consideration might be bargain prices for similar performance: for example, a $10,000 BD-4 rather than a $30,000 Mooney, or a 5151 Mustang for $10,000 rather than full-sized P-51 Mustang at $300,000.

Maybe you want to be able to do most of your own maintenance — thus saving money on expenses. Similarly, you might wish to avoid the huge cost of an aviation engine and associated parts by using an auto conversion or two-stroke powerplant.

Whatever your reasons, you will have approximately 11,000 custom aircraft to choose from, comprised of roughly 500 types in the USA.

How About an Ultralight?

For many shoppers, this type of aircraft could be adequate. For a complete description of ultralight regulations and limitations, see the chapter entitled "Regulations."

But for most of us, the ultralight's limited load-carrying capabilities, short range, low cruising speed, and inability to carry passengers are restrictions that are unacceptable.

Should You Consider a "One-Off" Design?

Another special consideration is the self-designed, or *one-off*, homebuilt. Some of these can be excellent values due to low prices and performance tailored to a specified portion of the flight envelope. Nonetheless, only very knowledgeable purchasers should stride into this possibly deep jungle, as there could be many hidden pitfalls. For the non-builder owner, there is the question of where parts could be purchased for this unique aircraft. And design questions such as stress loading, material compatibility, fastener ratings, and aerodynamic stability are only a few of the possible traps facing the unwary explorer. Some of the one-off designs that have been my steeds during experimental flight testing were nothing more than glorified death traps.

How About a Partially Completed Kit?

Some of the best values can be found in the purchase of a project that is being abandoned by a builder. Prices for these orphans tend to be considerably lower for two reasons: there is far less demand for a non-flying plane among those who don't want to build, and those who do want to build their own plane for the challenge and thrill of it don't want to complete a partial project.

This leaves astute buyers, who have some time and building skills, to clean up—in more ways than one. The best purchase I ever made, financially, was an almost complete Baby Great Lakes that a busy lawyer could find no time to complete. His loss was my gain.

The same considerations found throughout this chapter apply to partially completed projects as well. Review them carefully.

Moreover, there is a hidden pitfall with this type of project: namely, do not underestimate the amount of time remaining 'til completion. An enterprise that looks 90-percent complete is probably only half done. Wiring, engine installation, instrumentation, priming, painting, and paperwork exact a large time toll.

In your planning, don't forget the initial flight restrictions and test flying phase, complete with trouble-shooting and repairs. Until these are complete, you will not be free to introduce friends and family to the raptures of sport aviation, nor will you be able to fly to distant destinations.

Consider Your Needs

Firstly, you should determine what type of aircraft is suitable for your current and forecast needs—not to mention your flying skills.

It would be unwise, for example, for a newly licenced pilot, using an 1800-foot gravel strip and flying to nearby grass strips, to buy a high performance, cross-country plane like a Questair Venture. While the Venture is a terrific design, and has published data that indicate the 1600-foot field length is adequate, the landing gear, propeller clearance, and landing distances make it entirely unsuitable for short, rough strips. Put into that sort of environment, such a plane might spend more time down for maintenance than in the air. One might expect rock chip damage to propeller and airframe, along with wear and tear on the landing gear downlocks, doors and attach points, etc. (For more criteria, refer back to the chapter entitled "Selecting the Bird You'll Build.")

Information from high-time pilots and members of various flying groups will help you narrow the field down to suitable aircraft for your considerations. Be sure to obtain most of your advice from groups such as EAA chapters, since many private pilots look upon experimentals with disdain—mostly due to a lack of knowledge. Additionally, aviation magazines with their pilot reports will provide a source of relatively unbiased assessments.

Also, talk with owners of the design you are considering, to obtain their impressions of flying characteristics and repair requirements.

Where to Shop

By letting your fingers walk through the the classified sections of aviation publications, you can see what the asking prices are, and at the same time you may find just what you're looking for.

While aircraft "blue book" pricing is generally not available for custom-built aircraft, the publication *TRADE-A-PLANE* is a virtual bible to serious shoppers. The selection is so large on any given aircraft, it is possible to get a good idea of average asking prices.

In addition to *TRADE-A-PLANE*, *Kitplanes* and *Sport Aviation* magazines have extensive listings of homebuilts for sale.

In Canada, there are numerous magazines listing aircraft for sale, such as *Canadian General Aviation News* and *Canadian Homebuilt Aviation News* (available to members of the Canadian Owners and Pilots Association), and the *Recreational Flyer* from the RAAC. (See Appendix D for magazine subscription information.)

Incidentally, the current rate of exchange for US and Canadian dollars makes Canadian aircraft very attractive to US buyers, as they are effectively discounted, at this writing, by about 15 percent.

Another great place to shop is local aviation bulletin boards, where you might find an aircraft that not only suits your needs, but its care and condition may be well known by locals. If you can find a good plane in your vicinity, you can avoid the costs and time involved in distant searches.

Then, of course, there's your local EAA chapter, as well as experimental aircraft conventions and shows.

Consider the Power Train

Pricing for a given aircraft type is dictated by the model year, the options installed, and TBO (time between overhauls) of the major components such as engine and propeller. While an aircraft with a high-time engine may seem like a financial bargain because you want to fly it only for a hundred hours before trading, consider the resale value to the next purchaser.

For instance, recent quotes for an overhaul on our BD-4's Lycoming O-320 engine ranged from $8,500 to $11,600, not including possible camshaft and crankshaft costs. This equates to approximately $5 per engine hour in value, based on the 2000 hour TBO. Therefore, a Christavia with a zero-time engine priced at $20,000 is a better value than a $14,000 Christavia with 100 hours remaining on its Lycoming, if all other factors are equal.

Of course, all those other factors seldom are equal. The quality of an overhaul is of paramount importance. Low-cost, low-quality work by poor shops often results in engines that will fail, or at least require work before the expiration of the TBO.

Since we are talking experimentals, it may be that the overhaul was accomplished by the builder. If so, what are his qualifications, his level of workmanship, and exactly what was replaced during the teardown? If the quality of parts and labor is low, you might be better off with a high-time engine that could then be overhauled by a reputable shop.

Check the ADs

Determine whether all Airworthiness Directives were complied with. Compliance isn't mandatory if the engine is not an aircraft engine (Lycoming, etc.) or if the engine has no nameplate identifying it as an aircraft engine. However, safety dictates that you ensure that the ADs have been complied with.

The point here is simple. The quality of the work and condition of the engine are the main factors to consider, not the time that appears to be remaining until TBO expiration.

The same is true with propellers that have overhaul times based on hours and/or calendar years. The latter requirement catches many unwary buyers who note that a prop has only 50 hours on its 2000 hour overhaul, only to find that it has reached its five-year recommended overhaul date. Check with your local FSDO to learn the limits of a given propeller and its TBO. As a new owner, you may be required to have a perfectly serviceable prop removed and expensively over-hauled, just because five calendar years have passed. While this rule may be revised before long, Buyers Beware!

Contact the Clubs

When you have narrowed the selection down to one desirable aircraft type, get in touch with clubs of that design and ask if they have back issues of their newsletter that you could peruse, talk with owners and builders, and take one of them to help inspect prospective purchases. The chapter entitled "Flight Evaluation Checklists" has some suggested questions to ask builders.

Chat with the Designer

You might want to call the designer to ask him what portions of the aircraft have given problems to builders. This will alert you to areas that should receive special attention during the inspection to ensure structural integrity. Armed with this knowledge, a more detailed and accurate inspection will ensue.

Inspecting Your Prospective Purchase

If you've gotten serious about a particular aircraft, have an aircraft mechanic (in the US an A&P, or in Canada an AME) inspect the plane to ensure it is in airworthy condition. The inspection should cover the entire airplane, including (among other things) an engine compression (leak-down) check. Also, the mechanic should confirm that all mandatory modifications have been complied with. He should not only see that they have been signed off in the logbook, but he should also establish, where possible, that the actual modifications have been completed – properly.

In some cases, inspections of certain components are recommended at various time intervals on that aircraft or engine type. Although compliance may not be mandatory, it is wise to increase your safety margin by ensuring that your aircraft is as airworthy as possible.

Other paperwork commonly overlooked includes the weight and balance calculations. If the basic weight is considerably over that of the prototype, either the building practices were poor, or too many options were added, or perhaps the owner made modifications to the structure he isn't telling you about. Similarly, compare the balance calculations to the norm for the type. Any discrepancies here should end the inspection!

Then there's the inspection for a valid Special Airworthiness Certificate, or in Canada, a valid Flight Permit. These forms no longer have yearly expiration dates, but aircraft that have been inactive for a long time may have a form with an expired date. If the aircraft you are considering has an expired Airworthiness Certificate, the FAA will probably want to inspect it again before issuing a new Special C of A. In Canada, one simply reapplies for an updated Flight Permit.

Operations and Limitations

A very important piece of paper, the Operations and Limitations, specifies the uses that are approved for that airplane. These were issued to the builder by FAA (or Canadian DOT) and should be inspected for limitations that might not be acceptable for you and your planned applications.

For instance, the plane may be fully equipped for night and IFR flight, but restricted from doing so in the operational restrictions. If you were buying the plane for cross-country transportation, you might want to reconsider the plane or the usage. Similarly, you wouldn't want to buy a Christen Eagle for airshow demonstrations, and later find that the Operations and Limitations stated "no aerobatics." These restrictions are not written in stone, however, and if you are still really keen on a particular plane, you can petition the FAA (the DOT in Canada), to have them inspect the aircraft and process the applicable paperwork to amend the limitations.

With a little practice, you may be able to eliminate some planes by making your own detailed inspection prior to hiring an A&P. At other times, for distant aircraft, you may wish to call a mechanic on the plane's airfield to conduct an inspection. If the aircraft fails to pass with flying colors, you've saved yourself the expense of traveling to that prospect. A relatively small amount invested at this point could save thousands later.

Watch for Conflicts of Interest

Your choice of mechanic should exclude an individual who might have a personal interest in the aircraft or even be the one who performs the normal maintenance on her. For instance, my partner and I trusted a distant A&P who recommended a supposedly airworthy aircraft on which he had recently done the annual. We bought the plane for $7,500. The same fellow then proceeded to find so many snags on the aircraft during a 100-hour inspection that we ended up investing another $13,500 to bring her up to standards.

Also, check the history of sales before inspecting a plane. If it has had a lot of turnovers and very little flying, perhaps there is something scary about her. Frequent trips to maintenance facilities with attendant bills could also warn of persistent problems.

Inspection Tips

Scrutinizing the logbooks for indications of accidents and rebuild activity is also wise. If your dream has had a major "prang," it is necessary to ensure that the frame was not bent or misaligned. Determine whether jigs were used during the repairs to guarantee the aircraft will fly straight and true after restoration. Beware of the cosmetic rebuild that puts the best side forward while hiding structural damage.

Quality is More Than Skin Deep

Because the aircraft is homebuilt, a few more factors are important. For instance, who built the aircraft, and what is the quality of workmanship? Don't judge the construction quality by the plane's external appearance—it could have been painted by a professional. Look inside everywhere you can, to judge the builder's craftsmanship. A mirror will allow you to look around corners at structural joints for voids, poor surface joins, dry glue joints, or poorly installed fasteners, etc. Let common sense be your guide in appraising hidden internals.

Similarly, composites that appear very sound could in fact have poor bonds between layers or improperly cured structures.

Be very careful with older wooden structures—especially if they have been stored outside—for two reasons. Firstly, dry rot can easily destroy the integrity of the structure; secondly, older types of glues not only lose strength with time, but are subject to the effects of moisture. Glue joints should not appear dry or overly thin, as can happen when clamps are applied too tightly. Of course, small gaps will occasionally appear in the wooden structure, but these should be few and far between.

With the very high quality of composite or formed aluminum kit components, it is likely that the finished product will be more structurally sound and blemish-free than a rag-and-tube design.

Be sure to ask if there were any modifications of the original design, and try to assess whether these might affect the aircraft's airworthiness.

How Skillful are Those Who Did the Work?

While these cautions may appear to throw wrenches into your search, there is a way to minimize the risk. On talking with the seller, observe his attitude to help determine his aptitude. During the inspection, ascertain his skill level on the portions that show. Poor builders tend to produce slap-dash results everywhere, whereas good builders tend to produce excellent results everywhere.

If the engine was rebuilt, who did the work? Find out if the overhauler is respected, and discuss the engine with him. Where did the engine come from and what was the time remaining in the engine log? If the powerplant was removed from a wreckage, was there any damage to internal parts and did it sit around in the prevailing weather for a considerable period of time, perhaps sustaining interior corrosion?

The Problems with Inspections and Inspectors

Who did the annual inspections? How qualified were those people to accomplish the inspections? Remember, since the builder and subsequent owners may have accomplished these tasks, it would be wise to get a general idea of their qualifications.

In Canada, a builder or subsequent owner can do all of the work on an experimental — regardless of qualifications. In the US, the original builder is issued a Repairman's Certificate for his plane, allowing him to accomplish all of the maintenance tasks and the associated sign-off in the logs. While FAA currently allows subsequent owners to perform maintenance on the aircraft, once a year the original builder or an AI must check the work and sign it off.

As a result, you should determine who actually did the work. Did a rather unqualified previous owner perform the inspection and an unscrupulous inspector do a "Papermate sign-off," or was the work really accomplished, and in a professional manner?

You can see that in the case of a homebuilt, it is doubly important to have a qualified mechanic to protect your interests — and your life.

Doing the Walk-Around

During your walk-around, with the magnetos off, pull the propeller through a number of rotations to confirm that the compression on all of the cylinders is approximately even. (Hopefully, the aircraft doesn't have a live mag!) If compression is not equal, or you can hear "air leaks," there could be a leaky valve or an otherwise low or dead cylinder that will require attention. The inspecting mechanic should catch these problems on the engine leak test as well.

With all engine cowlings off and fuel on, check for cracks, chafing, and signs of leaks in the fuel and primer lines. Inspect the carburetor for control linkage security and safety wiring, as well as fuel leaks from brittle gaskets. Intake and exhaust manifolds should be securely fastened and free of cracks or signs of leakage. (Look for sooty, darkened or discolored areas near joints.)

Ensure that the spark plugs are secure and their wiring is in serviceable condition. Ditto the magnetos.

Look over the general condition of the engine; check for freedom from corrosion and absence of significant oil leaks. A clean engine is often an indication of good maintenance practices. Metal engine mounts should be free of cracks and serious rust and their rubber mounts should not be brittle or cracked.

After you are satisfied with the condition of all of the engine compartment's contents, check the engine cowlings and its fasteners for security when you reinstall them.

If the fuselage looks good enough to continue your inspection, take off the interior and exterior access panels. With a flashlight, probe every accessible nook and cranny for signs of corrosion, cracks, or structural repairs that could indicate unreported accidents. Check controls and linkages for excessive play and absence of frayed cables where they curve over pulleys. While inside the structures, look for signs of cables or push tubes rubbing against the main structure. Welded joints should be smooth beaded with minimum oxidation, lumpiness, or sagging filler.

Rivets should be tight and their holes free from elongation.

Viewing the unpainted areas of aluminum should show smooth, sanded edges and scratch-free surfaces. Paint should be well bonded to the surface with no corrosion under tell-tale lumps or bubbles.

Look Everywhere

In the case of fabric covering, punch test the material in a lower area where water or condensation tends to collect, to ensure that the fabric meets at least the minimum standards. Don't forget to scrape the paint and dope off the area(s) to be tested, to avoid misleading readings on the pressure tester: you are interested in the strength of the fabric, not the fabric/finish combination.

Remove the floor boards and seat back(s) to gain access to the lower and aft fuselage areas. If the builder isn't receptive to showing his craftsmanship in these areas, it's time to go on to the next aircraft.

Check landing gear and brake hydraulic lines for signs of chafing, leaking, or cracks.

Similarly, electrical wiring should be inspected at all accessible points, as should all circuits and breakers during the flight portion of the evaluation.

The battery should be secure, with the correct caps, vented externally and with adequate electrolyte that shows a full charge in all cells.

Tires should have adequate tread and inflation and be free of cracks and cuts — especially in the sidewalls. Similarly, wheels should be free of corrosion and cracks.

If shock absorption is courtesy of bungee cords, ensure that they are free of nicks, fraying, and oil or dirt collection.

Attachment points for the gear are areas of possible damage. Inspect this area carefully, especially in a retractable.

With all covers removed, inspect the wing for irregularities in the skin in an attempt to locate internal damage. The quality of composite surfaces and some aluminum, depending on the finish, will give further judgments on the general quality of the workmanship.

Rock Your Wings

Rocking the plane by the wing tips may also locate, by sound or tactile sense, possible damage to spars and attach points. If wing tanks are installed, check for leaks after this shake-up, as well as telltale stains near drains, inspection plates, etc. With your flashlight, inspect as much of the wing's interior as possible, including the security and condition of all control pulleys, cables and bell cranks.

Similarly, ensure that the control surfaces have complete and fairly frictionless travel. If the wings can be removed, check the attach points and quality and correctness of locking devices.

The tail surfaces should undergo a similar inspection.

Also, look for rock damage under the horizontal stabilizer, and check for excessive play on hinges and attachment points of the tail feathers.

Wooden propeller inspection should include possible cracks, scrapes, nicks, finish separation and, where installed, security of screws on leading edge metal covers. Don't forget to look for damaged wood fibers under the retention bolts due to over-tightening.

Composite blades should be free of structural cracks that could lead to a major delamination and departure during flight. Aluminum props should also be free of nicks that could result in blade separation, and all blades should track very close to each other. A simple way to test for this is to place a chair so that it is just touching the back of the propeller, and rotate the other blades, by hand, to confirm they also just touch the chair. Blade tips should track within an eighth of an inch of each other to ensure relatively vibration-free flight.

You should also measure the propeller diameter to ensure that it has not been cut down to a substandard size — thus reducing efficiency considerably. A propeller shop will give you the information you need when you tell them the serial and model number.

One other risk is the pitch being twisted beyond the original limits specified for that model, or repeated re-pitching, which stresses the blades.

While the preceding will give you a guideline to follow, it will be wise to keep your wits about you and your eyes wide open for anything that appears suspicious.

The Evaluation Flight

Be sure to check the operation of all of the equipment. For instance, in the case of the transponder, a flashing reply light is not enough to confirm operation. Ask ATC for permission to "ident" to confirm the complete function, and request an altitude check if there is a mode C encoder.

Similarly, checking only for a dead or poor magneto isn't enough. Be sure to perform a "live" mag check on shutdown, for everyone's safety around the propeller. Remember how? With the throttle closed to slow idle, turn the mags to off for a brief moment, then back to both. The engine rpm should drop, confirming that both mags were in fact off. It is not uncommon to have a grounding wire break, leaving a magneto live — and deadly.

During the flight, be aware of cabin size and comfort, noise and vibration levels, visibility, maneuverability on the ground and in the air, plus your overall impression of the plane.

Confirm proper operation of brakes, flying controls, trim, flaps, lighting, avionics, instrumentation, and engine controls.

Methods of estimating performance include verifying takeoff acceleration and distance required, rate of climb, cruise, and top speeds. If engine temperatures and pressures do not stay within normal operating limits, this is indicative of a worn out powerplant. While these are not completely accurate tests, due to varying conditions, they will at least indicate whether performance is in the ballpark.

During the stalls and slow flight portion of the flight, look for significant out-of-trim conditions or rapid wing drops that might indicate an out-of-rig condition.

And be sure to refer to the next chapter, "Flight Evaluation Checklists." It will help you remember those important details.

The Inherent Value of Homebuilts

The cautions and cavils we've mentioned do not necessarily mean that homebuilt aircraft can't be good values. As a matter of fact, six of the author's dozen aircraft have been homebuilts—and they were always the best performers and better values. In terms of value, much has changed in the last decade; these planes are now easily insured at reasonable premiums, and resale value tends to hover near the cost of materials to build—or higher, depending on the quality of the project.

And typically, the new homebuilt kits provide far superior performance and aesthetic appeal when compared to their factory-made brethren.

– 8 –

Flight Evaluation Checklists

For Buyers and Flyers

If you, like me, are absent-minded, you will find it easy to overlook various aspects of an aircraft during a flight test. As a result, you may miss a number of problem areas that could prove costly. The following evaluation checklist will be useful when test flying someone's experimental. Carrying a photocopy and filling in the blanks during the flight will provide you with a permanent record of the performance and of your initial impressions on any aircraft you test.

By now, you have read the chapter on buying a used homebuilt, and had an A&P (or AME in Canada) inspect the aircraft and declare it safe for flight before you strap in. You might also want to discuss the owner's flying qualifications and currency before trusting him with your life. You can ask others in the local area about the owner to obtain details on his flying, and about the aircraft as well.

While it may not seem tactful, you may also want to inquire about the owner's insurance coverage. See the chapter on insurance for more information. If the plane is single place and the owner won't let you fly it until it is paid for, try to settle on a qualified – and objective – pilot in the area who is mutually acceptable to both parties. Then give him/her a copy of the checklist to fill out for you.

First Flight Considerations

If this is the first flight of a newly completed homebuilt, or a flight within the plane's first 40 hours of experimental testing, you should be aware that more than two out of every five homebuilt aircraft accidents in the US happen during this time. The FAA attributes the causal factor in most of these 250 prangs per year to inadequate pre-flight preparation.

Use extra caution, since this homebuilt aircraft, as the name implies, was not necessarily constructed to factory standards of workmanship, nor was it test flown by a factory test pilot to ensure conformity.

Today, you are the test pilot. Assume your duties with a high degree of caution, professionalism and preparedness.

A PRE-PURCHASE EVALUATION CHECKLIST

Preliminary Data

Aircraft type
Registration
Date
Owner
Address
Ground Evaluation
Ease of completing walkaround inspection
Oil inspection access
Accessories
Gear locks & shocks
Tire size
Fuel drains for all tanks?
Lighting — nav, anti-collision, taxi/landing
Cabin
Ease of access
Cabin size, spaciousness
Baggage capacity, accessibility
Harness system
Seat comfort, adjustability
Any protruding items?
Canopy/door hinge & latch security

Cockpit Layout

Room for desired avionics?
Noteworthy instrumentation?
Lighting—panel, map, cabin
Access to all controls for all positions?
Adequate fuel system selector
Header tank?
Fuel quantity
Ignition control selections
Fuel load as tested
Empty or basic weight & weight during flight
Ease of starting—special techniques?
Sound level at idle
Smoothness of idle
Parking brake? How applied?

Taxiing and Runup

Taxiing visibility
Maneuverability
Brake effectiveness
Shock absorption of gear
Runup procedures
Control feel in all axes

Takeoff and Climb

Brake strength at takeoff power
Sound level
Vibration
Rudder effectiveness
Tail liftoff or nose gear rotation speed
Takeoff distance
Pitch changes on gear retraction

Rate of climb
Visibility
Control feel
Engine temperature during climb
Oil pressure and temperature

Cruise

Maximum and cruise speed calculations
Altimeter
Outside air temperature
Maximum level indicated speed
True airspeed
Power setting
Indicated airspeed
Fuel flow
Control feel
Pitch stability static
Pitch phugoid
Trim sensitivity and authority
Non-trimmable control pressures?
Vibration level
Visibility
Sound level
Cross-country comfort
Stability
Maneuverability
Roll rate
Gust turbulence handling
Gust penetration speed (yellow line)
Velocity Never Exceed (red line)
V_{ne} demonstrated? Any flutter?
Maneuvering speed handling
Aerobatics recommended?
Aerobatics flown

Airwork, Approach, and Landing

Rate of speed decay with power reduction
Published gear extension speed
Published flap extension speed
Pitch change on gear/flap deployment?
Slow flight stability with gear/flaps down
Slow speed handling characteristics
Any stall warning buffet?
Indicated airspeed of clean stall
IAS of gear/flaps down stall
Any pitch and roll yaw at the stall?
Sensitivity to secondary stall
Sideslip characteristics
Power-off rate of descent & indicated speed
Recommended base leg speed
Final approach speed
Threshold crossing speed
Steep approach capability
Effectiveness of flaps
Crosswind capability
Braking action & effectiveness
Directional controllability in crosswind
Additional notes

After-Flight Conclusions

After you've checked for signs of fuel and oil leaks, review the aircraft's performance during your flight. If the plane was rigged improperly, you may notice the performance numbers weren't as good as published for the prototype or other builders' planes. This problem may be remediable after further inspection and minor modifications — but then again, it may not. Before you decide to buy, the aircraft should be tweaked for optimum efficiency and re-flown until you are perfectly satisfied with its operation. Then, if you decide to buy, read the chapter entitled "Buying and Registering Your Aircraft" that includes a generic bill of sale.

LEARNING FROM THE BUILDERS

Here's a questionnaire that will enable you to learn a great deal about the aircraft you are considering, and other aircraft as well. Run off a bunch of copies, hand them out at a local EAA chapter meeting or experimental aircraft fly-in, and ask builders for their input. This data will be the very significant, as it will be provided by individuals with firsthand knowledge of the building and flying characteristics of the airplane you're contemplating.

Name_____

Address_____

Phone _____

Aircraft type _____

Engine_____Horsepower___Time SMOH____

Propeller_____Pitch ___Diameter____

Is this your first homebuilt aircraft?_____

If not, what else have you built? _____

What was the total cost of your project?_____

What was the most difficult part to build? _____

Rate the quality of the following (Poor, Fair, Good, Excellent):

   1: Plans_____

   2: Materials provided_____

   3: Construction manual_____

   4: Factory support_____

When did you start the project?_____Finish it?_____

How many hours to build?_____

How many hours have you flown the aircraft?_____

Please detail the specifications and performance you've observed:

Empty weight_____Gross weight_____Fuel capacity_____

75% Cruise power: Speed (mph)_____Fuel consumption_____

Stall speed: Clean_____Flaps/gear down_____

Rate of climb: Solo_____At gross weight_____

Was the aircraft built from plans or kit?_____

If plans-built, please list the parts you bought pre-formed:

_____

_____

_____

_____

Where were they bought? _____

_____

_____

_____

Why did you choose to build this aircraft type? _____

_____

_____

_____

_____

If you modified the plans, what did you change, and why?

_____

_____

_____

_____

What avionics have you installed? _____

_____

_____

_____

What, if any, special equipment have you installed?_____

_____

_____

_____

Have you had any problems with the aircraft? _____

_____

_____

_____

What qualities of the aircraft do you like? _____

_____

_____

_____

What do you dislike? _____

_____

_____

_____

Do you have any advice for other builders? _____

_____

_____

_____

_____

_____

_____

Section Two

Engines, Autogas, and Avionics

9

Go-Power

From Traditional to Modern

After choosing the plans or kit for the aircraft of your dreams, your next big decision will be selecting the powerplant that will have the honor of pulling you through the troposphere. We'll try to help you make that choice by looking at some of the benefits — and the costs — of engines for aviation use. In this chapter we will appraise the handling and selection considerations involved with two-stroke and automotive conversions, and provide a listing, complete with technical details, of the various powerplants currently available on the piston-powered aircraft engine market, with addresses and phone numbers of the companies that manufacture and/or distribute them.

Again, I remind you that, because of the changes that take place constantly in this industry, some of the information may no longer be valid by the time you read this book.

The Traditional Route

Lycoming, Continental, and others have provided aircraft powerplants for many decades. The benefits of the current horizontally opposed Lycoming and Continental air-cooled engines are their reliability (with some notable exceptions) and the fact they produce their horsepower in an rpm range that allows them to be directly coupled to large, efficient propellers.

Unfortunately, there has been little change in their design. They utilize old technology and have an extravagant thirst for fuel, with the result that the auto engines of today are considered by many to be superior in every way to these traditional aircraft engines.

The major law of economics is supply and demand. The fact that North America produces hundreds of thousands of auto engines yearly, compared to a few thousand aircraft engines, means that there is a great deal more money available for research and development. This leads to quantum leaps in performance in the auto conversions.

Additionally, the accessories mounted on the traditional aircraft engine are also old technology. In effect, we should pity the flyers of factory-builts, because they do not have the option of using a modern auto conversion. Recently, the major aircraft engine manufacturers modified some of these older designs and/or produced liquid-cooled versions. The jury is out as to whether these newer variants will be judged as desirable in the marketplace.

While the manufacturers have been forced to update these engines for market acceptability, many aircraft engines are joining the endangered species list or becoming inordinately expensive to buy, overhaul, and service. No wonder that builders have been increasingly turning to other options.

Let's have a look at some of the modern options available to power your project.

The Benefits of Auto Conversions

Although there have been major aircraft performance gains in the last few decades, most have been based on engine advances – not airframe improvements. Technological improvements in powerplant performance and reliability have allowed designers to really optimize aircraft efficiency. These advances include improvements in metals, combustion patterns, exhaust scavenging, ignition systems, reduction drives, fuels, turbo/supercharging, carburetion, and fuel injection – to name a few.

Progress has been so rapid that aviation engines, due to their lengthy and expensive certification processes, have fallen behind automotive and two-stroke engine developments.

The fact that aluminum blocks and heads are less than half the weight of cast iron makes the aftermarket automotive products very attractive. Besides, automotive engines, complete with all accessories, can be purchased from salvage yards for less than $1,000, and if necessary, rebuilt for hundreds, whereas aviation engines cost $3,000 to $10,000 used, or tens of thousands of dollars when bought new from the factory.

Many incredible praises and extravagant claims have been made for auto conversions in the past, making some buyers wary. Nonetheless, it is true that years of refinement have led to some very reliable, quiet, and smooth-running car conversions. Other benefits include readily available parts, ease of maintenance, cheap mufflers, and super fuel efficiency. In addition, there's the modern, reliable, solid state ignition with computer-controlled timing that senses the engine's load and adjusts accordingly, along with lightweight designs that rival and surpass aircraft engines in horsepower produced per pound.

Not surprisingly, then, this writer has observed a rapid rise in the number of builders who now consider their family car's engine a desirable alternative to the high-priced aircraft engines.

The demand has resulted in a handful of companies that have chosen to invest in the development of new powerplants that are optimized through the use of modern materials and production techniques.

There is a wide variety of conversions now offered to the public. A few of these make good aircraft engines. You must look beyond the hype and determine which conversions might be suitable for you.

If They're So Good, Why Isn't Everyone Flying Them?

Firstly, most conversions have not been marketed adequately—yet. Also, many buyers are waiting on the sidelines for the conversions to prove themselves.

Secondly, there is some question whether auto engines—that normally operate in cars at approximately 30 percent power output—will endure at 75% aircraft settings. Also, reduction units are required in these conversions in order to efficiently torque propellers through the atmosphere. The direct drive conversions that operate in the 3200 to 5500 rpm range will be lucky if they can transmit 60 percent of their horsepower into effective thrust at the propeller.

While the strong trend to lighter engines prevails, many auto engines nevertheless are quite heavy by the time all cooling and accessories are added. Since few are designed to hang on a firewall, an engine "bed" must be engineered into an experimental configuration.

Some carburetors don't behave very well when their installation is tilted to angles never achieved on the highway. If you aren't planning aerobatics, this may not be a problem; however, it is a consideration.

Unless you are building a P-51 or other "scooped" aircraft, the radiator mount may be a very unattractive blivot on your dream machine. Some builders get around this problem by building a plenum chamber in the engine cowling for cooling. This setup also allows air to flow over the accessories mounted on the engine, providing them with the necessary cooling.

While I have no love for magnetos, a device that came to us from the Stone Age, the need for an electrical system to drive the solid state ignition generally found on auto conversions is a slight safety risk, since most of these systems require at least 1.5 volts or so to fire. (Actually a small low-capacity battery is more than adequate for this task — with a backup that is easily switched on line in case the primary source fails.)

Builders will also find that the typical engine instruments purchased from your aviation supplier are not necessarily compatible on an auto engine. (Guess you'll just have to buy those cheaper automotive gauges.)

The good news is that starters, water pumps, alternators, generators, oil pumps, and the solid state ignitions normally installed on auto engines seem to provide no problems in aircraft use — although a high quality shielded ignition harness is recommended to prevent radio interference.

There Are Pitfalls

You are well advised to suspect the horsepower claims of many of the conversion salesmen. The exaggerated declarations are quickly disproved when the aircraft they power fail to produce adequate performance.

For those of you who wish to design your own auto conversion, a test stand with thrust measurement is highly recommended. One Washingtonian has upped the thrust for fellow Sea Hawk owners by more than 30 percent, with propeller and engine refinements courtesy of thrust measurement.

Internally, many auto engines currently use the much weaker, but cheaper, cast crankshaft rather than forged steel. Often camshafts have to be reground to produce longer "overlaps" in the valves and other modifications that will produce more torque at lower, propeller-efficient rpms. If the heavy flywheel and crankshaft torsion dampers are removed, it is possible the engine will suffer from torsional resonance that could eventually tear it apart. Designers have to test for vibrations and ensure that long-term difficulties won't ensue.

So there are many pitfalls involved in auto engine conversions. While they are not insurmountable, it behooves the shopper to search diligently and obtain assurances that a given engine will be suitable for his project. The proliferation of engines under 500 horsepower makes the current market a feast for builders. However, beware of indigestion.

Two-Stroke Powerplants

One of the most controversial entries into the homebuilt aviation field is the two-stroke engine. Recently graduating from ultralight use, this type of engine seemingly is either loved or hated by its operator.

These installations are not new to aircraft, as GM had a two-stroke four-cylinder engine flying successfully in a Cessna C-37 during the 1930s. More and more automobiles are furnishing shelter for these engines that provide power on every second stroke.

This prodigious power production—coupled with very light weight and low cost of purchase, maintenance, and overhaul costs—have made these engines very popular recently. Other benefits include cleanliness, due to the absence of a wet oil sump, and the capability of easily burning inexpensive auto gas. What's more, these engines provide excellent reliability and tremendous thrust per pound, as long as they are maintained and flown correctly.

A common problem is the tendency of builders to attach propellers that are too big (in terms of pitch and/or diameter) in the mistaken belief that they can fly faster. Similar to lugging a four-stroke, this overloads the engine. Excessive heat builds up, the pistons and rings deform in the cylinders, and the engine seizes.

This scenario is easily avoided with CHT (cylinder head temperature) and EGT (exhaust gas temperature) gauges. Don't fly without both of these useful gauges, and be sure they're both serviceable and accurately calibrated. Otherwise, it could cost you an engine, or at least an overhaul.

Tips on Two-Stroke Treatment

The following suggestions have resulted from interviews with well-known designer Molt Taylor and Avid Flyer salesman Ray Fletcher—a man with thousands of hours of two-stroke experience in the remote mountainous areas of western Canada. These pointers will help you attain maximum performance and longevity from your two-stroke engine.

Ray suggests running the fuel/oil mix no leaner than 50/1. In fact, he mixes an even richer blend at 40/1. Feeling that most flyers don't warm up the engines enough, he recommends no medium or high power applications until the CHT warms up to at least 100 degrees. However, it will be necessary to idle in the 1500-3000 rpm range to avoid the propeller/piston slapping phenomenon called four-stroking. This destructive situation is easily noticed as a rough-running, throbbing condition which disappears once the throttle is advanced above the low idle range.

During flight, know the EGT and CHT limits and keep within them. A common engine cooling problem occurs when fan-cooled engines have incorrectly tensioned drive belts. Once that rubber ribbon starts slipping, it is only a matter of time before it — and then your engine — self-destruct.

Additionally, do not fully close the throttle during prolonged descents. This allows the engine to "supercool" and the plugs to foul up. Instead, leave enough power on to give approximately 4000 rpm. In a two-stroker, this is not much residual thrust, since the tuned muffler system is designed to produce almost all of its power in the 5500-6500 rpm band.

If you are in a rush to get down, Ray suggests cross controlling the rudder and ailerons to produce sideslips. By this means, expensive engine repairs and downtime can be avoided.

Another common problem is overheating due to inaccurate engine ignition timing. Frequently check to ensure that the spark is occurring at the right time. Follow the engine manufacturer's instructions for this and all other routine maintenance; it's actually fun and very simple.

Features to Look for in a Two-Stroke

Although it is unlikely we will find all the possible attractive features in one engine, let's have a brief look at the desirable traits. While a carburetor system is good, fuel injection provides easier starting and uniform mixture management.

Liquid cooling is preferred, as it reduces hot spots, thus allowing more power to be produced with tighter ring/cylinder clearances. Also, the liquid coolant acts as a barrier to the outside, thus effectively reducing combustion noise.

To reduce plug fouling common at lower power settings, and for ease of starting, an electronic ignition should be installed — preferably dual ignition with a variable spark capability to optimize power output under varying loads.

The fuel metering system should have some method of modifying the mixture changes with altitude — that is, a mixture control or automatic altitude compensator. Engines suffer significant power losses as they climb with increasingly rich mixtures.

Modern two-strokes derive a very significant power increase with tuned exhausts. A minor drawback: this effectively produces almost all of the engine's power over a band in the 5000-7000 rpm range. Yet in order to maximize the propeller efficiency, a speed reduction system such as a gearbox will need to be installed to bring drive shaft speeds into the 2000-2800 rpm range. (Approximately 30 percent of the thrust can be lost to noise and compressibility effects when props are turned at higher speeds.)

The job of having to mix oil and gas is disagreeable and prone to error for many; consequently, an oil injection system would reduce the effort and increase the safety factor.

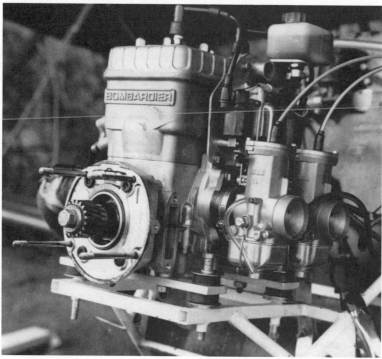

The beauty of a two-stroke, such as this Rotax 532, is its simplicity, ease of maintenance, and low costs.

For those desiring to perform aerobatics or relatively wild gyrations, consider a system that boasts inverted flying injection. (Also consider some training from an expert. See the chapter on pilot skills.)

A tuned-length exhaust is not only desirable for increased power, but also for noise reduction. There are some very quiet installations. One should get some idea of the sound pollution a given engine produces, lest it limits one's flying opportunities in a noise sensitive area. Many airports do not allow noisy ultralights to use their facilities.

Engine mounts should be of the dynafocal type or some other "nodal" design that effectively cancels almost all vibration. This avoids wear and tear on sensitive aircraft instruments — not to mention sensitive pilots.

If you wait long enough, history has shown that someone will bring to the marketplace the desired product. A case in point is the Rotax 582 engine, a much refined version of the 532, that boasts many of the attributes mentioned in this section.

Other Engine Types

Turbines, rotary and orbital models, pulse jets, turboshafts, radials, diesels, scotch yoke, Dyna-Cam, and combinations of the above offer builders a huge selection to choose from. Each claims revolutionary benefits — and each has its problems. The gripe list includes high fuel consumption, poor combustion chamber seals, leaky cylinders, high weight per horsepower, noise, and vibration.

The Search for a Suitable Engine

Look for a company with a strong history of success, especially with the model of engine you are considering. You want them to be around when you need maintenance parts or an overhaul.

Select an engine with a proven high power-to-weight ratio (better than one hp for every two pounds), and a low specific fuel consumption (SFC) at cruise in the neighborhood of .40 to .45 pounds of fuel per horsepower per hour. Typical horizontally opposed air-cooled aircraft engines have high SFC's in the .55 range.

Engines that are easily overhauled (no special tools required), are also desirable.

Relatively vibration-free operation should be ensured, and quiet operation will allow you to fly in noise-sensitive areas.

This Rotax 912 four-stroke engine produces 79 hp.

Obtain a list of users from manufacturers or dealers and determine what successes and problems individuals have had with the powerplant. Ask for suggestions to safeguard reliability and prolong engine life. Another good source of information is your local experimental builder's club.

Take courage. As more and more of these engine variations appear and are tested, we will benefit from improved performance through advanced technology. I tell many builders to go ahead and build the airframe first. By the time the project is ready for propulsion, advances in technology will likely provide a better powerplant than can be currently found in the marketplace. All you have to do is wait for it.

A Listing of Engines

In this section, we describe and list products and suppliers so that you can contact the engine sources directly. Of course, it wasn't possible to list all engines available in North America, but almost all of them that are included have proven their reliability in flight testing, or are new to the market but show significant promise for homebuilders.

All of the companies have been contacted and asked for their most up-to-date information in order to supplement the research. However, some of these offerings are so new, little is known of their reliability and the parts capability of the company. Where possible, we have attempted to ensure that the information is accurate by confirming performance with individuals operating these engines.

But the inclusion of a manufacturer is in no way an endorsement of his products or of the service he provides.

You should establish the reliability of suppliers and their products before committing to any purchases. When talking with the sales personnel, ask for the phone numbers of builders and their aircraft types, and discuss with them the engine's suitability for your project. This will help you avoid becoming an experimental guinea pig.

For additional help, contact EAA of Oshkosh, Wisconsin in the US, and RAAC of Ajax, Ontario in Canada, for a chapter in your area with individuals who can provide expert help in your selection.

Also, many of the auto conversions are complete engines with accessories from the supplier, while others simply supply the portions of the powerplant that convert the intended use from car to aircraft. Builders, therefore, have to locate suitable blocks, heads, and internal workings on their own.

Performance Automotive Wholesale. For Ford and Chevy V-6 and V-8 engines, try Performance Automotive Wholesale Inc, 21122 Lassen Street, Chatsworth, CA 91311. 818-998-6000.

Aviation Electric's V-8's. I had the extreme pleasure of flying George Morse's liquid cooled eight-cylinder 266 cid modified Oldsmobile engine during the winter. This was enough to make me a strong believer in the liquid-cooled auto conversion.

With parts commonly available at your local GM dealer, these engines promise to be inexpensive and easy to maintain. While the original 215 cid aluminum block is no longer manufactured in North America, the Rover factories in Great Britain and Australia keep turning out these lightweight engines. One of your neighbors has probably worked on the same engine.

With outputs of 200 to 250 hp, these powerplants are suitable for many aircraft. Morse's conversions are considerably more refined and thus more expensive than many, but then they are also much more optimised for aircraft use — and thus more reliable.

To give an idea of how advanced auto engine conversions can be, the following will detail some of the features on the engine that has powered the Prowler for hundreds of hours.

Twenty-one inches wide and twice as long, this V-8 has eleven drives from the Morse-designed accessory case on the rear of the engine. These drive accessories include two distributors, two water pumps, hydraulic pump, 55 amp alternator, vacuum pump, and fuel pump.

The Morse-crafted 1.67:1 gear reduction treads oil in its bath, transmitting 250 hp to the propeller while the engine cruises at 4350 rpm. Typical of the innovation in design, Muncie helical gears have been donated by a car transmission to drive the propeller that has been extracted from a Cessna 206.

Fuel is efficiently atomized courtesy of the Bendix PSH-5BD pressure carburetor and the wing-mounted coolant radiators have been liberated from a Cadillac air conditioner system and mated with Volkswagen thermostatic controls. (Why use aircraft parts, a convert asks, when automotive are cheaper and often superior?)

For those who desire 300 to 400 hp, a light Rodeck-Block Chevy 350 is now mounted in the Prowler. It should provide performance that will eclipse all of the horizontally opposed engines currently available. And on the bottom line, it will cost less than 50% of the aviation equivalent.

Remembering that cast iron is more than twice as heavy as aluminum, extensive use of the latter metal has significantly reduced this auto conversion's total weight. For instance, the 250 hp Oldsmobile F-85 tips the scales at 420 lb, including all normal accessories. (A 230 hp Continental O-470 weighs 488 lb with cooling baffles.)

The lightweight Chevy auto conversion will easily produce 350 hp and 700 lb of thrust at the propeller with its 1.67:1 gearbox reduction system. This is an increase of 73% in propulsive energy over even the converted Oldsmobile engine. Surprisingly, the Chevy will weigh less than the 488 lb fully baffled Continental O-470, yet it will produce an extra 100 hp on a lower fuel flow.

Mizell Enterprises. This company converts the aluminum block V-8 engines found on the Buicks and Oldsmobiles of 1961-1963. Although this version of the engine is no longer in production in North America, the Rover automobile manufacturing plant in England still produces this lightweight but powerful engine. Mizell takes these engines and converts them into "V-8 Specials," using a toothed-belt reduction drive or direct drive. Other alternatives include a supercharger and a gearbox reduction giving a complete systems weight of 386 lb.

Interested parties can reach them at 15749 Harvest Mile Road, Brighton, CO 80601. 303-654-0049.

Steve J. Wittman. The dean of homebuilders, and the man the Oshkosh Airport was named after, Wittman has a $30 set of plans that will allow craftsmen to build an inverted direct drive version of the aluminum block 215 cid V-8. After considerable flight testing, he has found that his version produces 130 hp at 3700 rpm with a 62" x 48" metal prop and a basic engine weight of 335 lb. This is enough power to fling his Tailwind W-8 at a maximum speed of 189 mph! Contact Steve at Box 2672, Oshkosh, WI 54901.

Geschwender. Building high performance Ford V-8s for aircraft since 1967, Fred Geschwender produces complete ready-to-run conversions only. His products use a Hy-Vo chain reduction drive or belts, and include the 2.8 liter V-6 of 230-250 hp, the 680 lb V-8 of 602 cid that produces 650 hp, and the 460 cid 430 hp V-8 weighing 735 lb without aluminum heads.

His high quality reduction systems use heat-treated aluminum and have proven their reliability in low level ag spraying operations on many aircraft. After much experimentation, he has settled on Holley four-barrel carbs and dual electronic ignition systems developed by himself and Magnavox. Fred's latest address is c/o Roth Flying Service, Route 2, Box 4, Milford, NE 68405. Phone 402-761-2322.

Engines by KFM. Actually, KFM (Komet Flight Motor) is a division of a firm called Ital-American Motor engineering of Zingonia, Italy. The company introduced three new engines at the 1981 Oshkosh extravaganza and has gained considerable acceptance since that time.

The largest powerplant is the four-stroke four-cylinder horizontally opposed 1832 cc Model 104, weighing 165 lb and rated at 77 horsepower at 3900 rpm for takeoff. Their Model 112 weighs 119 lb with all accessories and produces 62 hp at 3400 rpm. The Model 105, a two-cylinder version of the engine, produces a maximum of 39 hp or 35 at maximum continuous, and weighs 100 lb.

These powerplants come complete with full inverted systems, constant speed propeller mount, dual electronic ignition, vacuum pump, and full electrics including alternator and starter. Perhaps the most exciting news is the fact that these air-cooled engines are certified and offered by the company at prices similar to converted Volkswagens.

The Model 107 is a two-stroke two-cylinder opposed hummer that provides 22 hp at 6300 rpm. Options for this compact 294 cc powerplant include a built-in belt reduction drive and aft mounted electrics.

Designed especially for ultralights and homebuilt aircraft, the KFM engines are built by the Aircraft Motor Division of IAME at Via

Lisbona 15, 24040 Zingonia, Italy. The phone number is 35 88 30 22. The contacts in North America for the two-stroker are Wicks Aircraft Supply of 410 Pine Street, Highland, IL, 62249. 618-654-7447. Also Donald Black, 8775 Skylane Drive, Brighton, MI 48116. 313-229-6164.

Dyna-Cam Industries. This company markets a 210 hp turbine-like engine for rotary and fixed wing aircraft that can boast FAA type certificate approval Number 293. With the manufacturer claiming "vibration free operation," the 373 cubic inches produce 650 foot-pounds of torque!

Fuel injection and dual ignition provide a super-efficient specific fuel consumption of .40 lb/hp/hr at cruise settings. This is 10 to 20 percent better than most competing engines. A slim 13" diameter frontal dimension and 42" length combined with a high power-to-weight ratio of .7 lb/hp should make the engine a popular choice for high speed aircraft.

The unique design, with its six pistons servicing 12 cylinders, is said to have 50 percent less parts than other engines and 40 percent less friction horsepower. The pistons roll back and forth on a four-lobe sinusoidal shaped cam, thus producing power in both directions.

Flown successfully in a Piper Arrow, the engine is expected to be in production in the not-too-distant future, with later versions forecast to produce 350 hp (1100 ft/lb torque turbocharged) and 450 hp (1400 ft/lb turbo/intercooled). Replacing a 200 hp Lycoming in the Arrow, Dyna-Cam claims their engine installation was 40 lb lighter and took less than half the space. The company also states that the engine was able to turn a very wide blade prop with ease, due to the diesel power and torque that is inherent in this engine.

Since the power shaft has 12 power pulses per revolution compared to three in a conventional six-cylinder engine, the stress loads are 50 percent less and the powerplant "produces much smoother and quieter operation" according to the company. A two-stroke diesel design is also undergoing evaluation.

For further details on this amazing engine, send $50 for their video and technical data kits ($55 for addresses outside the US). Additionally, $10 can be sent for an complete investment info pak. Dyna-Cam Engines is located at 105 N. Irena Ave., Unit 1, Redondo Beach, CA 90277. 213-543-2917.

Kawasaki Motorcycle Engines. The TC 440A is a 72 hp liquid-cooled engine weighing only 82 lb. It boasts high quality engineering using modern materials, electric start, and a streamlined configuration. For those requiring more thrust, the Hitachi turboed engine found on the Kawasaki 750 cc bikes is a real screamer. Complete with altitude- and temperature-compensating spark and fuel injection systems, this engine is well suited for aviation use.

For those looking for a smaller, air-cooled engine, the TA 440A produces 38 hp and has been well proven on ultralight aircraft. Contact your local motorcycle emporium for availability.

Rotary-Aero Technologies. After three years of R&D, this company has developed two aero conversions of liquid-cooled Mazda rotary engines with reduction systems.

The single rotor RO-40A apparently weighs only 190 lb while producing 120 hp through the planetary gearbox at a propeller speed of 2260 rpm. The 255 lb twin rotor RO-80A, on the other hand, uses an offset chain reduction transmitting 225 hp at 3200 propeller rpm.

Burning regular car gas and including dual CDI ignition, alternators, and starters, these engines burn from 4.5 to 7 gph at cruise settings. Optional systems include constant speed propeller provisions and turbocharging. For details on the Aerotek engines, contact the factory at 19365 S.W. 89th, Tualatin, OR 97062. 503-692-0722.

Teledyne Continental Motors. By way of liquid-cooled engines, this major aircraft engine manufacturer has taken bold steps to improve their offerings and product performance in recent years. Continental is not only working on the Wankel with the Norton folks, but also developing a line of engines called the Voyager series — after the successful around-the-world non-stop un-refueled record-breaking flight of the Voyager, which used the liquid-cooled Teledyne Continental engine as one of its powerplants.

Current production in the IOL (injected/opposed/liquid-cooled) series includes the O-200 and the O-550, with 110 hp and 350 hp respectively. Additionally, an air-cooled version of the 550 engine produces 280 hp and can be found in the new Questair Venture kits.

A new engine, the 45 hp GR-18 has recently been found nesting in Developmental Research Corporation's Skyeye R4E-50 RPV. The exciting news about this Norton-produced liquid-cooled rotary is its 50 lb all-up weight with starter and reduction gearbox. Builders hungry for such an engine can lurk around the Hansen Airport in southern California waiting for one of these birds to fall out of its nest.

Interested readers can contact Continental at P.O. Box 90, Mobile, AL 36601. 205-438-3411.

Airboat Drive Units. Manufacturers of drive units since 1960, belt-driven models are available for ratings of 100-400 hp in reduction ratios of 1.762 to 2:1. Designed specifically for Volkswagen and GM engines, thousands of these drives are in use on air boats and other machinery. For details write R.D. 2, Box 262, Franklin, PA 16323. 814-437-3351.

Canadian Airmotive. Their 90 hp highly modified turbocharged three-cylinder engine employs triple solid state ignition, integrated carburetor heat, direct drive 20 amp alternator, Continental style engine mounts, hollow prop shaft for controllable propellers, and liquid cooling for efficiency.

Converted from an automotive design, the company says the installation burns 50 percent less fuel at cruise and weighs 100 lb less than a Continental C-85! A unique torsional vibration isolation system and a helicopter-like one way clutch apparently result in a very smooth power spectrum. An integral cam drive reduction unit provides a 2.23:1 ratio. Electric start, four hardened main bearings in a four-stroke engine with overhead cam are just a few of the features of this powerplant that entered the market in December 1989.

For further information, contact Canadian Airmotive at 7400 Wilson Ave., Delta, B.C., V4G 1E5, Canada. Phone 604-946-3131, FAX 604-270-6048.

Air Drive Service Co. Bringing nine years of engine engineering experience to the market, this company has been successfully proving their three offerings in racing cars and boats.

The engines are liquid cooled with the following accessories: water pump, gear reduction, alternator, high energy capacitance discharge ignition, and electric starters. Available are a carbureted 60 hp 90 lb single cylinder version, a fuel injected twin weighing 115 lb and producing 90 hp, and a 120 hp version tipping the scales at 135 lb.

These two-stroke powerplants are the result of two companies — Air Drive and AMW — combining forces to redesign the engines for aircraft applications. Contact Air Drive at 12140 Washington Blvd, Whittier, CA 90606. Phone 415-582-3322 and 213-698-6321, FAX 415-582-0551.

Norton Motors. In conjunction with Teledyne Continental Motors, this once-great motorcycle company is working on a series of robust, lightweight liquid-cooled Wankel rotary engines for the light aircraft market. They have a considerable head start over other companies because this project began years ago when research was accomplished to find a suitable motorcycle engine for the future.

The engines are envisaged in single rotor, double rotor, and multiples thereof to produce 50, 100 or more horsepower. Because the Wankel is so compact and streamlined, cowlings would result in improved cruising speeds for existing and planned aircraft.

With the backing that Continental should be able to provide, this series of powerplants could be a main contender in the aircraft engine business if reliability and performance expectations are realized. The P64 of 90 hp, with propeller, gearbox, and other accessories, weighs in at 116 lb.

Norton can be contacted at phone number 05 43 48 01 01 or write Lynn Lane, Shenstone, Lichfield, Staffs WS14 0EA, UK.

Renault Aluminum V-6. This commonly available engine of 163 cid produces 120 hp at 5500 rpm. With its overhead cam, fuel injection, and electronic ignition, the 150 ft/lb torque peak occurs at quite a low 2750 rpm.

Those who wish to engineer their own conversions can find these quality powerplants in DeLoreans, Volvo 264s, Peugeot 604s and Renault 30s. For converted engines and belt-driven reduction systems, write to the Robin S.A. aircraft company at Aerodrome de Dijon-Val-Suzon, Dardis-21121 Fontaine-les-Dijon, France, or telephone them at 80 31 61 01.

Custom Aircraft Research and Development. Airline pilot Ed Lubitz has some low cost, simple solutions to powerplant problems in the 80-100 hp range. Because his engines are perfectly (dynamically) balanced during production, they are virtually vibration-free, relative to standard air-cooled production aircraft engines.

Readily available — and certainly affordable — auto engine conversion parts and plans for Ford 1600cc Escort, Fiesta and Pinto engines can be obtained from Custom Aircraft. The company says "the heart of our unique installation is the timing belt reduction unit which lets the stock engine run at an efficient rpm while it keeps the prop working in its best range, below 2000 rpm." Lubitz wryly states that "it is attached directly to an unmodified Escort engine which Ford has been kind enough to spend several million dollars developing into the highly dependable and efficient powerplant that you can find at your local Ford dealer or perhaps even in your own driveway."

Twenty-one pages of plans are available for the conversion, as are the following products for those who wish to avoid machining work: basic drive kit, spindle assembly, distributor mount, starter and front engine mount, shock assembly, and high performance camshaft. This last item allows the engine to produce a conservative 100 hp at 5000 rpm while turning the 74" propeller through the belt reduction at 2000 rpm.

At 270 lb dry, Ed admits that "we are paying a weight penalty by using a standard auto engine." However, the low cost, and relatively easy modification steps, make this type of installation very attractive to aircraft with adequate clearance to swing this prop size.

Interested? If so, give Mr. Lubitz a call at his hangar: 519-648-2176 or home: 519-653-8307 to receive friendly facts on his ten years of trouble-free flying with this installation in his Pietenpol Aircamper. Or write to RR #4, Bright, Ontario, N0J 1B0, Canada.

Diverse Mechanical. This four-cylinder four-stroke in-line liquid-cooled Hawk AE engine includes all accessories, produces 40 hp, and weighs approximately 100 lb. It would be suitable for lightweight aircraft and for owners who have low fuel consumption and miserly operating costs in mind. For further details, phone Walt Costa at either 714-737-4230 or 714-970-6601.

Lou Ross. Lou and his sons Chris and Matthew have shipped over 40 auto conversions for installation in Lancairs, BD-4s, Sidewinders, Zenair Zeniths, Mini-Imps, Q-200s, GP-4s, Taylor Birds, and Kestrel aircraft, to name a few. Most of their publicity to date has surrounded their flying Mooney/Mazda rotary conversion and the planetary gear box reductions they will construct to suit builders' installations.

The patriarch, Lou, is the tool design engineer and machinist. He states, "Ross and Sons has accumulated valuable information that we wish to share with all those who wish to avail themselves of our experience." Business has expanded so rapidly that they have recently moved to a new 3400 sq ft production facility in an attempt to keep up to the flow of orders.

They are even prepared to help builders select a suitable engine/drive combination. Phone to obtain pertinent and important details for your installation.

Ross and Sons provide conversions and gear reductions for three Mazdas: the two-rotor 12-A (optionally turbocharged) and 13-B, as well as the single-rotor version of the 13-B. For those who are concerned that a rotary turning 5200 rpm is prone to failure, the Rosses point out that the actual rotors are only turning at 1733 rpm. This is due to the internal gearing of the Wankel engine design that has the output shaft rotating three times faster that the rotors.

Recent negotiations with Jim Feik and Will MacKenzie of Flight-Motor Systems have resulted in the construction of an all-aluminum

4.5 liter Chevrolet V-6 engine. This relatively light but high powered powerplant would be suitable for large and very fast aircraft.

Ross and Sons are also providing completed conversions for the following engines: Buick V-6; and Ford V-6; Buick/Olds 215 cid V-8; Subaru four-cylinder liquid-cooled (82 hp and 92 hp with high compression, and 115+ hp with turbo); BMW two-cylinder air-cooled; BMW k 5 liquid-cooled three-cylinder; Honda Civic four-cylinder; and the k 100 BMW four-cylinder of 75 horse power. Incidentally, that last engine, the 75 hp BMW, uses a 3.17 reduction ratio or 2.17 for reverse direction drive.

The Ross family seems to be filled with boundless energy in their efforts to convert suitable aero engines for homebuilt use. As if to prove this philosophy, Lou has recently begun to market his four-cylinder Bourke "Scotch-Yoke" engine and planetary reduction drive plans and components as well.

For further information contact Ross-Aero at 3824 East 37th Street, Tucson, AZ 85713. 602-747-7877.

Revmaster Aviation. These folks have been supplying bored and stroked VW engine conversions with controllable pitch propellers to homebuilders for many years. The 145 lb 75 hp R2100 employs dual Bendix magnetos. Accessories at extra weight—and extra cost—include starter, flywheel, alternator, oil cooler, turbocharger, constant speed prop, vacuum pump, and fuel pump. (The total for the appendages listed exceeds 70 lb.)

Using the Rev-Flow injector carburetor and 100 avgas, the engine is rated at 1000 hours before overhaul. Details are available from Revmaster at PO Box 2084-7146, Santa Fe Avenue East, Hesperia, CA 92345. 619-244-3074.

Corvair Auto Engine Conversions. Four-stroke six-cylinder air-cooled engines were produced on Chevrolet Corvair Cars from 1960-1969 with normally aspirated outputs of 80-180 hp. Souping-up these powerplants can produce another 60 hp and turbocharging results in 300 hp. The latter, with gearbox reduction, weighs less than 250 lb.

For more information on this engine series, send $10.95 for Richard Finch's book "How to Keep Your Corvair Engine Alive" to Finch Books, 340 Birch Street, Titusville, FL 32780. For information or plans on building an inexpensive gear reduction for Corvairs, contact Bud Rinker at 169 El Sueno Road, Santa Barbara, CA 93110.

Sport Plane Power. By the time you read this, the company may have its 100 hp BMW motorcycle conversion off the road and in the air. This four-cylinder liquid-cooled engine is well known for its reliability and long life during operations on the highways. The fact that a number of companies are converting this engine is an indication of its potential. To contact this operation write to 3659 Arnold Ave., Naples, FL 33942. 813-775-2214.

Bede-Micro Aviation. This is another company that is supplying Honda Civic conversions, in this case for BD-5 aircraft. The 1200 cc turbocharged engine weighs approximately 180 lb complete with all operational systems. With a claimed 85-135 hp, depending on the version, these engines have provided reliable power for dozens of BD-5s. 1484 Carmel Drive, San Jose, CA 95125. 408-293-3023.

Mosler Motors. Mosler supplies its its two- and four-cylinder four-stroke engines of 35 to 82 hp to a wide range of homebuilders and airframe manufacturers, from ultralights on up. The MMCB (Mosler Motors Counter Balanced) two-cylinder powerplant evolved from the now-defunct Global engine, but the manufacturer states that it is "a completely different animal." In the fall of 1990, the 35-hp engine won a variety of medals in the Ultralight World Championship Competition held in Hungary by the Federation Aeronautique Internationale. Contact Mosler at 140 Ashwood Road, Hendersonville, NC 28739. Phone 704-692-7713, FAX 704-692-2008.

Orbital Engine. Causing quite a sensation at its 1989 Oshkosh introduction, this revolutionary engine uses an orbital combustion process that is claimed to reduce carbon dioxide emissions by 30 percent, nitrogen oxide by 80 percent, and carbon monoxide pollution by 90 percent.

The company is converting a closed GM plant near Tecumseh, Michigan to produce this powerplant that it says will qualify for clean air emission restrictions anywhere in the world. Further, the company states the three-cylinder design has a much improved fuel efficiency approaching the 50 percent level. No address or phone number on this company was available at this writing.

Arrow Engines. Using a basic core, the Arrow series of air-cooled geared engines varies the horsepower from 34 to 110 by varying the number of cylinders from one to four. Additionally, they have marketed a conversion of a Moto-Guzzi four-stroke twin V with an output of 55 hp.

This company is looking to broaden its market penetration, with the result that we can expect to hear about new products from them in the near future. The US distributor is Arrow America,2965 Carrier Ave., Sanford, FL 32773. Phone 407-321-2372.

Emdair/Westlake Engines. The horizontally-opposed Emdair CF-112 A/B with dual ignition has recently been introduced to the market with an integral epicyclic gearing that provides a propeller rpm of 2500 while the engine turns at 3600. Who says you can't have your cake and eat it too?

This design results in a reasonably high power output, since horsepower is a function of rpm, while ensuring the propeller can be efficient due to its relatively low tip speeds. The CF-112 and CF-092 air-cooled powerplants have been designed to meet "the full international airworthiness requirements, namely the European JAR-E and US FAR Part 33."

Both powerplants are four-strokers based on the same basic design. The CF-092, previously rated at 70 hp, has been uprated to 100 hp with the addition of a front case supercharger that supplies air directly to each cylinder. A third engine in the lineup, the F-150A, is rated at 90 hp.

The group sports such features as dual electronic ignition, fuel injection, built-in electric starter, four valves per cylinder, plus drives for a diaphragm pump and 35 amp alternator. The rotational direction is standard anti-clockwise rotation (viewed from front). Only the exhaust muffler and 12-volt alternator are optional extras. The engines weigh from 112 to 130 lb.

The CF-092 has been flying in DeVore Aviation's Sunbird since October 1987. With its compression ratio of 9.5:1, high octane unleaded or 100 LL avgas is necessary (fuel consumption: 3.6 gph at cruise). The CF-092 measures 15.8" in length, 27.5" in width, with a height of 19.6".

Contact Howard L. Allmon of Flite-Lite Inc., PO Box 3187, Miami, FL 33159-3187. 305-472-5863. Or visit them at their shop at 3775 NW 145th St, Blvd 411, at Opa Locka Airport. Internationally, Emdair Ltd. is located in England at Harbour Road, Rye, East Sussex, TN31 7TH, phone 0797 22 34 60, FAX 0797 22 46 15.

Gobler Hirthemotoren. The Hirth family began aircraft engine manufacturing in 1930 and even produced engines under license for Continental Motors as early as 1952.

Firm believers in the benefits of air-cooled engines, Hirth uses four technological advances to provide high power output while still providing good reliability. The Nikasil process molecularly converts the inside five thousandths of the cylinder with a very tough coating that prolongs engine life. Chrome steel crankshafts, refined exhaust port design, and newly designed pistons of superentectic alloy contribute to a maximum operating cylinder head temperature of 320 C (608 F). The "high squish" design cylinder heads also contribute to the very high power output of these light weight powerplants.

Let's look at some specifics. At the top of the model line is the four-cylinder horizontally opposed F 30, producing 110 hp at 6500 rpm on 11 gph fuel flow. A detuned version of the F30 produces 95 hp (DIN) at 5700 rpm and 87.8 ft/lb of torque on a fuel consumption of 7.5 gph. The cruise consumption based on 70 hp would be 5.4 gph according to the charts.

Other engines are as follows: the 25 hp F22, the 30 hp 263, the 40 hp F23, the 55 hp 2703, and the 70 hp 2705. All of these powerplants include a 123-watt alternator system, relay and rectifier, electric start, exhaust manifold(s), spark plugs, intake manifold, fuel pump, and customs and brokerage fees from Edmonton, Alberta, Canada.

Accessories and their approximate prices are as follows: single tuned exhaust system, $132.50; belt reduction drive system, $294 for F22 and 263 or $337 for others; engine mounts, $40; recoil starter, $125; dual fuel pump $24; propeller adapter hub for 75 mm circle, $53; and direct drive hub $45.

As far as popularity is concerned, over 100,000 of the 260 series have been produced, and hundreds have been installed in gyrocopters and single-place aircraft including self-launched gliders.

The 95 hp 80 lb version of the F30 is strongly recommended for the BD-5, as it mounts readily in the small, confined engine compartment and is adequately cooled thanks to the high temperature capability of the Nikasil cylinders. Total installed weight with all accessories in BD-5 is 108 lb. Many readers will recall that Jim Bede had hoped to power his BD-5 kits with a Hirth engine until contract arrangements fell through.

Apparently, contact with the factory is not recommended. However, their address is Postfach 20 Max Eyth Strasse 10, Benningen, West Germany, phone number 071 44 60 74. The distributor for North America is Hirth Engines International, 21 Airport Road, Edmonton, Alberta, T5G 0W7, Canada. 403-454-2547. This company also lists prices on cog belt reductions for many auto conversions.

Ateliers JPX. This high quality series, based on the Volkswagen four-stroke horizontally opposed engine has been certified in Europe and is installed in numerous production aircraft. The company also produces a series of air-cooled engines comprised of singles and horizontally opposed twins, of up to 26 hp.

The factory is located at Z.I. Nord, BP 13, 72320 Vibraye, France. The North American Distributor, Zenair, is located at Huronia Airport, Midland, Ontario, L4K 4K8, Canada. 705-526-2871.

Lycoming. This listing couldn't be considered complete without mentioning this major supplier of generally reliable aircraft engines — although they're relatively expensive compared to automotive powerplants. With ratings of 115-425 hp, these engines will be attractive to builders of medium or large aircraft who want well-proven products — regardless of cost.

This is not to say that a run-out engine in very good condition can't be a best buy.

For instance, a 200 hp IO-360 that has been removed by a commercial operator at the TBO might be a very fine investment at a few thousand dollars. For those of you who feel this type of powerplant should be at the top of your shopping list, contact the company for further product information and prices for the more expensive factory-remanufactured or new engines. Their address is Williamsport, PA 17701. 717-323-6181.

Limbach Engines. An excellent and mature company, Limbach started with the basic VW engine and improved it so much that there is very little left that is VW.

Limbach's "conversions" have accumulated thousands of flight hours in hundreds of aircraft types. They are so reliable that they have been certified in Europe under the Joint Airworthiness Regulations JAR 22 (similar to FAR 23 in the US). According to the company, "Virtually all modern European-built, commercial industry, motorglider aircraft have been Limbach powered". The German craftsmen have been machining these marvels for over 25 years and have chosen in the past to make the engines more efficient and reliable rather than using stroking and other stress-related techniques to produce torque.

Herr Peter Limbach uses the finest quality materials and components, designed mostly by his son and chief engineer for the company, Peter Limbach, Jr. Limbach states that "engine heads, cylinders, pistons and crankshafts, as well as other critical engine parts are made to Limbach design specifications by some of the very best suppliers from Germany and elsewhere."

The dive in value of the American dollar relative to many other currencies, however, has resulted in a rather expensive engine. Nonetheless, prospective purchasers should consider the ratio of the dollar versus the engine quality in their decision making.

At any rate, four-cylinder four-stroke horizontally opposed engines are available in three series: 1700cc, 2000cc and 2400cc. They produce 56 to 90 hp. Their stroked L 2400 EB1 type-certificated model produces a continuous rating of 84.5 hp at 3000 rpm with its Stromberg-Zenith carb sipping 3.5 gallons of 96 octane fuel hourly. A Hoffmann variable pitch propeller is also available for this 181 lb single magneto version.

Limbach Aircraft Corporation is reached at P.O. Box 1201, Tulsa, OK 74101, 918-832-9017, or at the factory: Limbach Flugmotoren GmbH & Co. KG, Kotthausener Strasser 5, D-5330 Konisgswinter 21, West Germany, phone 022 44 23 22.

Konig Motorenbau. While not as popular as the Rotax engines, these air-cooled ultralight powerplants are well known for their fairly quiet, relatively vibration-free operation. Available in 24 to 48 horsepower versions, this series offers builders high power output at low weight. Contact the factory at Friedrich-Olbricht Domm 72, 1000 Berlin 13, West Germany for further details or call 493 03 44 30 71.

Javelin Aircraft Company. David Blanton has been working with aircraft for decades, and during the last 12 years has become a very outspoken advocate of the liquid-cooled auto engine for aircraft. His Ford conversions are flying in such diverse aircraft as a BD-4, Glasair, RV-4, Prescott Pusher, Thorpe T-18 and Sport Racer, to name a few. By mid 1988, 480 builders were installing Blanton's 230 cid V-6 in their homebuilts. Of these, 42 are for four-place Cub-like aircraft, 22 for Defiants, 21 for T-18's and 19 for the ever popular BD-4 design.

His current projects are the Model 116 of 125 hp, essentially a 1.9 liter Ford Escort engine, and the Model 230V6, a 3.8 liter Ford powerplant. For the latter, Blanton originally claimed 260 hp, but has reduced this to 230. Independent dynamometer tests have indicated that the engine is actually capable of producing about 190 hp. The V6 is available with conical, bed, or beam mounting.

A recent addition to his offerings is a beam-mounted Model 351V8 capable of 380 hp. Additionally, Blanton provides plans and toothed-belt reduction parts to customers for the many Ford conversions that his company supports. Reductions for the above noted engines are 2:1 for the Escort (this is the only recommended ratio) and the 230V6 driving a McCauley MFC 8467 propeller for seaplanes.

For high-speed aircraft, the V6 calls for a 1.6:1 reduction that yields a propeller rpm of 2625 at takeoff and 7.7 gph fuel flow at a cruise speed of approximately 200 mph. The 2.82:1 ratio is used to turn four-blade propellers on replica fighters with beam or bed mounts. In the case of the big V8, a 2.25:1 reduction is used for ag or high speed aircraft using beam mounts. A "hi-drive" version is available for aircraft such as the Spencer Aircar.

According to Blanton, these auto conversions require very little modification for aircraft operations. After all, the reasoning goes, if the engines were safe enough to take our families to church, they should be suitable for our recreational flying. As far as the technology and desirability of the V6 is concerned, the Canadian engine factory produces more of these engines in a month than an aircraft engine manufacturer produces in a lifetime!

Incidentally, Ford's "slimline" supercharged fuel-injected V-6 will be capable of 310 hp to cruising altitudes. This could produce some very high cruising airspeeds in some of the very sleek aircraft currently on the market.

For further details, contact the Javelin Aircraft Company Inc. at the Municipal Airport, Augusta, KS 67010. 316-733-1011

Bombardier-Rotax. With considerable experience in ultralight aircraft, Rotax is becoming a major contender in homebuilt aircraft powerplants. These two-stroke engines can gloat over their very high power-to-weight ratios. They have the added benefit of optional "tailor-made" gearboxes in varying ratios that multiply the torque and thus the effective thrust of the propeller.

While the engines must be kept tuned to avoid internal damage, for the builder/flyer who loves to tinker and overhaul his engine after approximately 300 hours, these machines are an excellent, low-cost alternative. With a user base of thousands of operators, Rotax has done a commendable job at increasing the time between overhauls by continually modifying engine problem areas as they are discovered.

The excellent selection ranges from 18 hp to 79 hp. Some pilots have been surprised at the high fuel consumption of these two-strokers. However, Rotax has been perfectly honest in their power-vs-fuel-consumption charts. To obtain the high power output, an air-cooled engine requires a considerable "burn rate" in order to aid the cooling process. Even the 64 hp liquid-cooled two-cylinder Rotax 582 uses more than 6.3 gph to produce its rated horsepower at 6500 rpm. The charts indicate that cruising at a conservative 5500 rpm will burn 4.4 gph and produce 52 hp.

Readers should note that Rotax publishes this data without the air silencer or exhaust system attached in the case of the 582. The old saying "you can't have something for nothing" comes to mind.

Muffled and silenced air-cooled engines include the 277 (19 hp), 377 (26 hp), 447 (35 hp), 503 (36 hp), and the 503 2-V (approximately 42 hp). The engine packages come assembled with integral fuel pump, exhaust system, rewind (manual) starter, and oil tank in the case of liquid-cooled engines. Options include air intake silencers, electric starters, five gear box ratios, muffler, propeller hub, rectifier-regulator, radiator, and shielded spark plug protectors.

Relatively new to the market are the 537 (97 hp) liquid-cooled snowmobile engine and the brand new 912, displacing 1200 cc. The 537 is a modified 532 that produces rated power at 8000 rpm and includes an oil injection system. However, the former distributor, Ron Shettler, advises that the powerplant is a snowmobile engine and therefore not optimized for aircraft use. Then there's the 582, an advanced 532 with oil injection and dual ignition.

The four-cylinder 79 hp four-stroke (yes, you reliability enthusiasts, I said four-stroke!) 912 is the first Rotax specifically designed for aircraft; it weighs only 132 lb with all accessories. The company plans to certify this powerplant so it can replace all of those older, expensive Continental and Lycoming engines that are becoming rare. With a 75% cruise consumption of four gph, these rather revolutionary engines will overcome previous objections to the fuel-guzzling habits of air-cooled two-strokers. Look for a turbocharged version to be available soon.

By the way, the 912 liquid-cools the heads while air-cooling the remainder of the engine. This minimizes weight and provides a high power-to-weight ratio of .6 hp/lb. (Not bad for a four-stroker.) The use of a dry sump lubrication system allows builders to mount the engine at various angles.

Benefits of the series are their relatively low purchase price and the very low cost of parts for overhauls. Incidentally, there are excellent books and videos available showing how to inspect, tune, and rebuild these easy-to-work-on powerplants.

The factory's address is Postfach 5, A-4623 Gunshkirchen, Austria, Phone 072 46 27 10. The sole distributor for North America is R. Shettler Enterprises Ltd, 901 Kal Lake Road, Vernon, B.C., V1T 6V4, Canada. 604-542-4151.

BEC Aircraft Engines. This company's first engine, called Stage One, is to be normally aspirated, fuel-injected, dry sump lubricated, and capable of 160 hp at 6500 rpm and 150 ft/lb of torque at 5000 rpm. The forecast "wet" weight of 370 lb includes reduction gearbox, starter, radiator, coolant, oil, and exhaust system. While this may appear to be rather heavy, with a ratio of 2.3 lb per horsepower developed, future Stage Two through Four Wankels will be turbocharged to produce better ratios.

Benefits claimed for the BEC engine are: smallest frontal area of any engine in the horsepower class, fewer moving parts to fail, lower vibration levels, relatively low overhaul costs, a TBO exceeding 2500 hours, and liquid cooling to avoid large operating temperature variations. The 18-inch diameter Stage One engine is 28 inches long. The company hopes to be able to obtain STCs in the future to install the Wankel on factory-certified aircraft.

BEC staff wooed builders at Oshkosh with a converted Mazda 13B rotary that produced 190 hp at 6300 rpm on a dynamometer. There is an ongoing search for funding for this project, and at this writing the engine has not flown.

For further details phone 619-232-3341 or write to P.O. Box 2060, Chula Vista, CA 92012.

Outboard Motor Conversions

A number of builders are being propelled through the skies with outboards in the 125 to 140 hp range. In fact, the older RotorWay Scorpion helicopters used a four-cylinder 140 hp liquid-cooled outboard.

The benefit of these powerplants is their aluminum construction, allowing high power output for light weight. They often feature an individual ignition system for each cylinder, such as Suzuki's 140 hp 1773 cc quad ignition scheme. It seems that the Suzuki and Mercury outboards are the most popular for conversion. For further details, visit your local outboard dealer.

10

Should You Use Auto Gas?

It's a Controversial Subject

Perhaps, like me, you have been amused, confused or confounded by the conflicting claims and alarms of proponents of mogas (automobile gasoline) versus avgas (aviation fuel). Let's first examine a few facts that are often masked by the considerable amount of hype published on the topic.

Some Fuel Facts

Leaded auto gas and "marked" — or "purple" — leaded outboard motor gas are all the same fuel, plus or minus dye for coloration.

Aviation gas is a different animal, but not by much. Before the second World War, there was a great deal of difference between automotive and aviation fuels. Back then, mogas was a relatively unstable mixture of hydrocarbons. Avgas was produced by catalytic cracking and Alkylation with the result that a superior, more stable concoction emerged.

Throughout the '50s and '60s, mogas improved to the point that it matched the octane ratings of aviation fuels. In the early '70s, the superior auto fuels known as "unleaded" were introduced after the naphtha reforming process was developed, allowing refineries to provide highly stable hydrocarbons with octanes equivalent to 80/87 avgas.

Essentially, the major difference between the two fuels is that mogas has more volatile additives to improve starting. This results in a fuel that will be more susceptible to carburetor icing and vapor lock compared to avgas. These additives may also be injurious to certain seals in your fuel system.

Because greater amounts of these "aromatic additives" are added by refineries in the cold months to improve starting, if you are going to use mogas in your aircraft, it would be best to use summer blended fuels throughout the year; less of the harmful additives are blended in during the warmer months.

Having said all that, it is necessary to add that I have only heard of a few high performance engines having problems with vapor lock — on hot days in tight cowlings — and this could likely be avoided with insulated fuel lines.

Homebuilt planes legally can use whatever fuel they choose, because they're experimental aircraft. However, it is always best to hedge one's bets. I recommend that, if possible, you conduct ground and flight tests to ensure that full power is being developed with auto fuel. Incidentally, you'll do well to use the "marked" gas for your plane if you can buy it for less; why pay an automotive road tax to fly the aircraft?

If your aircraft has two tanks, I recommend that you initially fill one tank with auto fuel and the other with aviation fuel. During flight, after temperatures and pressures have stabilized in cruise, switch tanks and record any changes in engine performance, temperatures, and pressures. If the auto fuel works perfectly well under all weather and flight parameters, there is no sense in paying up to 100 percent more for aviation gasoline.

There is a great deal of misleading or incorrect information in print concerning fuels currently available. The only way you will feel secure about using mogas will be to know the details involved in octane rating, fuel additives, vapor lock, and the possibilities of carburetor icing.

Octane Rating

The octane rating of a fuel is a numerical indication of its ability to resist detonation. Detonation is the destructive force that occurs when the fuel/air mixture spontaneously ignites before the spark plug fires. This uncontrolled explosion puts very heavy stresses on all of the engine components, from the pistons to the crankshaft. Valves can also be damaged if they're in the wrong portion of their travel as the unplanned explosions occur.

Detonation can be caused by a hot spot in the cylinder that acts as an ignition source (perhaps a glowing carbon particle), or it can be caused by low octane fuels igniting on their own when the compression/heating stroke occurs. The wildly expanding flame-front and gases pound down on the piston, which is trying to move up inside the cylinder. In cars, you hear this as a rattling or "pinging." This is your warning to back off of the accelerator and/or buy a higher octane fuel.

However, in the noisy aircraft environment, you won't hear the pinging, and thus you will be unaware of the destructive forces unleashed in your engine. So it is necessary to ensure that the fuel you use has adequate octane for all flight parameters before start-up.

To further complicate the matter, there are two methods of measuring the octane rating: the Motor Method (MON) and the Research Method (RON).

Because the RON method results in a number about 10 units higher than the MON, the former was used exclusively in advertising until the government insisted that the average of the two methods should be used. The averaged number is now called the AKI (Antiknock Index). This means that the same fuel of yesteryear has a rating about five points lower at the pumps today. Incidentally, avgas octane measurements are similar to the MON method.

As a matter of record, when the EAA checked unleaded mogas around the country in their intensive undertaking to obtain STCs for it, the average MON was 83.7 — well above the aviation engine requirements for 80/87 rated engines. (In fact, no mogas exists in the US with a MON of less than 82.) In the EAA's tests, the 80-grade avgas always detonated before the mogas did.

By the way, unleaded fuels are considerably cleaner and relatively free of contaminents compared to leaded fuels. This is yet another benefit to their operation in aircraft.

To vary these AKI ratings, gasoline manufacturers use additives such as TEL (Tetraethyl Lead), MTBE (Methyl Tert-Butyl Ether), alcohol, and other witches' brews they concoct in their laboratories.

Let's have an in-depth look at the well-known and commonly used "index improvers."

Tetraethyl Lead (TEL)

TEL has all but disappeared from mogas, with levels down to 0.1 gram per gallon or less in "leaded" mogas. Aircraft fuels still have much higher amounts of TEL, from 0.5 to 4 grams per gallon. This lead has a tendency to deposit itself on the valve seats during engine operation.

While this may sound terrible, it has the great benefit of acting as a cushion between the pounding valve and its seat. The large reduction of lead quantities in the so-called "low lead" aviation fuels has resulted in early failure of valves in many aviation engines when pilots switch from normal 100 to low lead 100 (100LL).

Running aviation engines at high power settings—and compared to cars, all airplane power settings are relatively high—and using unleaded fuels can greatly increase valve seat erosion, or recession. This is sufficient to destroy cylinder heads in as little as 100 hours of operation. Lower power settings, say 65% cruise or less, will increase engine life 100% to 600%. In case you wonder why cars and other modern engines have no problems with the unleaded fuels, it's because they have induction-hardened valve seats.

Unfortunately, most of our aircraft engines are ancient in design and construction, and because we use such a small amount of fuel compared to the national car fleet, the oil refineries no longer consider us important enough for them to blend a fuel that would be really perfect for our heavier-than-air machines.

Continuing the saga on low lead aviation fuel, a Texan friend operating a Continental O-300 that was designed for 80/87 fuel has been having valve failures due to excessive lead deposits that occur with the much higher lead content found in so-called low lead 100. These deposits can prevent the valves from fully closing, with the result that hot exhaust gases burn out the seats and valves.

Incidentally, adding TEL to gas does not increase the AKI in a linear manner. In other words, the first gram increases the octane rating considerably, the second gram less so, and anything after the third gram results in a minimal increase in the index.

Just to round out the fuel question, if you are operating a two-stroke engine in your aircraft, go right ahead with the unleaded fuel, as that powerplant has no need for lead.

Other Questionable Fuel Additives

As TEL amounts have been reduced in mogas, other additives have taken its place. Manufacturers make many claims about the gas improvers; however, most should be taken with a grain of salt, according to independent tests.

Prior to extensive flight testing, it was believed by some that the olefins, such as ethylene, would create gummy deposits in the fuel system. However, it appears that this hasn't occurred. The only significant question is what the AKI or octane rating is.

One major factor that should be of concern to aircraft owners is the effect of some of the "aromatics" added to the fuel to help it vaporize more readily. Some of these rather active ingredients can be very detrimental to the sealing compounds used in aircraft fuel tanks. This problem is reduced due to improved sealing products now on the market that are resistent to auto fuel. Before sealing your tanks, ensure that the compound is impervious to current mogas, perhaps by performing your own tests on a sample sealed joint.

Another ugly additive is alcohol. While few companies presently use this additive, their numbers seem to be growing. Alcohol is a cheap way to add to the octane rating; surprisingly, it raises the RON more than the MON.

Because alcohol has only half the energy of straight gasoline, it effectively leans the fuel/air mixture from optimum levels. This then requires the carburetor mixture to be enriched to provide good starting and adequate power at full throttle, which results in poorer fuel economy. As if this weren't bad enough, it also attracts water and causes corrosion of metal carburetor parts and fuel tanks.

Moreover, alcohol causes swelling and deterioration of synthetic rubber compounds such as are found in pumps, carburetors, and fuel lines.

Other car gas additives can include corrosion inhibitors, carburetor detergents, anti-oxidants, and chemicals to control deposits on intake valves. While these compounds are not specifically named in the standards or specifications published by each manufacturer, their benefits would appear to outweigh the fact that they are not identified.

Vapor Lock and You

The more volatile a fuel is — usually due to additives — the higher the vapor pressure. As atmospheric pressure decreases, the vapor pressure increases.

As a result, hot climates or high altitudes are more likely to increase your chances of vapor lock. This occurs when the gas effectively boils and the resulting air can no longer be pumped by the fuel system. A degree of fuel starvation, varying in severity, will then occur in the engine, resulting in lower power or complete engine stoppage.

This tends to be more of a problem on the ground on hot days, in heat soaked engine cowlings, and occasionally at altitude in tightly cowled installations where the fuel lines are not able to be cooled adequately by the ambient airflow.

Because gravity feed systems do not need to suck fuel with pumps, they are less prone to vapor lock. The bubbles that might form have a tendency to flow up the lines where they dissipate in the tanks. Logically, a pressure fuel system would be best if the pump were mounted in the tank pushing fuel to the engine, instead of an engine-mounted pump that could end up trying to suck air.

Other methods of avoiding vapor lock are to insulate any fuel lines within a few inches of the hot engine, along with the use of anti-syphon check valves.

Reid Vapor Pressure (RVP) is the measurement used to determine volatility of a fuel batch. It is simply the pressure exerted by a measured volume of an air/fuel mixture at 100° F. The higher the percentage of light hydrocarbons such as pentane and butane, the higher the RVP.

The maximum allowable for avgas has been 7 psi ever since the standard was established. (Incidentally, the standard was set in error as recounted by S. D. Herron when he was investigating engine malfunctions in the USAF many years ago. It turns out the problem was carburetor icing, not vapor locking.) Auto fuel RVPs average 10-14 psi in the winter and 8-10 in the summer.

During their auto fuel flight testing, the EAA team conducted their trials at altitudes as high as 22,000 feet. To ensure a worse than possible scenario, AMOCO prepared a special batch of super-volatile car gas with an RVP of 16. The aircraft engine performed flawlessly, with the test pilot reporting that it was no rougher than normal 100 LL aviation gas. Since an RVP of 16 is well beyond auto gas blend limits, it is unlikely that aviators will have this type of problem with mogas.

Moreover, the two engine stoppages that happened during the hundreds of hours of EAA testing occurred when the aircraft was operating on 100 LL aviation fuel!

As mentioned earlier, gas blended for winter operations in cold climates has a greater amount of volatile additives and therefore should not be used in warm weather. It is also worth noting that the RVP drops with storage, vibration, temperature changes, and simple aircraft refueling. It is unlikely that you will ever be able to find a fuel sample with a vapor pressure at the top limit.

A Formula for Safety

If you are concerned about using a given batch of fuel and if you know what the RVP is, then you can use a guideline calculation developed by Al Hundere of Alcor. The formula to determine the safe outside air temperature in degrees Fahrenheit is: Temperature = 120 -[6 x (RVP-7)]. Thus, a winter sample of motor gas with an RVP of 14 would be safe up to a temperature of 120 -[6 x (14-7)] = 78° F. A summer batch with an RVP of 10 would be safe and stable for use with OATs up to 102 degrees F.

The success story continues for the use of mogas in aircraft. The CAA in Great Britain approved car gas up to 6000 feet in 1982, Australia has followed suit, and even the ultra-conservative DOT of Canada has stuck its neck out with a trial flight test program for factory aircraft. Auto fuel is already legal in homebuilts, although DOT prefers aviation fuel in aviation engines.

Well, Should You or Shouldn't You?

The temptation to use mogas instead of avgas is great — especially considering the substantial savings in operating costs that can be realized. According to EAA, it has worked well for a large number of aircraft owners. On the other hand, some pilots have reported problems. As always, you're the captain, and it's your call. If you decide to go the mogas route, keep these considerations in mind:

1) Ensure that the fuel has an equivalent or higher octane rating than required for your engine.

2) As a general rule, use the unleaded super grades of fuel. They are also cleaner.

3) Avoid prolonged high power settings. This technique will increase valve seat and cylinder head life.

4) Never use fuels that may have alcohol added.

5) When possible, use fuel blended for the hot weather months with lower RVPs, thus reducing the possibility of carburetor icing and vapor lock.

6) During construction of the aircraft, use fuel cell sealants and fuel lines that are impervious to auto fuel.

7) Be sure that your fuel system — particularly carburetor seals — are not susceptible to swelling or disintegration in car gas solutions. There are ADs and SBs that can be checked for this information.

8) All fuels should be filtered when being added to the aircraft tanks to avoid water and other contaminants.

11

Those Black Boxes

Choose the Radios That Fit Your Flying Style

Years ago, when I was the sales manager and chief pilot for a Cessna sales organization, it amazed me to see our customers ordering transponders, marker beacon receivers, audio panels, ADF, DME, ILS, and double nav/comms for planes that lived on farm strips and were never flown into busy airport environments.

When asked if they knew what the avionics accomplished, they invariably shrugged. When asked why they wanted these expensive arrays, they indicated that they saw them in the brochures or a friend had all that gear hung around the cockpit of his Baron.

These good folks didn't need a lot of fancy avionics for the kind of flying they were doing.

On the other hand, if you're planning to fly IFR, or even VFR into busy terminal areas, you might want to go the whole nine yards. Just be sure you have the panel space – and the budget – for whatever electronic goodies you fancy.

You will be selecting the type of plane you intend to build or buy in accordance with the kind of flying you intend to do. I suggest that you use the same sensible approach in choosing the radios and other equipment that will be on board your craft.

Basic Boxes

For those of us who have cash flow limits, not to mention an instrument panel smaller than the Space Shuttle, we will have to be selective with our purchases. Miniaturization allows the avionics systems of today to be half the size and twice as capable as yesteryear; ditto the relative prices. For strictly sunshine flying in low-density areas, I recommend a starter set with three basic pieces: a communications transceiver, a loran, and a transponder.

The Comm Transceiver

This is the most likely unit for you. Even if you don't fly into control zones, a comm radio will be very handy for obtaining weather, as well using unicom frequencies for airport advisories and traffic reporting.

For those on the strictest of budgets, or flyers of planes with no electrical system, a handheld VHF transceiver might be the answer. Except for their lower transmission power of 1 to 3 watts, they are as capable as, and sometimes more multi-featured than, the units that live in the panels of many planes. Many of the portables even have VOR navigation capability. However, a recommended option is an external antenna that will allow you to double or treble your radio's range, compared to the rubber ducky it comes with.

The handhelds, priced in the $300-600 range, save panel space as well as money. Models are offered by Bendix/King, Narco, ICOM, and others. Sporty's Pilot Shop markets an inexpensive house brand.

However, panel-mounted radios are more convenient to operate, and there are some compact units that are easy on the panel space. These include the Terra TX 720, Bendix/King KY 96A, and Val Com 760. Prices range from about $800 to $1,200. (Note that in all cases I refer to list prices. Discounts are readily available.)

Loran

Now, here is a real handy-dandy Long Range Navigation (LORAN) device that makes a pilot look good.

Forget about the line-of-sight problems common with VORs and DMEs, forget the bent legs, inaccuracy and tuning hassles of ADF, forget the maintenance costs involved with those systems. Loran has the answers. Distance to checkpoint, heading to checkpoint, groundspeed, time to go, all this and more, instantly calculated! The loran will graphically show you how far you are off the predetermined track and will display a new heading to fly for a direct track from your present position.

It seems there is nothing a loran can't do. However, good airmanship dictates that the pilot follow the navigation proceedings with a chart, in case the loran goes on vacation at an inappropriate time.

An additional caution: not all lorans are certified for IFR use. If flight in instrument meteorological conditions is your desire, choose carefully.

II Morrow's Flybuddy loran is one of the lower priced panel-mounted units that features a database..

For owners of more than one aircraft, or folks who share their avionics with others, there are portable lorans, listing at around $500 to $750, from Voyager and Azure Technology. Most of the panel-mounted sets are standardized at 2" high by 6.25" wide. These are offered by such manufacturers as II Morrow, Foster, Northstar, and Bendix/King, at prices ranging from $1,500 to nearly $6,000. The more expensive sets have databases containing the locations of airports and navaids, as well as other information.

VOR

Since the USA and southern Canada are laced with VOR transmitters, pilots of experimentals might want to consider a receiver in a nav/comm unit, if funds permit. This would provide a backup to your loran, and crosstrack reference information during navigation. Unfortunately, VOR transmitters are seldom located exactly where we want to go, and while we thought they were great years ago, loran's capabilities have eclipsed the VOR's popularity. Nevertheless, for instrument flying you will need at least one VOR receiver.

Transponder

A descendant of Selective Identification and Friend or Foe systems from the second war, this little black box responds to primary radar signals from the ATC system on the ground, to identify you and your position. With mode C capability, even your altitude is painted on the operator's radar. If you are planning to penetrate the growing web of TCAs, you will need a mode C transponder to protect you from the sting of the spider (FAA or DOT). New and used units typically cost $500 to $1,500.

ADF

If you fly in the northern three quarters of Canada, or just like to listen to the radio while obtaining navigational information, you might want to invest in an ADF. Modern units are one third the weight of the older units with the motor driven loops. Personally, I'd rather carry a Walkman unit and a few good tapes directly plugged into a portable intercom, and navigate with a map and/or loran.

In Conclusion

Unless money is no object, don't get caught up in an envy-driven frenzy to surpass the expenditures of your aviation neighbors. Analyze your travel itineraries and your planned penetration of terminal control areas, and buy only the radios you require.

Dick VanGrunsven and his prototypes RV-4 and RV-6 are a good example. He carries the minimum radios and flies all over the States to demonstrations and air shows. Part of the reason that the RV series is so fast is the light weight of the structures—the minimum of anchor weights in the panel.

The author flew his BD-4 across Canada and the US with a "one and a half" nav/comm, then delivered his Stinson to Alaska with nothing more than a comm. I'm saving my money for my next experimental and honing my navigation skills instead of buying expensive avionics.

You may have a different view. If you like bells and whistles, and have the money and panel space to satisfy your desires, there are moving map displays, weather and collision avoidance systems, and other sophisticated equipment to command your interest.

A couple of final thoughts: To give your radios a long and happy life, provide ample cooling. And bear in mind that your life could depend on your avionics functioning reliably, especially if you fly IFR—so if you're not an aircraft electronics expert, find a good avionics shop for your installation.

Section Three

Flight Evaluations

– 12 –

How They Really Fly

The Author's Impressions

The following pilot reports will allow readers to assess various aircraft types and their suitability as a project or personal plane.

The evaluations are organized alphabetically by manufacturer's name, followed by the model name(s). If you want to look up a particular model and don't know the manufacturer's name, check the index in the back of the book, where you'll find, for example, "Venture. *See* Questair Venture."

For your convenience in determining quickly which designs are offered as kit and plans, kit only, and plans only, we've categorized the various models in Appendix E.

Regarding Performance Claims

Each flight evaluation is followed by a chart that details the various performance parameters as specified by the factory. In my own flight evaluations, I may have reached different conclusions. And remember that variances in building skills will often produce considerably different numbers in speed and empty weights. Few builders are able to obtain the low empty weights claimed in the charts after they have added avionics and personal equipment.

Also, pilots may be hard pressed to safely match the takeoff and landing distances given by the manufacturers, as most of them do not do not include an obstacle clearance factor.

Unlike production aircraft, homebuilts have few standards that allow for reliable comparison, because the designers might be using different parameters. For instance, one aircraft might have its maximum level airspeed shown in the chart as the "Top Speed" while another might publish its diving velocity never exceed (V_{ne}) as the top speed in the charts.

Engine Variations

In some cases, the charts show alternate engines. This will allow you to single out the powerplant that will best suit your performance needs. Keep in mind, the power output of many of these engines is the maximum possible. The deletion of tuned exhausts or addition of air filters or forced air cooling fans can reduce output significantly. As mentioned in an earlier chapter, the use of overly coarse propeller pitch will also reduce the power — and perhaps overload the engine.

Pirep Criteria

Construction materials and design goals, as well as construction and flying difficulty, are assessed in the pilot reports to provide you with the facts you need in your decision making. This information, followed with your own interviews of builders, pilots, and the factory personnel, will allow you to make an excellent project choice.

All prices are in American dollars and measurements are in pounds, feet, inches, US gallons, and statute miles per hour. (While airspeed stated in knots is now the accepted standard for production aircraft, the homebuilding fraternity still seems more comfortable with mph.)

Of course, the author and publisher have attempted to validate all information provided. However, it is very likely that changes have taken place in this dynamic industry since this book went to press. For this reason, as well as other factors I have mentioned, we cannot be responsible for the accuracy of the specifications.

Companies that have not been cooperative in providing information have been judged as poor in support and been eliminated from the listings. However, the absence of a manufacturer or its planes does not mean that either is not up to the standards set for these evaluations. It simply means the author has not yet had the opportunity or pleasure of flying those products.

Finally, you will notice that the evaluations vary in length, due in part to the differing complexities of various designs as well as the amount of background information provided by each company on its products.

Aces High Cuby II

A Cub-Like Homebuilt

Cor Wester first displayed his dazzlingly finished two-place side-by-side at the Toronto Sport Expo in 1988, and later reassembled the aircraft in approximately one hour at the London Ontario turf strip for my evaluation. This aircraft was designed by aircraft maintenance engineer (A&P in the US) Al Jasmine of Calgary, Alberta, Canada. It is a rugged but lightweight (360 pounds empty) taildragger that has been static tested to a stress factor of +4 and -1 G. The factory will completely build the ultralight version at extra cost in Canada.

While powerplant options from 42-64 hp exist, we flew with the 42 hp air-cooled 503 for our flight test.

The Cuby II was much easier than most Cub-like homebuilts to get into, and gave better-than-average comfort in the bucket seats mounted in a 38" wide cabin. A very large baggage compartment aft of the seats would be suitable for almost any amount of possessions — within the weight and balance limitations, of course.

The twin-cylinder two-stroke Rotax started readily and idled smoothly above 2000 rpm. Taxiing was accomplished with zig-zag turns for improved visibility on a bungee-restrained conventional gear that transmitted all of the contours of the turf to my rump. The brakes were designed at Cor's Aces High company and were able to hold the aircraft at up to one-half to two-thirds throttle.

Takeoff was accomplished in 300 feet at an indicated airspeed of 30 mph. The climb-out was steep enough to leave the spectators' mouths agape.

I'm pleased to mention that the delightfully balanced rudder was smooth and linear in response — the best I've felt in an ultralight or homebuilt. Controls were moderately light, but the aircraft requires an elevator trim system — added to subsequent kits — to "unload" the stick over the Cuby's speed range. (The company now provides elevator trim plans and materials.) Considerable force was required to overcome the tail-heavy feeling at anything but descent power.

At 2100 feet and 60 degrees F, we indicated 65 mph at 5000 rpm and 75 at 6000 rpm with the standard 68 X 32 laminated maple climb propeller. Visibility was generally good, and stalls occurred at 25 mph indicated (factory specifications claim 30 mph), with no apparent pre-stall burble or buffet. The actual break was a non-event as the nose gently and slowly lowered itself slightly below the horizon. Ailerons remained effective.

Having no flaps or other drag-producing devices, we resorted to the time-proven sideslip to steepen our approaches, up to 1200 fpm. Touch and goes in the Cuby were so much fun that several abbreviated circuits ensued, with a half dozen landings accomplished in ten minutes.

With a claimed payload of 600-640 lb, its short field performance, improved brakes, and a large baggage area, this homebuilt seems quite attractive at a complete kit price of approximately $11,900, depending on the current rate of exchange. Additionally, the Cuby has proven very successful on skis and floats for the bush pilots in our midst.

The Cuby's wings fold back for easy towing and storage.

Varied options make the Cuby II versatile for use on land, water, and snow.

Specifications

Aces High Cuby II

KIT PRICE:	$9,163
NUMBER OF SEATS	2 side by side
BUILDING TIME	approx 1000-1500 hrs
ENGINE TYPE	Rotax 42-64 hp
RATED HORSEPOWER	50 Hp Rotax as tested
EMPTY WEIGHT	360-400 lb
GROSS WEIGHT	1000 lb
USEFUL LOAD	600 lb
TAKEOFF DISTANCE	200 ft (300 off water)
LANDING DISTANCE	300 ft
CRUISE SPEED	70-75 mph
TOP SPEED	85 mph
FUEL CAPACITY	5-10 gal
RANGE	150-300 sm
REMARKS	Steel tube and fabric construction

Performance figures provided by the factory

The Commanders

What's it Like to Fly a Gyroplane?

The airshow crowd was amazed as the Commander Elite executed precision maneuvers beyond the capabilities of the other show performers. Knowing that my gyroplane training was about to begin in her, I was both enthralled and apprehensive at what appeared to be dangerous feats. Later that day, the capabilities of these unique aircraft would prove that the airshow demonstration was well within the gyro's normal flight envelope.

According to Air Command's founder and former president, Dennis Fetters, "The FAA certifies the gyroplane to be *structurally* the safest in general aviation," based on Dr. Benson's gyrocopter designs of yesteryear. These craft "have the perfect record of no structural failures causing accidents in their over-30-year history." Further, he states the Commander has also been upholding this claim. (To be sure, there have been pilot-induced accidents; more on that shortly.)

Are Gyroplanes Popular?

Safety, low cost, and minimum runway requirements have made gyros so prevalent that they are almost fashionable, with over 1000 of the Air Command gyros sold by the factory in the last five years. If that isn't popularity, what is?

In an attempt to understand this craze, I went flying with the president and chief demonstration pilot. Decades of commercial flying in rotary and fixed wing aircraft did not fully prepare me for the fascinating blend of characteristics experienced during my first gyro flight. In many respects, it combined some of the best characteristics of both types of flying — albeit with a few minor drawbacks.

Fling Wing Safety and Construction

Designer Dennis Fetters personally demonstrated the Rotax 532-powered Commander Sport with its optional enclosure fairing.

Although the aluminum framework with its stainless steel "instabushings," plastic inserts, and rotor blades is the same as on the 447 ultralight single-place, the additional weight of the larger engine puts the two-place in the experimental category.

As we were preparing for our introductory/instruction flight, Fetters cautioned that no one should ever try to fly a gyroplane without instruction. After our half-hour episode, I agree. If you were to crossbreed a helicopter and a fixed-wing aircraft, the flying characteristics that would result would be a blend of both parents, yet quite unique in their own right.

The very forgiving engine-out glide, short field landing capability, and slower speed of the gyro should make it a very safe aircraft. However, a fairly high accident rate has historically been the norm.

A close look at the statistics shows that most crashes have been a result of inadequate training or pilots flying beyond the gyro's flight envelope. In other words, the prangs were avoidable. Fetters feels the recent introduction of economical, efficient two-place gyros for instruction will drastically reduce the accident rate.

The designer uses a potpourri of materials to optimize the benefits of each.

We were able to easily preflight the Commander as all components are readily visible—no requirement to remove 40 cowling screws to inspect this engine. The McCutcheon rotor blades are made of E and S glass with a leading edge aluminum spar. While they are balanced at the factory, adjustments—including tracking—are easily accomplished by minor changes to the four bolts that hold the blades on the hub. Having pre-flighted numerous types of blades in the past decades, I was delighted to note the high quality of these offerings.

Equipped with the optional $528 prerotator with its rubber engine-pulley drive and basic rotor brake, this version has the capability of fast spool-up and deceleration of the fling-wing system.

Does Something This Homely Fly, or Does the Earth Repel It?

Because the engine pull-cord was mounted behind the cockpit, it was easier to start the liquid-cooled Rotax before strapping in. Settling into the roomy cockpit with full dual controls and side-by-side seating, we fastened the long seat belt that crossed both occupants. The intercom and helmet system removed most of the Rotax's cacophony, allowing Fetters to fill in the gaps in my understanding of gyro characteristics.

I was delighted to note that the stick and rudder pedals did not work in reverse to helicopters or fixed wing aircraft, as some companies' gyros do! Imagine trying to reverse your control instincts after hundreds or thousands of hours of automatic inputs.

The direct-connect nosewheel steering was very accurate and easy. The left hand throttle controlled the engine/propeller rpm and thus our taxi speed. Eventually, we reached the distant ultralight runway threshold where the joystick-mounted motorcycle handle was gently and increasingly squeezed to increase friction on the prerotator system.

This clutch-like device slowly accelerated the rotor to the 200 rpm used for takeoff distance reduction. According to the published specifications, the takeoff run without the prerotator engagement requires an additional 467 percent of ground run. One can often see prerotator-less gyro pilots reaching up to spin the blades by hand to reduce the takeoff distance. This can be somewhat exhausting.

Advancing the throttle to maximum initially resulted in the Rotax bogging down. Fetters quickly aborted the demonstration takeoff, complaining that this had never happened before. A suggestion that it was not uncommon for these two-stokes to load up after prolonged idling led him to slowly advance the throttle to maximum, whereupon the 532 cleared itself and we commenced our run again.

"A 150-Foot Roll is Possible"

Because the rotor is tilted aft, the relative wind racing through the blades caused them to accelerate quickly. At 45 mph we rotated the nosewheel off the ground with gentle aft stick, and the gyro lifted off in a gentle climb after a 500-foot run. Fetters claims a 150-foot roll is possible under ideal conditions with normal sized pilots and a well-tuned engine. Due to a rotor system phenomenon called "flap-back," a little forward pressure was necessary to overcome the tendency to nose-up over-rotate.

With a rate of climb that may have approached 500 fpm we worked our way up to pattern altitude, climbing at 45-50 mph. During turns, we had to lower the nose to ensure we didn't lose too much airspeed, thus negating some climb performance. Speed control is of paramount importance in gyros. Go too fast or too slow and the aircraft won't climb.

The 13-lb enclosure fairing eliminated almost all of the slipstream, and the visibility was as good as, or better than, that found in dozens of helicopters. As a matter of fact, it gave me that "no visible means of support" feeling. Steep turns to the right initially made me wonder why I hadn't worn my parachute. With approximately 1000 hours on gyros, Fetters made perfectly balanced turns, overcoming my fear of being skidded out of the cockpit to oblivion below.

My Turn

When it was my turn (no pun intended), I found the controls were light and responsive without being overly sensitive, basically a blend between helicopters and planes.

The addition of the $695 fiberglass fairing with its balancing horizontal stabilizer streamlined this Commander enough to add 20 mph to the normal 45 mph cruising speed. "The fairing has reduced control sensitivity in all axes, making it better for student training," declares Fetters.

The maximum throttle speed produced a noisy, fuel-guzzling 75 mph. However, all-out speed should not be much of a consideration to gyro pilots, who are more likely to be attracted by the simple freedom of flight.

Helicopter-Like Procedures

Departing the circuit, we cruised out to an open field, where my instructor demonstrated the true maneuverability of the Commander without creating consternation around the airport. Vertical power-off autorotational spins, and sideways and backwards flight were only a few of the helicopter-like procedures that Fetters was able to perform.

Because the unpowered rotor system is always being driven by the relative wind, it was necessary to maintain a minimum speed of about 18 mph in level flight to keep our wings rotating at an adequate speed to maintain lift. In descending flight, the airflow rushing up through the blades was able to give us a parachute-like descent, but the rate would be too high for the structure to sustain in a vertical sink to touchdown. Contrary to popular belief, even helicopters avoid lengthy vertical descents because rotor systems are less efficient with no forward speed. Airflow through the disk, as a result of forward speeds of 10-15 mph or so, produces approximately 30 percent more lift in typical rotorcraft.

Thanks to rubber isolation mounts, properly placed for maximum damping, the engine vibration was so muted that I have no recollection of sensing any. However, a one-per-rev vertical vibration indicated the blades were not quite flying in the same geometric plane. This out-of-track condition is common in helicopters, giving the crew a little vertical jiggle every time the rotor system makes a gyration (approximately 300 times per minute).

This can be easily eliminated by making a small adjustment at the rotor blade attachment point, according to Fetters. Of course, one would have to know which blade to slightly lower or raise to be in track with the other. Apparently, the blades are perfectly balanced (laterally) during manufacturing to preclude the possibility of a side-to-side jiggle.

Knowing that the black poly-painted frame was designed for 9 G impacts, we confidently returned to the circuit to sample my first landings. Turning final at cruise speed, then reducing the throttle to a medium idle (to stop the engine's spark plugs from loading up), caused the speed to drop off quickly to the minimum approach speed of 45 mph. The nose had to be lowered a great deal to maintain speed, giving a visually steep approach.

Coincidentally, this provides a strong airflow into the autorotating blades, storing up a great deal of kinetic energy for the landing flare. While this high-drag glide seems somewhat challenging, the actual touchdown is very elementary and gentle.

Just Level Off

Unlike a helicopter, where the autorotative flare requires a great deal of manual dexterity and judgment, the gyro needs simply to be leveled off just above the ground, whereupon the speed and rate of descent quickly decay, to give a feather-like touchdown at approximately 10-15 mph in a calm wind.

The rotor system, strongly tilted backwards, acts as a very effective air brake in the flare and after-landing roll. This allows the gyro pilot to land in a very short distance. In fact, this type of aircraft can be landed in a small percentage of the distance required for takeoff. Repeated landings and takeoffs were elementary and somewhat similar to "running" operations in wheeled helicopters. This running takeoff/landing technique is commonly used, even on skid-equipped choppers, when their loads are too heavy to permit hovering operations.

Using wheel brakes to constrain our momentum, Fetters reached overhead to the rotor hub, flipped a small teflon tab against the mast, and over a period of a minute or so, this basic, reliable system dragged the rotor blades to a gentle halt.

One of the biggest differences in the Commander gyroplane compared to the typical helicopter is the absence of "time-lifed" parts on the Commanders. The use of Oil-lite bushings (oil-impregnated brass) results in an "inspect and replace if needed" form of preventative maintenance.

This allows monumental financial savings, not to mention a reduction in the effort required to keep the machine serviceable. Helicopters typically average six hours of maintenance for every hour flown when overhauls are included! With their freewheeling rotor system, it would appear gyros would require only slightly more effort than fixed wings to be kept serviceable.

Conclusions

The blend of rotary and fixed-wing characteristics seems to have produced the best of both worlds in many respects. With short field and slow flight capabilities approaching helicopter performance, combined with operating costs and maintenance requirements that are closer to fixed wing, these modern gyroplanes have a lot to offer.

If aerobatics and long range cross-country flights aren't your bag, you might want to consider these aircraft that gave birth to modern-day helicopters.

In the past, there were such drawbacks to this product as a mediocre construction manual, absence of an operations manual, and substandard customer service. There has since been a change of ownership and we hope that these problems are being rectified.

The new company is offering one- and two-place Commanders with a variety of Rotax and Arrow engines.

Specifications

Air Command Sport Dual Commander

KIT PRICE	$7,600
BUILDING TIME	28 hrs
NUMBER OF SEATS	2 side by side
ENGINE TYPE	Rotax 582
RATED HORSEPOWER	64
EMPTY WEIGHT	347 lb
GROSS WEIGHT	750 lb
ROTOR SPAN	22 ft
TAKEOFF DISTANCE	150-700 ft
LANDING DISTANCE	0-30 ft
CRUISE SPEED	55 mph
TOP SPEED	90 mph

Air Command 532 Commander Elite

(Performance specifications are for the one-place version)

KIT PRICES	$6,800 one-place
	$8,495 two-place
BUILDING TIME	28 hrs
NUMBER OF SEATS	1, or 2 side by side
ENGINE TYPE	Rotax 582
RATED HORSEPOWER	67
EMPTY WEIGHT	275 lb
GROSS WEIGHT	775 lb
ROTOR SPAN	22 ft
TAKEOFF DISTANCE	100 ft
LANDING DISTANCE	0 ft
CRUISE SPEED	65 mph
TOP SPEED	110 mph
FUEL CAPACITY	9 gal
RANGE	195 sm
REMARKS	Info kit $10

Performance specifications are a combination of those observed and factory claims.

The Avid Aircraft Series

The Intrepid Birdman

Within a few days of qualifying for his private pilot license 21 years ago, Ray Fletcher bought a Cessna 170 and flew it across Canada to his ranch. However, requirements of his expanding cattle operation kept him hog-tied with work (so to speak). Having no further use for the factory-built, he sold it after three years.

But steer-spotting requirements and the ultralight revolution led Fletcher into purchasing his second aircraft, a Lazair. He found the lightweight twin perfect for local, low-speed, low-altitude herd reconnaissance. However, his need for a go-anywhere sport aircraft that had reasonable cross-country capability as well as rough field potential led him to the Avid flyer at the Light Aero Inc. factory near Boise, Idaho.

Fletcher was so impressed with company president Dean Wilson that he not only bought an Avid Flyer, he also took on a dealership for Western Canada and sold more than 500 aircraft in seven years. Fletcher spends much of the rest of his time farming in the mountains of British Columbia's heartland.

You might say that Ray Fletcher is the type of man this aircraft was designed for — he goes everywhere in it and uses it for almost everything.

His photo album has one picture of his Flyer parked on a rock-strewn mountain meadow at the 6500 foot elevation. What is unusual is that the aircraft is mounted on wheel-less skis that Ray designed — and there's no snow in the photo! (It all melted during his overnight stay on the meadow). "The first 50 feet of the takeoff roll was a little rough," he says, "but once the wings started lifting, it smoothed out and she was off in 150 feet."

After that, Ray never took the wheels off the aircraft when ski flying. With their two inches of "penetration", there is no appreciable speed penalty leaving the wheels on, and he never knows what type of terrain will greet his next landing.

He built his own lightweight, aluminum box-channeled, Teflon-bottomed skis because nothing was available that would fill his requirements. With caps on the end of the channels, the structure can be used for storing fishing equipment or whatever. Ray tells me he has now landed on a glacier at the 8200-foot level and is looking for a higher conquest.

You can believe that Ray really knows his snow operations, as he states, "Reckon I've got more ski experience than anyone on ultralights." The Light Aero factory has now followed suit and has designed their own skis for $525, using steel channeling.

The Basic Plane

The Avid Flyer prototype first flew in 1983. Since then, many more have graced the skies with their constant improvements. Current factory shipments include the liquid-cooled 582 of 64 hp, although purchasers of older models might have the Cuyuna or Rotax 503 air-cooled engines.

For this evaluation, we flew the heavier, but more powerful, Rotax 532 Avid Hauler variant that Fletcher has just completed after years of flying his old Cuyuna-powered Avid Flyer.

They are available as six partial kits, and there is no crating charge when they are all ordered together. The wing kit comes with jig-drilled spars, stiffeners extension tubes, routed and glued plywood ribs, fiberglass wing tips, aircraft quality AN hardware, adhesive, rivets, primer paint, nitrate dope, and the construction manual. "Construction of the Avid is straightforward," Fletcher says, "with the ribs easily sliding over the spars, for instance."

While the company publishes limit loads of +3.8 G and -1.5 G, the wings have actually been statically loaded to +5.7 and -2.25 at the gross weight of 911 lb—lots of safety margin there.

The fuselage is 4130 steel tube with control system and door frames all welded. The rest of the package includes floorboards, firewall, butt ribs, rod ends, rudder cable, and AN hardware.

The tail group is comprised of welded 4130 steel tube, and the engine kit includes the carbs, gear reduction, air filters, mount, muffler/exhaust systems, radiator, hoses, clamps, header tank, surge tank, fuel pump, fuel lines, water temp gauge, regulator/rectifier, choke and throttle cables, propeller, spinner, cowling, and all fittings.

Finally, the finish and cover kit includes all the fabric system materials, seat belts, upholstered seats, shoulder harnesses, speed fairings, decals, etc., in short, everything except the final paint, an option left to the builder.

There is no crating charge when the Avid Flyer kit, complete with the 64 hp Rotax, is bought at the same time for $12,395 to $13,995, depending on the model.

Building time varies from 200-400 hours, depending on the quality of the craftsman's skills and choice of aircraft finish, according to Fletcher. In a reversal of the usual understatement of factory-claimed completion time, the company estimates 500 hours for completion.

New Options and Advances

The Avid Hauler was "conceived to meet the needs of those who desire to use the Avid as a traveling airplane, cable of carrying enough fuel, people weight, and baggage a reasonable distance." According to the factory, this hauler can carry a useful load of 660 lb. Heavier spars, fuselage, landing struts, wing struts, and more ribs have strengthened the structure enough to allow a gross weight of 1085. This increase in payload of 150 lb comes with the cost of a three-mph higher stall speed, a somewhat longer takeoff, and a reduced rate of climb when operated at gross.

To allow maximum utility for the Hauler and other Flyers, options include increased fuel capacity of 28 gallons and a detachable belly-mounted fiberglass cargo pod. The $595 streamlined pod, mounted at the center of gravity, is five ft long, two ft wide, 15" deep and rated for 200 lb. For $3,150, farmers can buy the pod with a 45-gal agricultural spray system that includes spray booms, nozzles, pump, valve and fan assembly.

Some quick weight calculations indicate that one would have to buy the Hauler version of the Avid Flyer, in order to carry this 450-lb or heavier payload — with minimum fuel. Of course, spray pilots wouldn't have to fill the chemical tank's reservoir to capacity. Nonetheless, the useful load of pilot, spray rig, fuel, and spray chemicals should not exceed 660 lb.

At sea level with the standard temperature of 59 degrees F, the Hauler would require 625 ft of runway to break ground and 885 ft to clear a 50-ft obstacle during gross weight operations.

While these runway requirements are considerably longer than you might expect, when the load and utility of the Hauler at gross is considered, this is excellent performance for the few dollars invested.

The Avid Flyer is very versatile on amphibious floats.

Optionally, for $2,095, a clipped "speed wing" is available that stalls five mph higher at 40 indicated, but produces 100-110 mph at cruise. Owners of the speed wing can, for an extra $525, purchase reinforcements to the tail section, wing and lift struts, all of which will make the Avid Flyer suitable for mild aerobatics.

Fiberglassed-foam 12-chambered floats at $2,095 are frequently requested options that reduce the cruise speed only two mph. However, at 50 lb each, they reduce the useful load by 65 lb with the landing gear removed. According to the factory, the Flyer gets off the water in one-third the distance of a 150 hp Piper Super Cub!

Let's Fly

The walk-around inspection was easy on Fletcher's Hauler, thanks to speedily removed access panels with cam-locks or Dzus fasteners on the cowling. Inspecting the large low-pressure 8.00 x 6 tires and their Cub-like bungee suspension was also straightforward.

The taildragger version has the axles moved forward three inches to reduce the possibility of nosing over during heavy braking.

The series have had their cockpits widened from 36" to 40.5" — a vast improvement. Adjustable slings on cushioned seats allow for wide variations in pilot height. The stainless steel rudder bars mounted on the birch plywood floors can also be moved to accommodate a wide variety of leg lengths. Lexan window panels provide very good visibility in all flight regimes. Additionally, the doors can be opened in flight and locked up against the bottom of the wing for increased ventilation or photographic missions.

On the latest model, the fuselage fuel tank has been replaced with a right wing fiberglass cell holding 18 gallons. Removable dual controls are standard, with the throttle in the middle of the shock-mounted instrument panel. Mechanical toe brakes are located on the left side only, and the stick controls activate push-pull tubes and bell cranks with ball bearing rod ends. Hydraulic disc brakes are an option.

The control installation static feel was very light and relatively friction-free. The Junkers-style full-span ailerons are also full-span flaps. The geometry of this system is such that the wings fold flat against the fuselage with the "flaperons" rotating upwards 90 degrees without the need to disconnect any controls!

Factory kits come complete with the liquid-cooled Rotax 582, with its 2.58:1 gear reduction driving a high efficiency 71" wood propeller. The Bosch flywheel magneto/generator apparently produces 140 watts of power at 12 volts to supply most electrical needs. An engineless partial kit is available at approximately $6,945, for builders who have their own engine.

Clear Prop!

The liquid-cooled engine started readily on the regular car gas mixture after a yank on the cockpit-mounted pull cord. Idling at 2000 rpm, we taxied towards Arlington's ultralight runway during their 20th anniversary fly-in. Ground handling, visibility and sound level were very good.

After completing the pre-takeoff check, the throttle was firewalled, the joy stick was pulsed forward to lift the tail, and almost immediately pulled back to produce a very short takeoff, consisting of a 200 foot roll into a 10 mph wind, followed by a very steep climb. (We were 300 lb under gross.)

As spectators awaited the impending stall, we ascended through pattern altitude at 1000 fpm and 46 mph before reaching the end of the 2000 foot runway! Our repeated steep climbs were eventually quashed

Even Avid Flyers powered by the small Cuyuna engine can climb at very steep, sustained angles.

by the airport manager, as he felt the demonstration of such remarkable ascents must be unsafe and a bad example to set for others who might attempt the same feats with lesser aircraft.

The cabin sound level was quieter than in the old air-cooled Cuyuna Avid Flyer, but the use of an intercom and headsets is recommended for good cockpit communications. The controls were light and quite responsive, making the Avid Hauler easy to maneuver in the confined valleys that Fletcher flies from. At the same time, the stability was more than adequate for cross-country flying.

While the 90-degree-per-second roll rate won't challenge the Pitts Special, it was very good for an aircraft designed to go places. Adverse yaw was plentiful, requiring generous use of rudder to initiate and roll out of turns. This trait was common for decades in aircraft, and simply requires a little pilot skill to produce smooth, skidless turns.

Leveling at 2500 feet with an OAT of 54 degrees F (12 C), full throttle produced 85 IAS, only five mph below the V_{ne} red line. Throttling back to 5500 rpm gave 75 indicated with a fuel flow of approximately 3.0 gph fuel consumption.

For the low end, we selected the first five degrees of flap at 70 mph and the full 35 degrees at 50 mph, with the stall coming at 35 mph indicated after a very light buffet. Standard recovery procedures resulted in minimal loss of altitude, even in aggravated attitudes. Horsing the Flyer around at low speed during stalls showed no ragged-edge characteristics.

Returning to the airport, Fletcher set up such a high approach, it seemed impossible that he could land on any part of the runway, never mind the displaced threshold.

Then the bottom fell out of the sky. Reducing the power to a high idle and selecting full flap, Ray pushed the left rudder pedal to the firewall and moved the stick to the extreme right. I was almost looking straight down in one of the most outrageous sideslips I have ever experienced.

Later, ground-bound spectators told me the aircraft seemed to fall out of the sky—sideways! Our glide path approximated that of a greased crow bar or a submarine with screen doors.

As he leveled the wings on short final, Fletcher had to add power to make it to the runway, a fact I found hard to believe. With such incredible approach control at one's foot/finger tips, coupled with low touchdown speeds, landings were easy and smooth.

Excellent braking and tailwheel steering make the after-landing roll both short and sweet. One small idiosyncrasy is the tendency for the tailwheel to touch first if one holds the Hauler off till the approach of the stall. However, this is no problem, as it is a very strong structure.

After our flight, Fletcher and I folded up the Avid Flyer for highway transport, and connected it to his trailer hitch in about ten minutes. He tows the rig at 50-70 mph, depending on the road conditions.

Conclusions

Considering the well-proven design, high quality construction materials, broad versatility, and large performance spectrum, this aircraft is a best buy for operations out of rough airfields. Compare, as the Light Aero folks like to do, the short field feats to a Super Cub's. Now compare the prices! With a saving of tens of thousands of dollars, most of us would be quite happy to invest a couple of weeks of our time to build an Avid Flyer.

Specifications

Avid Hauler

KIT PRICE	$12,795
BUILDING TIME	500 hrs
NUMBER OF SEATS	2 side by side
ENGINE TYPE	Rotax 582
RATED HORSEPOWER	64
EMPTY WEIGHT	425 lb
GROSS WEIGHT	1085 lb
WING AREA	122.5 sq ft
TAKEOFF DISTANCE	625 ft
LANDING DISTANCE	500 ft
CRUISE SPEED	85 mph
TOP SPEED	95 mph
FUEL CAPACITY	14-18 gal
RANGE	340 sm
REMARKS	Info kit $6

Avid Speedwing, semi-aerobatic

KIT PRICE	$12,195
BUILDING TIME	500 hrs
NUMBER OF SEATS	2 side by side
ENGINE TYPE	Rotax 582
RATED HORSEPOWER	65
EMPTY WEIGHT	390 lb
GROSS WEIGHT	911 lb
WING AREA	97.3 sq ft
TAKEOFF DISTANCE	125 ft
LANDING DISTANCE	500 ft
CRUISE SPEED	110 mph
TOP SPEED	125 mph
FUEL CAPACITY	18 gal
RANGE	600 sm
REMARKS	Info kit $6

Performance figures provided by the factory.

Barracuda

Willie's Wooden Wonder

Designed by Geoff Siers, a retired senior engineer with Boeing and a former RAF Spitfire Pilot, this retractable is all wood with a large engine and a very sleek profile — hence its name, Barracuda. True to its fishy namesake, this aerodyne exudes a slick, fast, predatory aura that is backed up by its performance.

The Barracuda was conceived as a fast cross-country airplane with aerobatic capability, according to Siers. Additionally, a large useful load, supreme comfort, fighter-like response and performance, and good manners at low speed were also considered desirable.

Well, Siers succeeded in his design goals.

The owner/builder of our evaluation machine, Dr. Bill Buethe, selected this aircraft type after a search for a suitable scaled-down P-51 Mustang. Powered with a 250 hp Lycoming IO-540-C4B5 from a Piper Comanche, this 2300-lb gross weight side-by-side speedster has a very high power-to-weight ratio (9.2:1) that gives strong climb performance and short takeoff capability. (Siers designed the 'Cuda for powerplants of 150-300 horsepower.)

The modified 64215 series airfoil allows some laminar flow on the gull wing and a reasonably fast cruise of 190 mph. This airfoil, the clipped wingspan of 24.75 ft, and the wing loading of 19.2 lb/sq ft, could result in a handful for beginners. However, as you will learn in our flight evaluation, the 'Cuda has no tendencies to bite.

'Cuda Construction

The wing and spar are built in three sections, with the center portion housing the main fuel cells, controls, seating, and landing gear. Outer sections are skinned with 3⁄32" mahogany over a box section spruce spar and 3⁄8" spruce ribs. The fuselage is similarly built in the "match stick" manner common with model airplanes, and is thus the height of simplicity.

Other than some welding on the 4130 chromoly steel landing gear, construction is rather straightforward. The retraction system is electro-hydraulic and the flaps are electrically actuated. After a couple of builders had a few gear problems at crucial times, it is now common practice to install mechanical linkages to allow the main gear to free-fall and the nose gear to be extended during emergencies. While the wings don't fold, two folks can remove them in less than an hour if long-term storage becomes important.

Bill Buethe's Barracuda, loaded with options as it is, weighs 1570 lb empty. 1500 lb is more typical. While I haven't seen a lot of 'Cudas at local airports, their popularity is indicated by the number sold already: at this writing, 535 + sets of plans, with more than 100 projects under construction. The excellent plans comprise 32 sheets measuring 24" x 36" and include a builder's manual.

All about Flying Fish

On a private field nestled high in a mountain valley in southern California, my wife and I found Bill washing the 'Cuda in anticipation of our gravel/dirt runway operations.

Our walkaround was easily accomplished, as N78WB stands quite high on its landing gear. This led to the problem of mounting her, since the center section flaps are not weight-bearing. One has to take a giant

Good stability and high control responsiveness make the Barracuda a very solid cross country platform.

step in order to reach the upper surface of the wing. Normally, Bill leaves the flaps down to ease the operation.

With double gullwing canopy halves open, access to the very comfortable seats can be accomplished gracefully even by ladies in dresses. The seats provide thigh support and would be very comfortable for average-sized individuals conducting flights of two or more hours.

Cabin width at shoulder level is 40" and good separation between occupants is provided by the center console with its complement of engine controls. This console has the added benefit of improved crash survivability, as protruding objects from in front of the occupants have been eliminated. A hat rack or shelf behind the occupants could hold loose articles, while a baggage compartment with 80-pound capacity is accessible via an external door. The member between the two cannot be cut, as it is a portion of the load-bearing structure.

Securing our four-point harness system and looking around the cockpit, I noted a well-stacked instrument panel that included an autopilot. Dr. Buethe files IFR regularly and considers this "Bonanza Buster" to be an aircraft for all uses. Access to controls is excellent, including the fuel selector system to the four wing tanks. In addition to the standard 21-gallon inboard tanks, Bill has installed two six-gallon outboards.

Starting the big six-banger was easy after the fuel pump was turned on to prime the fuel-injected engine. The sound level was quite low and the vibration low, too, considering the engine's size. Of course, this is partially due to the wood structure's capacity for absorbing noise and the relative smoothness of a six-cylinder powerplant.

Completing the pre-taxi and run-up checks on the paved pad, we released the parking brake and taxied uphill to the far end of the runway. Visibility was very good over the snout, and maneuverability was excellent with the steerable nose wheel.

Going Up

We applied power slowly so as not to pick up any stones or dent the shiny chrome three-blade Hartzell constant speed propeller. Nonetheless, acceleration was vigorous as we easily guided this charger with 250 ponies down the center of the field.

Unsticking at 65 mph after a 1000-ft run, and accelerating to best climb speed in the ground cushion, we retracted the gear and shot skyward at nearly 1800 fpm. At our 3000-ft altitude and 65 degree F temperature and with a takeoff weight of 2200 pounds, this is quite a respectable performance.

The landing gear typically require 6-10 seconds to tuck themselves — with the 5.00 x 5 wheels — into the deep wing, completely sealing behind the gear doors. Some owners have installed 6.00 x 6's without modifications to the wing, with the result that some of the "riggins" hang out in the airflow.

The din of the large Lycoming and slipstream were significant until Bill flipped the switch that inflates the canopy seal to seven psi. An awesome hush overcame the cockpit, negating the requirement for the headsets we had been wearing. (This retrofittable accessory is highly recommended for those having noisy canopy/fuselage interfaces on any aircraft.)

Climbing to 6000 ft for upper air work was quickly and enjoyably accomplished, thanks to the light control pressure required to elicit snappy responses in this steed that has descended from thoroughbreds. (It brought to mind the fact that Siers was involved in the Lightning fighter and Concorde transport programs.)

At Cruise

Leveling off at 24 square (approximately 75% power) the indicated airspeed settled at 185 mph whilst consuming 12.5 gph. Pulling back the "fuel drain rate controller" and setting 22" MAP and 2200 rpm resulted in a consumption of approximately 8.5 gph, and the dial settled at 140 mph. The maximum level speed for Bill's bird is 208 mph at 2500 feet. However, the fuel costs at this speed would make the national debt look like small change.

Control feel is very solid, with fairly light control pressures resulting in instant responses; in a word — fighter-like. Static pitch stability is rather neutral but adequate for monitored cross-country flight, especially with an autopilot. The roll rate is more reminiscent of a competitive aerobatic aircraft than a family homebuilt.

These control characteristics, combined with the rugged structure, make the Barracuda well suited for limited aerobatics. The rudder separation was well defined and there was very little tendency towards adverse yaw, thanks to the wise design decision to incorporate Frise-type ailerons.

Throughout the entire speed range and drag device selection, trim changes were negligible. As a matter of fact, it was unnecessary to trim from 70 mph after takeoff to 160 mph indicated in cruise. More good designing, or perhaps good luck. Bill's Barracuda was well rigged, as neither rudder nor aileron trim was necessary.

Combined with the low sound and vibration levels, these flying characteristics have led a number of builders to use their 'Cudas extensively in instrument flight conditions. As a matter of fact, Bill has been in such heavy rain, he lost a significant amount of paint on his leading edge — until he installed tape as a protective barrier.

Except under wings and engine cowlings, visibility is good. The tapered wing, with its relatively high wing loading, dampens the effects of turbulence measurably.

Undoubtedly, this would be a very fine platform for cross-country flights of 500-700 miles, depending on fuel tank options. The red line speed of 250 leaves plenty of margin above cruising speeds, and the limit loads of +8 and -4 G provide a large leeway for those who might botch an aerobatic sequence or doze off during a cross country.

Slow Flight

As you might expect from her clean lines, the 'Cuda was reluctant to slow down. Hanging the gear and flaps into the relative wind at speeds below 140 and 120 stabilized the airspeed quickly below 100 mph for slow speed handling trials.

Incidentally, Bill continues a drag reduction program that makes this aircraft sleeker every year and thus harder to slow down — not to mention faster.

The full span center section flaps are limited to 25 degrees of deflection, but they are quite effective at drag and lift production. Equally beneficial is the lack of trim requirement on their deployment.

At 80 mph indicated, she was rock solid while still light, but crisp, on the controls. Stalls were preceded by mild buffeting and moderate pitch-downs. No tendency of wing dropping for spin autorotation was noticed during numerous stalls. The clean, power-off break came at 65 and the landing configuration stall occurred at 60 mph with a smidgen of power on.

If the aft stick pressure is not applied excessively, there is no tendency to enter a secondary stall. Apparently the prototype was not spin-tested, so we skipped that portion of the program. However, if the stall characteristics are any indication, there should be no problem if a normal spin recovery technique is used.

Descending

Sideslips with maximum control deflection at 1.3 times the power-off stall speed showed a powerful rudder capable of generating abundant sideslip angles. Crosswind landings even in fairly strong wind conditions should pose no problems for proficient pilots.

Full-flap power-off sideslipping descents rival the glide angle of a brick. One has to remind oneself that putting aircraft with high wing loadings in conditions of low power/low speed can lead to final approaches with rates of descent that cannot be arrested during the landing flare.

...and Landing

With that self reminder, we turned the electrical fuel pump on and zipped back to the circuit to test the landing gear, hopefully short of destruction. On Bill's advice, speed was reduced to 90 mph with 20 degrees of flap and gear dangling on base leg. By the way, that gear snapped down and locked in a few seconds.

After a confined pattern in Bill's rather cramped valley, we turned final, subsequently crossing the threshold at 70 mph. Smooth landings followed each touch and go as I engaged in an orgy of ever-tightening fighter-break circuits until it appeared my conservative host might consider the activity excessive.

It was with great regret that I realized the flight had to come to an end. The concluding power-carrying approach led to an impressive demonstration of the braking capability of those Clevelands.

And then the plane had to be given back to her owner/builder, while I fleetingly pondered pretexts for asking for another evaluation flight. (Sometimes it's a long time between fixes for aviation addicts.)

Other Lean, Mean, Fighting Machines

The first plans-built Barracuda was completed by Jackie Yoder in just under 2500 hours. Operating at an increased gross weight of 2700 pounds, the extra 400 lb useful load allows him to fill the extended range fuel tanks and load extra baggage in the enlarged storage area. Turbocharging, 300 hp, and the use of an efficient Hartzell three-blade "Q-tip" prop results in a 235 mph TAS at 12,000 feet on 15.1 gph.

Jackie has invested $22,800 in his 'Cuda, including the zero-time engine. By way of modification, three sets of wing fences have been added to retard the span-wise flow on the low aspect ratio Hershey Bar wing. This has eked an additional 5 mph at cruise power settings.

Another builder, Dick Stiles, has $40,000 invested in his fully IFR-equipped 200 hp Barracuda. The IO-360 Lycoming flings the aircraft through hypospace at 190 mph on only 10 gph. Incidentally, Dr. Buethe warns potential builders not to use too light an engine, as the Barracuda would become tail-heavy.

Aircraft hardware and supplies are available through Aircraft Spruce and Specialty or Wicks Aircraft Supply. The former lists the complete kit for $832 and the spar kits for $506 in their catalog. Additionally, engine mounts, landing gears, engine cowlings, canopies, windshields, and rear window are available from the world-wide distributor, Dr. Bill Buethe.

Conclusions

Because this is not a kitbuilt aircraft, builders can expect to invest a lot more time (2000-3000 hours) and a lot less money ($15,000-35,000) than in a somewhat comparable kit aircraft.

Readers should also note that this design is nearly two decades old, so the performance does not compare favorably with more efficient plastic airplanes such as the Lancair and Glasair products. However, the Barracuda offers builders the opportunity to work with wood and build the complete aircraft from plans.

As a strong, comfortable, powerful, smooth, cross-country aircraft, this chariot is very well designed and relatively pilot-proof for the mid- or high-time operator. Good training aircraft for conversion to the Barracuda would include Mooneys, Grumman singles, and perhaps the Piper Tomahawk.

Because this airframe was designed to carry heavy engine options, builders might like to opt for an auto-engine conversion of the same approximate power to avoid the high cost and weight of the Lycoming engines. Imagine, a belly mounted radiator, coupled with the 'Cuda's flying qualities, would result in a low-cost, side-by-side mini Mustang. Come to think of it, it's just what the Doctor ordered.

Specifications

Buethe Barracuda

PLANS PRICE	$200
NUMBER OF SEATS	2 side by side
ENGINE TYPE	Various Lycomings (IO-540 used for specs)
RATED HORSEPOWER	180-300 (250 used for specs)
EMPTY WEIGHT	1500 lb
GROSS WEIGHT	2300 lb
WING AREA	120 sq ft
TAKEOFF DISTANCE	800 ft
LANDING DISTANCE	1000 ft
CRUISE SPEED	195 mi
TOP SPEED	220 mi
FUEL CAPACITY	52 gal
RANGE	805 sm
REMARKS	Info kit $10
	Pkg & prefab parts available

Performance figures provided by the factory.

Earthstar Gulls

An Amazing Aviary

Hidden on top of a peak in the mountainous area of west central California is an almost secret airport, and a collection of aircraft that are destined to become well known.

Perhaps even more remarkable is the "Gull" series designer, Mark H. Beierle. At first, it seemed that this was a rather young looking man to have designed so many successful flying machines. This, of course, was based on the incorrect assumption that he would have started designing and building in his twenties at the earliest.

Wrong! With 110 free flight and radio-controlled models to his credit, this industrious individual started with an EAA Biplane before he was even a teenager! (It was completed during his high school years at age 18.) Since then, he has increased his working pace and productivity. As an indication of his commitment to aviation, it should be noted that he selected a wife, Julie, who was majoring in aeronautical engineering at California Polytechnic State University.

A Love Affair

Living a semi-reclusive life at the 2000-foot level has allowed them to concentrate on the design and development of the constantly improving Laughing Gull prototypes. This is obviously a love affair. The first of the Gull series was flown in 1976, with improvements being incorporated in each aircraft on a monthly basis.

Before detailing the aerodynamic advances that Mark has used in his ultralight and homebuilt aircraft, let's have a look at his credentials and experience. He has worked with Teledyne Continental, Matrix, and General Dynamics on projects that included aircraft modifications, custom alterations, wind tunnel models, Cruise missiles, radar, and computer equipment.

As if this weren't enough for one man, he is also a tool and die maker. He used this latter skill to build tooling for the somewhat revolutionary Bourke engine and then went on to assemble one at age 21. Never content with older technology engines, he has experimented with rotary, turbo, Honda conversions, and two-stroke engines in his prototypes. While others talk about these various powerplants, Mark modifies, installs, and then flies hundreds of hours on them.

He has been so keen on seeking perfection in performance and safety features, that he didn't release his machines for sale until 1983 — at which time the prototypes had winged their way to over 800 hours of flight time. Incidentally, Julie and Mark have built five prototypes, each successive model including improvements in handling, performance, reliability, and safety features. The team's experience in this evolving string of aircraft has resulted in machines that rate very highly against their competitors.

It's no wonder that the folks who fly his products have nothing but praise for Mark and his planes.

Let's Look at His Gaggle of Gulls

The first of the series was begun in 1976 when Mark became discouraged with the light airplanes that were then on the market. His first efforts were similar to the state-of-the-art aircraft that are now on the market. Since then, his Gulls have set the standards and shown others where their future developments should be.

For instance, all six members of the flock, including the ultralight versions, can fold their wings in five minutes or less to give true roadability and enable them to be stored in the garage between their aerial migrations. The high quality Stits fabric system is used to cover their flight feathers. This results in a finish that is impervious to that fabric killer — ultraviolet rays. Mark conservatively rates the covering at 20 years; however, test panels indicate that this could be a lifetime fabric. None of that cheap-to-buy but expensive-to-replace "sailcloth" that one commonly finds on lesser ultralights and some homebuilts. You won't see these birds shedding their feathers in flight!

Only aircraft-approved hardware and metals are used. For instance, the cockpit roll cage uses chromoly steel to ensure occupant protection. Even the standard-equipment shoulder harnesses are FAA approved.

Additionally, the landing gear struts are pultruded fiberglass rod, engineered to reduce weight while providing the strength and ride-smoothing qualities necessary for the rough strip operations these avions were designed for. Other standard features include an enclosed cockpit for year-round flying, Lexan rather than lower-grade plexiglass windows, a heavy duty steerable nose wheel for improved maneuvering, and a roomy storage area to make cross country flight a practical proposition.

Gimme a Brake

Each of the Gulls has double-surfaced wings, true three-axis controls, and independent main wheel brakes — unlike many competitors in the lightweight category. Personally, I feel that it's ludicrous to have an aircraft that can take off in a couple of hundred feet, land at a low 25 or 30 miles per hour, and then run off the end of a thousand foot runway because the brakes are inadequate or non-existent. Unfortunately, many manufacturers skimp on brakes to reduce the empty weight and final cost. It's a bonus that the Gulls, with their capable brakes, will save running shoes and prevent broken ankles that are common with "Adidas brakes."

All of the fleet come with the innovative IVO composite propeller with its universal hub mount. The propeller is ground-adjustable, allowing the pilot to set his engine thrust for optimum performance, i.e., short field/high rate of climb operations versus high speed cruise or some in-between compromise.

Earthstar states that the individually molded blades are replaceable and interchangeable since they have an identical helix angle. They also claim that this type of propulsion is smoother and quieter both on the ground and in the air, compared to any of the other props they have tested. In fact, they were so impressed with the quality and performance that they have become IVO dealers and sell the two-, three-, and four-blade models at the deeply discounted prices of $190, $290, and $300 respectively.

(Mr. Ivo, you may recall, is that ingenious and brave individual who lived behind the iron curtain a few years ago. In order to escape, he designed and built his own ultralight and then flew it to freedom through darkness and military threat! But that's another story.)

Earthstar has announced a new prototype that has been improved with the addition of flaps and all metal (aluminum) wings and empennage. It also nestles a Honda Prelude car conversion under its streamlined fairing. Unfortunately, this later version of the Laughing Gull II is not included in the following flight evaluations, as it was under construction at the time of my visit.

For those who want to use their aircraft for agricultural spraying, the "Spray Miser" system is available—as are floats for amphibious operations.

THE HOMEBUILT LAUGHING GULL LG1H

This single-seater carries an additional 75 pounds of useful load or payload, compared to the ultralight it was refined from. This would allow a tall 200-pound pilot to carry 75 pounds or so of baggage over 300 miles at a conservative cruising speed of 70 mph. Rotax engines from 28 to 40 horsepower are available. To quote performance for the latter option, with its Rotax 447, we find that a 5500 rpm cruise results in a fuel consumption of 3.1 gph. (At the full rated power output of 7000 RPM, the consumption is 5.2 gph—proof positive that this is a fuel-cooled engine.)

With its power loading of 14.4 pounds per horsepower, this Gull climbed at 900 fpm during the evaluation. With a smaller wing than the ultralight version, there is an increase in maximum speed to 90 mph. (Ultralights are limited to a maximum level speed of 63 mph in the US.)

In the low-speed realm, the stall speed hovered around 27 mph indicated and the characteristics were very docile.

The Gulls have demonstrated the capability to climb to 14,500 feet. This is a good measure of efficiency, but these dizzying heights are pursued by few aviators—a noticeably high pucker factor invariably pursues flyers who venture higher than a few thousand feet above the terrain in these high visibility aircraft with their open feeling.

All in all, the LG1H is a safe, predictable, and efficient load lifter. The extensive design engineering and the quality of the materials used in the kit, along with the lengthy test hours on the prototypes, ensure a durable aircraft with relatively little maintenance requirement. It's an excellent value for recreational flyers who need true short field performance.

THE LAUGHING GULL II T2H

I had the opportunity to fly two prototypes with different powerplants—both of them liquid-cooled. Before giving a detailed comparison between the 64 hp Rotax two-stroke and the 65 hp Honda turbocharged CVCC engines, let's have a peek at the numbers on this two-place aircraft.

Depending on the powerplant option, this Gull has a useful load of 390-450 pounds, with a gross weight of 850. Takeoff at 40 mph requires approximately 200 feet, followed by a rate of climb of 800 fpm. Solo rates and angles of climb were impressive; getting to altitude was quick and steep.

Honda vs Rotax

Would you believe that both Honda and Rotax engines yield a cruise speed of 100 mph? The same lines that give the Gull series an attractive appearance also look good to the slipstream. These light aircraft have benefitted by evolving from third or fourth generation (what number are we at now?) ultralight/homebuilts, leaving much of their competition flying older, inefficient designs.

Now to those engines. Well, you can't eat your cake and have it too. The Honda purred easily to life by virtue of its electric starter system and settled into a smooth steady idle. The Rotax 532 LC, on the other hand, required four pulls on the rope instead of the normal two, then settled into the typical noisy idle that provides a massage through the pilot seat at no extra cost. (To be fair, the Rotax could have had the optional electric starter for an additional $150 or so.)

By virtue of its extra weight, the Honda required a little more throttle to get rolling, compared to the lighter 110 pound Rotax installation. This chunky CVCC would continue to penalize the Gull's performance during the remainder of the flight, with its 170 pounds or so of mass. With pre-takeoff checks complete, the Rotax-powered two-place provided very brisk acceleration. The more laggardly Honda was throttled up to five pounds of boost, maximum. (In an emergency, the throttle could be firewalled to produce a great deal more horsepower; of course, engine life and reliability might suffer.)

The lighter Rotax-powered Gull veritably zoomed to cruising altitude, while the Honda-powered plane dawdled on up. This was due in part to a reduced climb power of 3-4 inches of boost to allow the

Perched on a mountain top, the Gull flock await the opportunity to take you skyward.

turbo installation, with its much higher heat rejection requirements, to be able to cool itself. (This difference in performance tends to support the assertion by auto engine detractors that the output claimed by manufacturers is somewhat optimistic.)

This doesn't look too good for the turbo'd Honda, does it? Perhaps it would make a good wing tie-down weight? To be fair, Mark advised me a month after the flight that the fuel jet had been twisted in the carburetor, thus reducing the power output.

Actually, all of the rest of the benefits go to this four-stroker. You might ask, what's left? How about fuel consumption, reliability, availability and cost of parts—not to mention proven costs of operation? At rated power, the Rotax burns 6.8 gph of 50:1 mixed regular gas and oil. Reducing the rpm by 1000 to 5500 results in a consumption of 4.5 gph. Typically, the Honda would consume 3.5 gallons to produce the same thrust. (Both installations use gear reduction systems.) This means that the turbocharged engine would go the same distance on approximately 20 percent less fuel.

Actually, this is all penny ante data. The biggest news, derived from hundreds of hours of flight operations, is the cost of reliability. To be succinct, the Rotax has cost Earthstar twice as much to operate as the Honda's $5/hr—even though the Rotax was new and the turbo was taken from a tired car! The two-stroker's $10/hr operational costs have been due to numerous defects and replacement parts. Not only that, Honda owners can pop down to the local car dealership in most major towns to pick up parts or service information at reasonably competitive costs. Compare that to the relatively scant 532 service network. (These observations are courtesy of the Earthstar folks.)

To further complicate the decision-making process, there are a lot of other powerplants that would be suitable for your Gull—with modification. The Rotary Mazda, the liquid-cooled BMW motorcycle engines, and the VW conversions are examples. So, while you are burdened with a choice, the selection allows you to match the engine to your flying requirements.

Whatever your decision, you will be mating your option to a very fine, well-designed Gull that will soar with the rest of its relatives.

THE HOMEBUILT ULTRA GULL U1H

How does 135 mph on 28 hp sound to you? Not fast enough? Then try the larger engines and top 150 mph! Combine that with a docile stall of 32 mph and a super-impressive rate of climb exceeding 1500 fpm, and you have a single-place biplane that is guaranteed to turn heads everywhere you go! These much greater feats are a result of larger engine options, resulting in twice as much "horse pressure" hauling a gross weight of only 500 pounds through the airways. This is superlative-yet-economical flying by anyone's pocketbook. The $6,680 kit takes less than 200 hours to build, and when completed yields a very strong machine that can handle 6 Gs in both directions.

With a wingspan of only 20 feet, the Ultra Gull could perch in the garage between flights. Or if you prefer, make up a dolly and slide it under another aircraft's wing at the hangar, because this bird is only 10 feet long! And don't be scared by those apparently short clipped wings. Remember, there are two of them, with a total area of 100 square feet, resulting in a relatively low wing loading of 6.3 pounds per square foot. This craft would be no more difficult for the average pilot to fly than a Cessna 150.

Conclusions

It was easy to be impressed with the excellent handling characteristics of this fleet of flyers. The standard-setting quality of construction and materials ensures the highest safety margins for a pilot's personal protection and confidence. The cabin comfort and stability make one conclude that these would be good cross-country aircraft.

Low wing loadings, low drag, and light stick forces virtually guarantee that these Gulls will be able to soar with their avion brethren in summer thermals or fly at slow speeds for patrol work while sipping meager amounts of go-juice.

Mark does not openly approve of aerobatics in his aircraft, due to liability concerns (and his anxiety over untrained cowboys ripping their wings off and making messy spots in the landscape). Nonetheless, Mark did put on quite an airshow for me.

With a selection of six models, various engines for each, and a willingness to modify the kit makeup and designs to suit each customer, the Earthstar line is suited for all types of recreational flying. So there is quite possibly a Gull in the diverse flock that would suit your needs.

Specifications

Earthstar Laughing Gull LG1H

KIT PRICE	$5,590
BUILDING TIME	250 hrs
NUMBER OF SEATS	1
ENGINE TYPE	Rotax 447
RATED HORSEPOWER	40
EMPTY WEIGHT	280 lb
GROSS WEIGHT	650 lb
WING AREA	130 sq ft
TAKEOFF DISTANCE	125 ft
LANDING DISTANCE	135 ft
CRUISE SPEED	80 mph
TOP SPEED	90 mph
FUEL CAPACITY	5 gal
RANGE	300 sm
REMARKS	No plans for sale. Info kit $2

Earthstar Ultra Gull U1H

KIT PRICE	$6,680
BUILDING TIME	210 hrs
NUMBER OF SEATS	1
ENGINE TYPE	Rotax 532
RATED HORSEPOWER	65
EMPTY WEIGHT	232 lb
GROSS WEIGHT	500 lb
WING AREA	100 sq ft
TAKEOFF DISTANCE	140 ft
LANDING DISTANCE	130 ft
CRUISE SPEED	85 mph
TOP SPEED	150 mph
FUEL CAPACITY	5 gal
RANGE	Approximately 170 sm
REMARKS	Info kit $2

Performance figures provided by the factory.

Elmwood Christavia

A Man with a Mission

Designer-builder Ron Mason has lived decades of fascinating aviation experiences—from his first homemade hang glider of bamboo
and paper, which he flew off a cliff (read crashed) at age seven, to his
latest creation, the four-place Christavia Mark 4. In between, his training included Air Cadets and a stint as a pilot in the Royal Air Force.

Christavia's Beginnings

Let's consider this Plain Jane Aeronca-like aircraft with the
Maule-like performance.

It all started when Ron Mason decided to become a pilot with a
missionary support group called Mission Aviation Fellowship. According to Ron, the MAF is an interdenominational group whose
mandate is to look after the transportation needs of missionaries.
These aviators are comprised of over 400 families all over the world,
flying aircraft types varying from Cessnas to DC-3s.

During Ron's MAF piloting course, he became aware of the need
for a single pilot type of aircraft with a go-anywhere capability. After
questioning numerous missionaries, Ron filled two pages with the requirements necessary for a light aircraft that could operate from very
small strips to provide "aviation for Christ." Hence the Christavia.

Since no existing aircraft could accomplish all of the tasks on the
list with existing airfoil limitations, he worked for a decade to design
one that could.

Using a basic Radio Shack TRS 80 computer, he designed a program to look at all the existing NASA airfoils. Extrapolating the data,
he considered "what if" situations where the computer looked at the
direction parameters would go and then the program was allowed to
predict what would happen with further shape changes. After many
thousands of hours of development, the simple computer and the

dedicated designer achieved the epitome of home-made wings. Observers have called it a modified 4412 section or a Clark Y with camber under the wing.

Not so, says Ron. Suffice it to say, the shape has rather incredible low speed performance while still providing high cruising speeds on low horsepower. Consider the Christavia MK 1 with a 75 hp engine — stalling below 40 mph, yet able to traverse the jungles at 105 mph.

This tandem two- to three-place plane, with an empty weight under 750 lb, is able to carry its own weight for a useful load. Performance specifications like this are based on a wing with so much lift that it stalls at an angle of attack exceeding 25 degrees, power on.

Mason's airfoil passed initial flight testing at Toronto's Ryerson Polytechnical Institute wind tunnel. However, Ron felt that there was no substitute for in-flight testing, so he built a biplane and used the upper wing position to test the various new designs. Airfoil sections undergoing testing were made of easy-to-construct constant cord, aileron-less eight-foot sections. Tuft-testing was then possible through the complete flight envelope in all conceivable attitudes. There would be no surprises for aviators out over the rocks, jungles, or waterways of the world.

Thus, Christavia builders will receive a docile yet high performance wing that has been proven in a very complete and well-documented regime of developmental flight testing.

This Christavia MK 1 may look like an Aeronca, but it sure performs differently!

Since the April, 1983 first flight of the MK 1, over 300 sets of plans have been sold, with more than 50 currently flying. This is a much higher completion ratio than is normal, testifying to the ease of construction and the popularity of the design.

From Cherub to Archangel: The Christavia MK 4

When Ron designed the MK 1, his aims were short takeoff/landing capability, a small engine with low fuel consumption, a low stall speed, good cruise speed, good rate of climb, a large cabin area, low maintenance, and a high safety factor in the event of a forced landing. The Christavias also can easily be converted from wheels to skis to floats.

With the tremendous success of the MK 1, and the need for a lightweight bulky cargo hauler in the mission fields, it was only a matter of time until Ron went back to the drawing boards to create a four-place. Designed from its inception to FAR 23 (factory aircraft standards) by this mechanical engineer with 27 years of instructional experience, there was never any doubt that the finished product would be everything that was promised.

Similar to the MK 1, the MK 4 fuselage uses inexpensive milled steel tube and 4130 plate welded in flat sections on, say, your garage floor. The wings employ wooden truss-type ribs and Sitka spruce for the double spars. (Aluminum ribs and spars are optional.)

One major difference in the MK 4 is the addition of half-span wing flaps that are selected with a handle bar between the two front seats. The strut-braced wings are finished with Dacron (some builders might like to try the new inexpensive Hipec system) and the leaf spring landing gear uses 6.00x6 wheels with toe-operated hydraulic brakes. A parking brake is mounted on the very large IFR-capable instrument panel.

The adjustable front seats utilize a steel tube framework that is designed to crush down in event of a forced landing. Seat and shoulder harnesses are called for even on the rear bench seats. The large aft baggage area, with tie-down hooks, is rated for 60 pounds. For those who might like to carry larger and heavier loads, the rear bench seat can simply be removed.

Flight Manual Included

Calculating loads from the flight manual—yes, you read correctly; the excellent Christavia plans come complete, not only with a construction manual that teaches building skills, but with a pilot's handbook as well—the following CG limits are reached: the forward limit is 16" from the datum. This would be attained with two very heavy pilots up front, approximately 30 lb of fuel, and no rear-seat passengers or baggage.

The rear CG limit of 26" would be approached with full fuel, 350 lb of rear-seat load, a single (or perhaps married) 170-lb pilot, and the baggage compartment filled with 60 lb. However, using the fairly heavy well-equipped prototype as an example, it can haul full fuel, four people of 170 lb, and 56 lb of baggage. Compare this with other so-called four-place aircraft!

Ron says that engines from 135 to 150 hp may be used to power the Christavia 4. The prototype is powered by a 150 hp Lycoming O-320 engine sipping low octane gas from two 18-gal wing tanks. Provided with drains, vents, and a primer, the fuel system has an on-off valve

Materials packages that reduce parts-chasing time are available for the Christavia series at reasonable cost. Purists, or the budget-minded, may want to shop for their own parts.

located on the occupant side of the firewall with a shaft connecting it to a knob on the instrument panel.

As a testimony to the structure's strength, a Christavia was dropped on its landing gear from 20 feet without incurring major damage! Mason sets the load factor at + 4.3 and -2.4 G after testing the wings with static loads. This is calculated at the MK 4's gross weight of 2150 lb (standard empty weight is 1100 lb for builders). And he went a step further than most designers by analyzing the wing torsional loads that could occur due to gusts and control deflections.

To minimize weight and maximize strength, he did not include a wing folding mechanism. However, the wings are easily removed by two people in 15 minutes.

The hundreds of hours of flight testing included flying at speeds over red line in order to ensure safety for subsequent builders. Full spectrum stalls, unusual attitudes, and spins were also explored in depth (or should I say at altitude).

Time to Fly

Enough details. It was time to evaluate this aircraft for myself. Donning my crash helmet (just for the ride to the airfield), we motored out to the Belleville airport. Owner Jimmy Marker likes the homebuilders so much, he gives them free tiedown space. And Ron Mason and the Christavias are so popular with the locals, there are a fleet of MK 1's and the prototype MK 4 gracing the airfield. Somehow, a taildragger looks so much more natural on a grass field than a tricycle looks on the asphalt.

After the preflight inspection, we gained easy access to the MK 4 through the very large doors on either side of the cabin. These have an interesting hinge-axis geometry that holds them open to facilitate the loading or unloading of large pieces of cargo. Fabricated of aircraft-grade wood, the doors surround plexiglass windows that can be pushed in or out in an emergency.

The interior was very spacious with its 41" width (similar to a Cessna 172) and the individually adjustable foam-cushioned and leatherette-covered seats.

Firing up my favorite air-cooled engine — the Lycoming O-320 — and completing the pre-taxi checks was completely straightforward in this entirely conventional go-anywhere bush plane. While visibility over the nose was fairly good for a taildragger, this driver elected to do taxiing turns to clear the wooden propeller's arc from possible obstacles. The fully castering tailwheel geometry, combined with the toe brakes, allowed very sharp turns on the way to Belleville's 3000 ft turf runway.

When the time came, we didn't use much of it. The takeoff acceleration was vigorous and that new airfoil wanted us airborne by 40 mph. By the time we reached the end of the strip we were ready to turn crosswind at 500 AGL—and all this after a climb that likely exceeded a 30-degree deck angle, with a 10 mph crosswind. The initial rate of climb exceeded 1200 fpm! That 35.5-ft wing still gives 100 fpm at the 19,000 foot service ceiling. On 150 hp, this seemed amazing to me.

With that sort of takeoff and climb performance, it was likely that stalls would be gentle and at very low airspeeds—but would the MK 4 be able to top 100 mph in cruise? Would the exceptional low-speed handling be worth it if it took forever to go cross country? We would find out shortly.

During the cruise climb to 2000 feet, visibility was good and the sound level was moderate. The noise, muted by the good headsets and intercom system, was very reasonable for a cross-country flight that could traverse 400 miles or more.

The ailerons and elevator controls were lightly balanced and a pleasure to wave around in maneuvers. The rudder was moderately heavy—a balance I prefer. Since pilots' legs are stronger than their arms, the rudders should be heavier in order to balance the relative efforts. Otherwise, aviators would be waving their tails around the skies like whales during migration.

In Cruise

Light turbulence due to daytime heating persisted with the result that we weren't able to exactly pin down our cruise airspeeds. However, C-GIKQ is able to top 125 mph at full power and 120 mph at 2450 rpm (approximately 75% power and nine gph fuel flow). We could have extended our range to approximately 600 miles at an indicated 110-115 mph burning six gph at 2250 rpm.

Because the fixed rudder trim tab needed adjustment, I had to use a little pressure on the rudder to maintain the Christavia straight on its vertical axis. Elevator trim was linear and smooth in operation, with the control mounted overhead in the cabin. The MK 4 was a delight to throw into turns with the light controls and Frise-type ailerons; however, a little rudder was required to overcome the smidgen of adverse yaw.

Diving to the 140 mph V_{ne} resulted in no tendency towards control flutter. While the fight manual says aerobatics are prohibited, Ron will admit that "limited" aeros can be accommodated. However, pilots should be aware that the aircraft was designed as a utility workhorse, and thus does not have a lot of margin in the limit loads to allow sloppy recoveries—they could overstress the aircraft and subsequently the occupants.

Slow speed handling was accomplished at 60 mph with, it turned out, a large margin above the stall. Under these conditions, the Christavia was very maneuverable, and was able to negotiate very small radius turns—similar to an ultralight. Controls were very responsive, showing no tendency towards sluggishness.

Next, we entered the bottom part of the envelope for some stalls. One surprise was how low the airspeed indicator was when the nose dropped. Perhaps a second surprise was the effectiveness of the ailerons, even after the stall. More Mason magic in the wings. The power-off/flaps-up stall had very little warning buffet and occurred at 40 mph. Manually deploying the flaps to their 20-degree limit caused a slight nose-up pitch change and then reduced the stall speed to a Cub-like 35 mph. And this is a four-place aircraft!

Spin entry and recovery are conventional but not recommended on other than test flights, and not with four on board.

Landings

Well, there wasn't much more to do, other than to see if I could land her. With the addition of flaps, it wouldn't be necessary to incur those huge sideslip angles and 2000 fpm rates of descent the MK 1 was capable of—but those slips were a lot of fun.

So, we flew this multi-passenger ship back to the airport selecting the first 10 degrees of flap below 85 mph and the second below 80 mph. Then, powering along with a sedate 80 mph on final and 65 over the threshold, we floated for a considerable time, easily correcting for the crosswind. The extra speed above the 40 mph stall was carried for safety margin, to overcome the possible harmful effects of windshear and gusts in the turbulent air.

Even with the extra knots, we were always stopped in less than half the runway's length. For true short field operations, by using 10 degrees of flap the MK 4 can get off in 450 feet and land in 650 feet at gross weight, according to the flight manual. With the very low stall speeds, this writer has no doubt that this performance is achievable by most pilots.

The powerful rudders on the Christavias made the crosswind landings a piece of cake. They also created such sizable yaw angles that, when coupled with unlimited bank, substantial sideslips were possible.

A number of circuits and landings showed that this bird had no hidden vices when it came to returning to the nest. That spring leaf seemed to absorb any bad judgment or rough terrain as if it were planned that way.

A Hands Down Winner

Taxiing back to the Christavia fleet allowed a few minutes of wonderment concerning the MK 4's performance. If one were to compare published specifications between the MK 4 and Piper's Super Cub, the Christavia comes out a hands down winner — and both use the 150 hp Lycoming and carry 36 gallons of 80/87. The homebuilt carries triple the passenger load, cruises faster, stalls slower, uses less runway, flies farther, carries more useful load, and costs considerably less.

The only way to account for these superior achievements is to give credit to the advanced capabilities of the Mason wing. Look for this airfoil to vastly improve the performance of other aircraft if Ron releases the ordinates of the wing shape.

Pennies per pound, speed per shekel, or performance per piaster — no matter where you live, the MK 4 Christavia provides the maximum honest four-place aircraft for the minimum money.

Ron completed his prototype in 1986 for $8,300 Canadian ($5,893 US)! Now, how else can you own your own brand new four-place for that sort of money?

Currently, MK 1 plans are $125, the MK 4 plans are $200, and information packs for each aircraft are $10 each; and all monies from the sale of plans are donated to the missions. Builders are very happy with the plans and service from Ron, as indicated by the many Christavias already flying.

Complete materials kits are available from Aircraft Spruce and Specialty. A Mason-built nose cowling is available, and partial material kits are obtainable from third parties such as Grass-Roots Aviation of Oshawa, Ontario.

Specifications

Elmwood Christavia MK 1

PLANS PRICE	$125
BUILDING TIME	2000 hrs
NUMBER OF SEATS	2 tandem
ENGINE TYPE	Continentals and Lycomings or auto conversions
RATED HORSEPOWER	65-100
EMPTY WEIGHT	720 lb
GROSS WEIGHT	1500 lb
WING AREA	146 sq ft
TAKE OFF DISTANCE	300 ft
LANDING DISTANCE	600 ft
CRUISE SPEED	105 mph
TOP SPEED	118 mph
FUEL CAPACITY	15 gal
RANGE	315 sm
REMARKS	Partial kit from Aircraft Spruce

Elmwood Christavia MK 4

PLANS PRICE	$200
BUILDING TIME	2000-2400 hrs
NUMBER OF SEATS	4
ENGINE TYPE	Lycoming or auto conversions
RATED HORSEPOWER	125-180
EMPTY WEIGHT	1100 lb
GROSS WEIGHT	2150 lb
WING AREA	178 sq ft
TAKE OFF DISTANCE	450 ft
LANDING DISTANCE	800 ft
CRUISE SPEED	118 mph
TOP SPEED	138 mph
FUEL CAPACITY	36 gal
RANGE	400 sm plus reserves
REMARKS	Partial kit from Aircraft Spruce

Performance claims are those of the designer.

Kestrel Hawks

And a Low-Cost Training Program

Unanimously voted the Best Ultralight during its introduction at the Canadian Sport Aircraft Exhibition in Toronto (the author was one of the judges), the Kestrel Hawk has been designed to transform the pilot training industry in Canada – and perhaps in the US.

Claiming to have a unique concept in flight training with ultralights, Dave Saunders and Colin Phipps of Kestrel Sport Aviation plan to set up franchised flight training centers across the country. Under their plan, fledgling aviators will be able to obtain a private pilot certificate for approximately $1,500, a low price tag compared to the current $4,500 cost of learning on production aircraft. They state that, "Under-financing, unprofessionalism, and a backyard operation mentality have been some of the ultralight industry's problems in the past."

A Highly Qualified Design Team

Saunders has over 20 years of experience in the aircraft design and modification business. Phipps is known for his work as an aviation inspector with Canada's Department of Transport and his test piloting for DeHavilland. If the excellent quality of the first ten factory-built prototypes and the high degree of public interest are any indications, they may well accomplish their sales objectives.

Two Kits

In the US, the Kit Hawk exceeds the speed and weight limitations for ultralights, so it is offered in two experimental kits – the Sport Hawk and Float Hawk. Due to weather, I was unable to fly the Kit

The Kestrel series is available in land plane and amphibious configurations.

Hawk ultralight version; however, the quality of factory workmanship and materials is excellent.

The Kestrel series features a tandem two-place biplane configuration with a fully enclosed cockpit that is heated and ventilated for all-season flight. The streamlined, side-hinged canopy allows easy access to the cockpit while providing unrestricted visibility.

Sitting on a single 6.00 x 6 spring-mounted fuselage tire with a small, two-inch steerable tailwheel and supported by lower wing-mounted castering-wheeled outriggers, the 395-pound ultralight version is reminiscent of a powered glider. Indeed, with its wing loading of only 4.75 lb/sq ft and 171.5 sq ft of wing area, it is rather glider-like in design and would provide good soaring performance.

Designed by a California company to FAR 23 limits, the homebuilt kits employ skins of .020" and .015" 2024 T3 aluminum on the wings and fuselage. Aluminum wing spars and stamped ribs come preformed for fast construction. Using a "dual load path" fastener system for framework attachment provides a form of redundancy that should increase safety in the structure.

The performance of the Rotax 582-powered pusher belies its appearance. Claiming a takeoff distance of 175 feet and a rate of climb of 800 fpm with two aboard, the Kit Hawk is capable of a true airspeed of

85 mph in cruise. With maximum design loads of +4 and -2 G, based on a gross weight of 830 pounds, she should be able to take the normal loads imposed by turbulence and training with no problems. The two-place stall speed of 38 mph contributes to a published landing distance of 350 feet. Kestrel Sport Aviation feels their all-metal airframe will provide a long life, since it is designed according to standard aviation practices. Due to the rigidity of the Kestrel series, only "simple maintenance requirements" will be necessary to ensure serviceability.

Swing Wings Save Space

Another cost-saving feature is the design of the swing wings that can be folded in 15 minutes to an eight-foot width with the wings flanking the horizontal stabilizer. Mind you, the short wing span of 24.5 feet and overall height of 5.5 feet would allow the Kestrel to occupy a rather small enclosure at the airport or share a hangar with many high winged aircraft.

In the US, the experimental versions called the Sport Hawk and the Float Hawk are powered with the Rotax 582 with its liquid cooling and 64 hp. The latter includes fiberglass wheel/floats. These models are priced at $18,850 and $21,750 respectively. The amphibious model operates at an increased gross weight of 1050 lb, while still providing +4 and -2 G protection. The Sport Hawk grosses 950 lb and supports a maximum design load of +6 and -3 G at an operating weight of 725 lb. (Exterior dimensions of the Canadian ultralight and US homebuilt versions are the same.) The more powerful engine on the homebuilts provides cruise speeds of 85-95 mph and top speeds in the 100-105 mph range.

Float Hawk takeoff roll is 300 feet on land and 750 feet on water. Landing requires 350 feet and 500 feet respectively, according to the company. The Sport Hawk's land performance is equally impressive at 175 feet for takeoff and 350 feet for landing. These capabilities will allow operations out of short strips and small lakes, thus opening wilderness areas to many sport aviators.

Standard features on all Hawks include: airspeed indicator, altimeter, tachometer, CHT, EGT, fuel quantity gauge, 12 VDC electrical system, 60" x 48" Ron Shettler propeller, tiedown points, dual flight and engine controls, elevator trim, wheel brake, external fuel filler, lap belts, steerable tail wheel, exterior paint and a heating/demisting system.

A Detailed Look at Construction

The kits require approximately 300 to 400 hours of construction time, using a few hand tools and with minimal skill levels, according to Kestrel Sport Aviation. Builders are provided with major assemblies that are factory jigged and tack riveted.

The major steps necessary to complete the kit are as follows: *Fuselage:* install rivets, flight control system, fuel tank, engine mount and electrical wiring. *Empennage:* assemble horizontal stabilizer, fin, elevator, rudder and cover. *Wings:* assemble three wings using the sample included for reference on a flat 10' x 4' table. Then assemble ailerons, flaps and cover. *Landing Gear:* mount the main wheels and springs, install outrigger assemblies to lower wings, mount tailwheel and steering gear. *Powerplant:* install on mount, connecting fuel and controls then secure propeller. *Final assembly:* install instruments, bolt the plane together and apply paint coats.

Those with cash flow limitations will be delighted to know that the Kestrel series is available in partial kits as well. Additionally, a detailed assembly manual, video, flight and maintenance manuals are included in the package. With the exception of the instruments and paint, everything needed to build and fly the airplane is included, according to the company.

Enthusiasts seeking the utility of an amphibious sport aircraft for less than $22,000 should consider the Float Hawk — now available with the Norton rotary engine as well as the Rotax 582.

Specifications

Kestrel Kit Hawk

KIT PRICE	$19,750
BUILDING TIME	300 hrs
NUMBER OF SEATS	2 tandem
ENGINE TYPE	Rotax 582
RATED HORSEPOWER	64
EMPTY WEIGHT	395 lb
GROSS WEIGHT	830 lb
WING AREA	171.5 sq ft
TAKEOFF DISTANCE	175 ft
LANDING DISTANCE	350 ft
CRUISE SPEED	85 mph
TOP SPEED	100 mph
RANGE	800 sm

Kestrel Sport Hawk and Float Hawk

KIT PRICE	$18,850 and $21,750
BUILDING TIME	300 hrs
NUMBER OF SEATS	2 tandem
ENGINE TYPE	Rotax 582
RATED HORSEPOWER	65
EMPTY WEIGHT	450 lb
GROSS WEIGHT	950 lb
WING AREA	171.5 sq ft
TAKEOFF DISTANCE	175 ft (750 ft on water)
LANDING DISTANCE	350 ft (500 ft on water)
CRUISE SPEED	85 mph
TOP SPEED	100 mph

Performance figures provided by the factory.

Loehle 5151 Mustang

Maximum Mustang for Minimum Money

If you, like most of us, would like to be able to purchase your own warbird and thrash the air into submission, you should give serious consideration to the well proven Loehle 5151 Mustang replica. Since its introduction as an ultralight at the Oshkosh '85 extravaganza, and its growth to the experimental/homebuilt category, over 100 of the kits have been shipped to builders.

The big news is the availability of the new retractable-geared version of this P-51 facsimile. The numerical designation also refers to the $5,151 price tag, which gets you an engineless kit for a ¾ scale replica of the famous WW II North American design that served so successfully as a long range pursuit/fighter aircraft. For less than $7,500, the Rotax 503 engine can be included with the airframe package.

Easy to Build

Costing far less than any other Mustang look-alike, the licensed Loehle experimental is probably the easiest to build, with the current estimate at about 400 hours. Balsa airplane builders will be very familiar with the type of construction found on this wooden Mustang.

Similar to a "stick and tissue" model, this real airplane can be built by anyone with a modicum of shop skills. Designer Carl Loehle and his son Mike feel that the 5151 is very similar in construction to a Pietenpol and Volksplane with their slab-sided fuselage assembly.

Company president Mike Loehle's introduction to the aviation industry began with the purchase of the late Jerry Ritz's ultralight propeller company. The most recent expansion in products was his retractable option for the 5151 introduced at the Sun 'N Fun show with high speed passes that proved how enviable are the Mustang's lines.

Mike reports that he taught himself how to handle the taildragger after a half hour of taxiing up and down the runway—easy, he says, thanks to good rudder and tailwheel steering response.

The company offers a rudder kit to allow prospective purchasers an opportunity to build a portion of the plane in order to assess the skills involved. This partial kit is shipped complete with assembly drawings, pre-cut wood parts, hardware, and T-88 epoxy glue. The price of the rudder package is then subtracted from the total package price—a deal where nobody loses.

Stringers are used extensively throughout the structure, with geodetic or X-shaped reinforcements in the wing's main spar, rear fuselage, and empennage to give greater strength to these high stress areas. Additionally, these locations receive even greater structural integrity, thanks to a thin plywood covering that provides increased rigidity.

The prototype was static-tested to failure and beefed up to provide a comfortable safety margin. Items that are difficult to fabricate, such as spinner, canopy, propeller, and tip fairings, come completed from the factory. Noted author/designer and propeller expert Eric Clutton works in the Ritz portion of the factory, producing wooden props. The latest prototype employs a very deep 12" box spar and a thick NASA 4412 section to enable it to completely swallow the main gear.

The entire structure is covered with Dacron fabric of the 2.7 ounce-per-sq-yd weight, glued directly to the wooden capstrips. (You might want to consider the 1.7 ounce Stits SH90X weave of polyester for weight reduction as well as its ease of application to tight radius corners.) The building technique results in somewhat less rounded contours than all-metal construction would provide; however, the 5151 looks surprisingly similar to a real P-51.

To Cycle Gear, Pull Lever 75 Times

While Loehle wanted to avoid the problems associated with a folding gear, he eventually bowed to the customer demand for a more Mustang-like appearance. Hence the retractable. He says, "We're aiming the airplane at people who have never flown retractable landing gear planes, so we had to make it as simple as possible".

The result was a direct drive shaft with a ratchet activation. Cycling the gear up or down requires approximately 32 seconds and 75 activations on the lever. For safety, the main gear scissors unit goes over center for a positive stop, with a backup mechanical lock in the form of a 3⁄8 pin to provide fail-safe redundancy. The entire system is built strongly enough to support an aircraft nearly twice the 5151's gross weight. The landing gear uses chromoly steel struts with industrial wheels and balloon 4.80 x 4 tires to cushion landings.

Loehle Aviation provides mechanical drum brakes that are adapted from go-carts to provide low-cost stopping power — although improved braking is recommended by this scribe. Purists would likely note the non-retracting tailwheel in this mini-fighter, and the existence of an inlet under the propeller spinner for the air-cooled engine. The belly scoop on Loehle's prototype makes one wonder how a liquid-cooled 532 would fit the cowling with a remote radiator in the belly scoop — just like a real Merlin-powered Mustang. Those who want complete authenticity — that is, a full-sized Mustang — can join the line on the left with $300,000 or so. Personally, I'd say that for three percent of the price and twenty-five percent of the performance of the real thing, the 5151 looks like a best buy!

On the acceleration side, the 50 hp two-stroke two-cylinder 503 is considered by many to be the most reliable, proven engine of the Rotax series. Cruise settings provide an airspeed of 85 mph in the retractable and 75 mph in the fixed gear prototypes.

A Warbird for Weekend Warriors

Contrary to its high performance heritage, the 5151 has a tame stall speed in the low 30's. The light wing loading — in the five lb/sq ft range—contributes to a gentle, forgiving stall, making the 5151 suitable for short fields and short-time aviators.

In honor of the EAA's past-president Paul Poberezny, the retractable prototype has a paint scheme similar to Paul's full size Mustang. The 5151's useful load of nearly 300 lb enables this Mustang to carry a considerable combination of fuel and pilot.

Although the 5151 has the appearance of a high performance warbird, especially with the gear retracted, its handling is designed for the weekend warrior with little flying experience. Detailed plans and easy-to-follow instructions ensure the kit will be an attractive, low cost entry vehicle to the world of warbirds.

Specifications

Loehle 5151 Mustang (Fixed Gear)

KIT PRICE	$7,282 with engine, $5,151 without
	Retractable $8,577 with engine
BUILDING TIME	350 hrs
NUMBER OF SEATS	1
ENGINE TYPE	Rotax 503 for specs
RATED HORSEPOWER	48-52 depending on accessories
EMPTY WEIGHT	400 lb
GROSS WEIGHT	700 lb
WING AREA	135 sq ft
TAKEOFF DISTANCE	150 ft
LANDING DISTANCE	200 ft
CRUISE SPEED	75 mph
TOP SPEED	95 mph
FUEL CAPACITY	5 gal
RANGE	125 sm
REMARKS	Info kit $10, video $24

Performance figures provided by the factory.

Macair Merlin

For the Grass-Roots Aviator

The quiet town of Baldwin in Canada's central Ontario has a surprise in store for North America. At the airport there, a rare bird is nesting preparatory to proliferating its progeny country-wide. Baldwin has become a beehive of activity humming with the production of a Cub-like aircraft featuring spacious-side-by side seating.

It all started when John Burch, a commercially rated pilot without a cockpit job, incorporated Burmac Aviation to instruct aviation students on ultralights. However, as he grew increasingly disenchanted with the older generation wire-and-tube contraptions, he yearned for an U/L that would look and fly like a conventional homebuilt or factory aircraft.

Not able to find a suitable aircraft on the market, he set out to design his own. Since he wasn't qualified as an aeronautical engineer (most ultralight or homebuilt designers aren't), he researched the field

Full span flaperons and a high lift coefficient in the modified Lazair wing result in short field performance.

and borrowed the best features from half a dozen existing aircraft. Establishing a new company called Macair, Burch employed consulting services to help build his prototype.

Burch's criteria for the Merlin began with lower purchase and operating costs compared to factory-built aircraft such as the Piper Cub. Strength and rigidity were of paramount importance, as the aircraft was to be used on rough fields as a trainer. Crosswind and wind gust penetration were also targeted for improvement over earlier generation ultralights.

In these goals, John succeeded admirably.

The good looks of this aircraft won it the Pilot's Choice, Best Ultralight at the Aircraft Sport Expo 88. Those strut-braced tapered wings and the spacious interior, with its broad wooden instrument panel, were real vote-getters. The company's presentation was so well done that they also got the judges' nod for the runner-up in the Best Ultralight Presentation.

Macairs Everywhere

Macair plans to expand further, establishing a couple of service centers in North America, staffed by trained individuals prepared to offer a high level of service. Mr. Burch states, "We are a very strong company with controlled and steady growth. We have good backing, are financially sound, and are 100 percent jigged-up and ready to go." A tour of the manufacturing facility in town showed major production jigs and numerous aircraft under construction, with quality tools in abundance.

Available as a kit or fly-away ultralight, the Merlin could also be assembled as a 49-percent complete kit, qualifying as a homebuilt for pilots possessing a private pilot's license or better. During my May 1988 visit, John reported that they were going through the homebuilt certification process.

After the Sport Expo, the personable Regional Sales Manager, Kelly Trafford, prepared the Merlin for a series of three flight evaluations by the author at Baldwin's 2500-foot grass strip.

Roaming around the temporary assembly area (the company is building a new facility) allowed me to see the skeleton structures and assess the quality of welding. Macair's crew has combined proven designs with high quality workmanship to provide strong but lightweight fuselage and wing sections.

Merlin's Skeleton

Structurally, the fuselage is comprised of welded chromoly steel tubing, and the wings use aluminum spars and "D" cell construction with foam ribs. The lightweight Hipec covering system shields the Merlin from the elements.

The wing's genesis is from the very popular Lazair. This airfoil is responsible for the best low-speed handling characteristics the writer has ever experienced — short of rotary wing flight. The wing was apparently tested in Canada's National Research Council wind tunnel, and Macair quotes the design loads as +6 and -3 G. Additionally, the company chopped the wing span by four feet to further reduce wing stresses, while increasing the effective wing loading to 4.9 lb/sq ft, thereby reducing the Merlin's sensitivity to wind gusts.

By removing four bolts, you can fold the wings flat against the fuselage, allowing the Merlin to be towed. In this configuration, the widest portion is the eight-foot stabilizer, permitting the Merlin to be stored in a garage.

The gear legs on the model I flew were hand-laid unidirectional fiberglass. For production models, the company plans to fabricate a steel Taylorcraft-type gear that connects and pivots in the center with bungee cords and a welded drag strut.

A few defects in building practices and design were noted during the walk-around inspection. The fabric join on the full ailerons was at the leading edge, not aft as is standard aircraft practice. Also, numerous nuts and bolts were used to hold the upper and lower engine cowling in place, instead of quick release devices such as Dzus fasteners. The difficulty of access would result in few pilots pre-flighting the engine compartment.

John advised me that these deficiencies would be eliminated in future production aircraft. Furthermore, a higher quality fabric will be used with the Hipec system for subsequent production. One needn't be concerned about the design being well proven, since the prototype has amassed more than 200 hours.

I was happy to see how easy it was to enter the cabin, and to note that the generous 40" wide bench seat provided a roomy cabin environment. Though there was no seat adjustment other than with cushion variations, my 70" height and John's 73" were easily accommodated. A cavernous baggage area behind the bench would be suitable for lightweight, bulky items such as camping gear.

Your Choice of Options

Available as the M50 with the air-cooled Rotax 503, or as the Sport 65 with the 582 liquid-cooled engine, the Merlin has a number of options to satisfy grass-roots blue-jeaned aviators, who are, according to John Burch, Macair's projected market.

Our steed was the more powerful 64 hp Sport 65 with the optional three-blade ground-adjustable propeller. Manufactured by Precision Propellers, this is the first production model that John feels is reliable enough to use on the aircraft. Some other pitch-adjustable props have had a disagreeable tendency to fling blades when the bolts holding them weren't quite tight enough. According to Macair's staff, this design won't part with its blades even if the fasteners aren't torqued correctly.

Full Lotus floats have been very successful on the Merlin, giving the safety factor of being able to land anywhere. They have even been demonstrated landing on a paved roadway.

According to the specifications chart, the 582-powered Merlin has an empty weight of 485 lb and a useful load of 615. The air-cooled 46-52 hp version tips the scales at 415 to 420 lb empty, but with its reduced gross weight can carry only 465 lb useful load.

Let's Pull the Cord

The pull cord for starting the engine is mounted against the firewall. After turning the ignition switch on, one simply bends over, grasps the handle and pulls by sitting up. After John accidentally flooded the engine with the choke, six healthy tugs were needed to shake the two-stroke to life. Numerous other U/L's have the grip closer, with the result that once the pilot pulls the slack out of the take-up reel, there is only a half foot between the handle and the operator's chest.

After start-up, we idled above 2000 rpm to smooth out the vibration. We taxied to the end of the runway using the steerable tailwheel for very precise maneuvering—which could have been anticipated, given the small diameter tire and considerable weight aft.

Visibility over the nose was very good, due in part to the long tailwheel strut lifting the tail. The control yoke is a center-mounted Y-shaped column. While this seems unusual, it felt perfectly normal in the subsequent flight. The static control movements were free of system resistance, although the elevator was somewhat heavy, due to an oversized trailing edge spar (to be replaced on production models).

In the Air

Fire-walling one of the strong, large-gripped throttles mounted on each side of the cockpit provided animated acceleration from the 65 ponies up front.

With a gross weight of 1100 lb, the Merlin's takeoff run was less than 400 ft with two aboard. The best angle of climb speed resulted in a very steep departure that turned spectators' heads. Using good headsets and an intercom to communicate significantly muted the typically high sound level. Additionally, the noise level to ground-bound observers is very low in this tuned-muffler and liquid-surrounded two-cylinder installation.

Control feel and balance during takeoff were excellent in the 15 mph quartering crosswind and throughout the flight. With full span Junkers-style ailerons, the roll rate and control were excellent at all speeds. Even though the design incorporates differential ailerons, there still remains a moderate amount of adverse yaw during banking operations.

Avoiding the Meltdown

Timing the climb yielded a rate exceeding 800 fpm at 50 mph (best rate of climb speed is 40 mph). Unfortunately, we were unable to prolong our climb for more accurate checks, as the engine coolant temperature was approaching the red line after 1500 feet of altitude. John advised that the engine had only eight hours since new and that the timing needed adjustment due to the points breaking in.

Having heard from others that power output and performance is critical to timing adjustment on these high performance engines, I concluded that this was not a cooling problem related to the inclined radiator mounted on the belly. Operators should be cautioned that continued operation at these high coolant temperatures can easily lead to a powerplant meltdown.

To avoid overheating the engine, we leveled off temporarily to conduct slow speed trials. Since the published maneuvering speed is 45 mph, we reduced our indicated to 40 mph. Control forces were excellent and no trim changes were felt throughout the entire speed envelope.

For that matter, no trim system had been installed on this ultralight version, in order to keep the weight down. Steep turns and large control displacements created no undesirable results. Indeed, the Merlin was delightful to wheel around the skies and proved to be a winsome aircraft during the cavorting camera runs.

The modified Lazair wing, known for its exceptional low-speed performance, produced power-off stalls of 24 to 25 mph. The only pre-stall warning was a slight rudder twinge. A moderate amount of nose-down pitch accompanied the lift reduction, leaving no question that it was time to initiate the conventional stall recovery. Only a modicum of altitude was lost and there was no inclination towards a secondary stall.

The maximum level speed we attained with this out-of-tune engine was 85 mph. Tachometer readings of 6000 and 5000 resulted in airspeeds of 70 and 50 respectively. There was no tendency towards control flutter in a dive to the 100 mph V_{ne}. During all of this in-flight envelope testing, the powerplant/airframe interface was virtually vibration free, due to the use of dynafocal engine mounts.

Homecoming

Returning to the pattern with a downwind speed of 50 mph, we completed the landing check. This entailed fuel quantity and ignition switch only, as there are no flaps, retractable gear, fuel selectors, magnetos, trim system, or brakes!

Final approach was flown at 45 mph using sideslip to control descent angles. To avoid annoying residents or getting tangled up in the power lines at the end of the runway, a steep power-off approach is used for the north runway at Baldwin. The Merlin is limited by the rudder travel to only average angles of sideslip. Nonetheless, we were able to make steep descents over the wires to the button.

The demonstrated crosswind capability is 20 mph and directional control was excellent during numerous touch and go landings. Crossing the threshold at 35-40 mph resulted in smooth three-point touchdowns at approximately 25-30 mph.

Because of a need to keep the weight down for the Canadian ultralight empty weight limit of 430 lb, this Merlin had no brakes. So, while it is possible to get down in short order, the ground roll is considerable without an anchor to throw. Personally, the brake option at

$395 would be one of my first selections. Captain Ken's Corollary states, "an aircraft without brakes is an accident looking for a place to happen."

John may have been impressed with my judgment as I taxied to within inches of the building. However, he couldn't tell I was mentally dragging my feet while selecting the ignition switch off to eliminate the Rotax's residual thrust.

In summary, small improvements to the Merlin series will provide students and recreational flyers with an ultralight/homebuilt that is well-designed, safe, and relatively inexpensive to fly and maintain. Compared to other aircraft in the same category, this is one of the best, as Macair has combined characteristics which result in high marks throughout the score card.

The Kit

At $9,200 for the 503-powered kit, the Merlin is one of the lowest priced aircraft on the market. Alternatively, one could select the 582 liquid-cooled kit as per the flight evaluation. Optionally, one can add the eight-piece Instrument Package ($995), Sports Package (prop spinner, wheel pants, and stripe kit, for $365), and a three-blade prop ($395) for a total of $12,750, and get a rather complete, good-looking aircraft.

As well as improving the appearance, the extra investment buys a shorter takeoff run, higher rates of climb and cruising speeds, and perhaps a little more reliability with the liquid cooling.

Shipped with the aluminum wing "D" cells and spars complete, ribs formed, and aileron pieces only requiring riveting together, the Merlin kit requires only simple hand tools and 300 hours to complete. The fuselage with rudder pedals, seat frames, throttle and controls is already fully welded. Also included is the finishing system, which is comprised of glue, fabric, and ultraviolet base paint.

Specifications

Macair Merlin Sport 65

KIT PRICE $12,995
BUILDING TIME   300 hrs
NUMBER OF SEATS   2 side by side
ENGINE TYPE   Rotax 582
RATED HORSEPOWER   65
EMPTY WEIGHT   485 lb
GROSS WEIGHT   1100 lb
WING AREA   157 sq ft
TAKEOFF DISTANCE   150 ft
LANDING DISTANCE   250 ft
CRUISE SPEED   87 mph
TOP SPEED   100 mph
FUEL CAPACITY   12 gal, 24 optional
RANGE   210 sm
REMARKS   Info kit $5

Performance figures provided by the factory.

Marquart Charger

She Won't Stampede

During this decade of homebuilt aviation, it seems that designers have been pursuing honors for top speed and jet fighter-like handling. This is all well and good for a few pilots; however, for most of us weekend warriors, gentle and forgiving flight characteristics are preferred, and would provide pleasurable pastimes rather than hair-raising flights of fear.

If you don't consider yourself in the advanced aviator class, and if your heart pounds a little harder at the sight of a nostalgic biplane, consider the two-place Marquart MA-5 Charger as your next steed. Fernando Ramos did, and he is so delighted with his first that he is well along on the construction of his second.

Before we fly the Ramos red rocket, let's have a look at the development of the Charger. The MA-5 incorporates advances from the testing of Ed Marquart's prototype MA-3 Maverick. The popularity of the Charger design is evident by the more than 320 sets of plans sold to date, with over 40 currently flying. Incidentally, Remo Galeazzi, the winner of the Oshkosh Grand Champion award for plans-built aircraft, said the plans are so complete that "it makes your hair hurt."

Aimed at filling a requirement for a sporty biplane, Marquart's prototype first flew in October 1970. A month later, Oscar Tombolo's more powerful 160 hp Charger took to the air and in a short time galloped on to corral a dozen or so first place trophies. Since then, there has been a virtual stampede of these tandem-seated steeds.

Construction of the MA-5 uses conventional practices, such as the 4130 steel tubing throughout the fuselage and empennage, as well as spruce spars and wooden ribs throughout the equal span/equal chord wings. This latter design consideration allows all of the ribs to be fabricated on one jig.

The landing gear have widely spaced tires on 4130 sheet steel legs that form a tapered box with individual shocks. The result of this design is stable handling on the runway and smooth shock-dampening rides during boon-dock operations. For the many non-welders in the crowd, Marquart will provide the fuselage frame completed, at extra cost.

The fuel system uses gravity to provide reliable flow from the 18-gallon fuselage tank. Four-gallon "butt" tanks in the upper wings boost total capacity to 26 gallons. Some builders have increased the fuselage tank size to carry as much as 35 gallons. According to Ed, for reasons of increased safety, some owners choose to add a back-up pump such as the "wobble" style in case the engine-driven pump fails.

Pilots would be hard pressed to find many aircraft that are easier to pre-flight. Panels are easily removed in a couple of minutes to expose the entire front half of the Charger. Few aircraft allow this pre-flight access, although all should. Admission to this area allowed us to survey Fernando's award-winning Continental C125 installation, as well as the fuel tank connections, rudder pedals, and numerous accessories.

With a lot of the strength of the structure on the exterior in the form of flying wires, their availability for inspection is reassuring to owners. It is further comforting to note that Mr. Marquart has doubled the required number of flying wires, for that extra margin of safety through redundancy.

The Charger has gentle and forgiving flight characteristics.

Interestingly, some builders have modified the elliptically shaped vertical fin for appearances, although I would prefer to keep the most efficient wing planform in existence – a la the WW II Spitfire.

Because Fernando and I both show the effects of good living, it appeared that it would be a struggle to enter the holes of the biplane's cockpit. Wrong! The 10 degree sweep-back of both wings not only helps the CG travel and provides sexy looks, it also moves the upper intersection forward, allowing easy access to the front flying position.

The next surprise was the vast expanse inside. Six-foot-five pilots, considerably over 200 lb, have no problem getting into or acclimatizing to the MA-5. Also, because the CG is located in this seat, a passenger of virtually any weight could be carried – without any adverse effect on the aircraft's balance.

Helmet, Goggles, and White Silk Scarf

Donning the paraphernalia that adorn the open-cockpit aviator is all part of the ceremony of flight. The reassuring shoulder and seat straps, helmet, goggles, and scarf only add to the exhilaration.

After overcoming the small setbacks of a dead battery and a dangerous live magneto, the Continental was purring in front of Fernando's Corona, California airport hangar. Mr. Ramos, a high school chemistry/biology teacher, is not overwhelmed by small problems, as evidenced by his comment: "If you screw something up in a homebuilt, it is usually easy to fix."

Zig-zag turns increased the tail dragger's visibility, while the excellent brakes and the short overall length of 19.5 feet allowed us to maneuver in confined quarters with ease. (The wing span is 24 feet and the height 7.5 feet.) As we completed the run-up and pre-takeoff checks, I was keeping in mind the fact that most Chargers weigh more than the 1000 lb prototype. With a maximum legal gross of 1550, it seemed that we would be operating within a few ounces of the limit.

During the short takeoff roll I was surprised at the invigorating acceleration for such a small engine – must have had good compression. By the time we passed abeam the camera person, that large 170 square feet of wing area had us a couple of hundred feet over the runway, galloping upwards at 750 fpm at 90 mph – not too shabby for our weight and the fuel-miserly engine. Solo rates of climb with the slightly larger powerplants top 1500 fpm.

In this densely populated airspace, our look-out was aided by an almost unrestricted view – thanks again to those swept wings.

Hands-Off Flight

My next surprise was the light and delightful control feel. On the premise that it was a good idea to keep turning to ensure that we didn't fly into any other locals, I kept that steed turning from side to side.

This is not to say that the Charger is difficult to keep straight. As a matter of fact, it seemed that this plane could fly itself indefinitely, hands off, once it was trimmed. The combination of Frise-type and differential ailerons meant that one's feet could be left on the floor for banking turns up to moderate rates of roll. To really crank this thoroughbred around, a little light rudder input was needed to overcome the adverse yaw of that downward aileron.

With four of these slotted controls, one per wing, the MA-5 has a snappy roll rate. Rudders and elevators are balanced control surfaces that complete the harmonious symmetry. Unlike many exotic freedom machines that share these control responses, the Marquart craft adds a greater amount of inherent stability, making it an easy-to-fly cross-country plane as well. (Fernando has flown to Oshkosh twice from Los Angeles.)

Smell the Flowers

Allowing the rpm to steady at a conservative 2350 resulted in a true airspeed of 120 mph at 3000 feet. (The 150-160 hp engined MA-5s typically cruise at 125-135 mph on eight gph with a 78" diameter, 58 pitch prop.) While these speeds may not set any world records, this open cockpit smell-the-flowers form of flying makes high top speeds seem unimportant.

Although the clipped windshields reduced the raging slipstream to a scanty burble, it required good headsets and an intercom to conduct conversation over the naturally high sound level that was a byproduct of the open two-hole configuration.

Slow flight and stalls were next. The former holds no surprises, and if one encounters turbulence under these conditions or inadvertently stalls, the characteristics remain docile. After talking with other Charger builders, I deduced that it's necessary to hold Fernando's low-end airspeed reading suspect. Nonetheless, we found generally gentle manners when N77FR ceased flying at 60 mph indicated, power off, and 55 mph with 1500 rpm. Other MA-5 owners report average stall speeds of 42-45 mph indicated with no perceptible wing drop. The 2412 airfoil leaves a great percentage of lift in the wings at the onset of the stall, with the result that roll can easily be controlled with hand inputs to the ailerons during the stalled condition. Of course, the rudder also remains very effective.

This is also true of the design during spins, when the nose pitches steeply downward, but the rate of yaw is sedate. Centering the rudder and stick results in an immediate recovery from the stalled condition.

While my desire for longevity (and in this case, Fernando's feelings on the matter) forbade me from conducting a full blown series of aerobatics in this machine, its generous limit loads of +5 and -3.5 Gs indicate a strong aircraft. Of course, that evil spectre of liability precludes Mr. Marquart from declaring the Charger an aerobatic aircraft. Years ago, such a plane would introduce many owners to the thrill of well-executed aerial convolutions. Today, this same kind of forgiving-yet-responsive machine would be an excellent primary aerobatics trainer.

Flying final approaches at 75 mph produced touchdowns at 55 mph. With light braking, the MA-5 is easily stopped in 1000 feet. With its rugged gear and oversized tires, the Charger would be suitable for almost any backwoods landing strip.

A unique aspect of this design is its appeal to low- and high-time pilots alike. While it is a perfect taildragging and aerobatics trainer, it is also capable of all-out precision flying.

It Doesn't Come in Crates

If you've been entranced by the thought of owning an MA-5, it's time to come down to earth — where your tools are. This well-rounded performer does not arrive at your door in numerous crates as a 49-percent completed kit.

The good news is that the Marquart Charger comes in a relatively small package and costs only $125. This meager price buys you one of the best sets of plans on the market. Then all you have to do is collect all of the parts listed on the Bill of Materials and invest a couple of thousand hours building your dream machine. In other words, this is a fabricate-from-scratch homebuilt — like they all used to be.

For those of you who want to save time in lieu of money, a number of components are available from Ed's shop and other suppliers. While Mr. Marquart's work is superb, it is necessary to stand in line for his services — nothing is perfect in life. With his MA-5 jigs, he can weld up a perfectly aligned fuselage and tail feathers for you, if you can wait three months — or longer if the list grows. Last I heard, Ed was also able to supply builders with landing gear, interplane or cabane struts, and engine mounts.

While there are a few other two-place biplanes on the market, their construction is generally more expensive and the flight skills required to fly them are more demanding. This high-spirited mare is so trustworthy, she won't bite or stampede when you least expect it.

Specifications

Marquart MA-5 Charger

PLANS PRICE	$125; some materials pkgs avail
BUILDING TIME	1500 to 2000+ hrs
NUMBER OF SEATS	2 tandem
ENGINE TYPE	Lycoming
RATED HORSEPOWER	125
EMPTY WEIGHT	1000 lb
GROSS WEIGHT	1550 lb
WING AREA	170 sq ft
TAKEOFF DISTANCE	600 ft
LANDING DISTANCE	700 ft
CRUISE SPEED	116 mph
TOP SPEED	125 mph
FUEL CAPACITY	27 gal
RANGE	400 sm
REMARKS	Info kit $3

Performance claims are those of the factory.

Mirage Celerity

How to Make an Oregon Cedar Top 200 mph

Webster's dictionary's definition of *celerity* as "rapidity of motion; speed; swiftness" only begins to describe the attributes of this foam-over-wood speedster from Mirage Aircraft Inc. An opportunity to fly Larry Burton's design at the 1988 Arlington Fly-in provided significant surprises at the performance of this relatively new cross-country carrier.

Designer Larry Burton is a quiet and knowledgeable man with 24 years of machine shop experience and a large collection of awards he won with his first aircraft, a Cavalier. One of his builders said of him, "To know the man is to believe in the aircraft." After a day with Mr. Burton, I share that opinion. Always suspicious of designers who are not aeronautical engineers (and of some who *are*), I grilled him on his product. He has really done his homework well, as he had excellent answers — even to the trick questions.

High Performance at Low Cost

While there are a considerable number of competitors vying for this market, the Celerity's niche is earned by her high performance at low cost. The materials used and plans-built concept result in an aircraft that can be completed with an investment of approximately $20,000 and 2500 to 3000 hours.

The plans are well illustrated, with numerous items such as wing ribs and fittings drawn to full scale. By the time this evaluation is published, Larry says a new set of plans will be available, as well as videotapes of construction techniques. Additionally, a construction manual leads the builder in step-by-step building techniques, and owners receive design updates via the Mirage Aircraft mailing list.

The blueprints show a strong, easily constructed airframe of wood that is covered with urethane foam, two layers of 3.8 ounce fiberglass laid at 45 degrees to each other, and Safe-T-poxy resin, to form a streamlined shape. This proven process provides excellent strength and bonding, while minimizing the builder's skin and respiratory irritation. The wooden structure benefits novices, because it is easy to build using standard shop tools, and it further provides a very high strength-to-weight ratio. Other benefits include wood's ability to absorb noise and vibration in the flying environment.

Larry's conviction that wood is the ultimate composite for construction led him to a steep, wet ravine where he selected a Port Orford cedar tree to become his 200 mph projectile. After a year of drying and aging, he began work with simple shop tools.

The fuselage framework is covered with 1.5 mm birch plywood, with lightening holes strategically cut in the skin to reduce weight. Exterior contours are formed when the wooden structure is covered with foam, sanded to shape, and fiberglass cloth is laid up with epoxy resin. This method of construction also gives knowledgeable builders the option of changing some shapes and customizing their aircraft.

Behind the "scissoring" canopy with its Glasair-style latches, a foam-core-and-fiberglass turtledeck adds to the baggage capacity and exposes very clean lines to the slipstream. Fiberglass canopy shells are available from the factory as an extra-cost option.

A Well-Designed Cockpit

Much thought has gone into the cockpit layout of the Celerity, and even the upholstery design and patterns were created by an interior designer, Darlene Heckenliable. The side-by-side seating provides a 40" inside dimension, resulting in a wide instrument panel sufficient for IFR needs.

Behind the seats and underneath the 12 sq ft hat rack area resides a large baggage compartment of 9 cubic feet that will handle up to 60 lb of portables. A window area aft of the canopy, combined with generous use of plexiglass, results in nearly 360-degree visibility.

Wing assembly utilizes the proven wooden box spar-and-ribs design. These are then covered with foam and fiberglass. This method results in a very smooth 23000 series airfoil that has minimum drag and maximum lift. The airfoil is actually a 23015 at the root, tapering to a 23010 with 1.5 degrees of washout. Set with 2.5 degrees of incidence, the wing fits into root fairings that are built as part of the fuselage to provide an excellent air seal. Removal or installation of the wings requires approximately one and a half or two hours.

The fiberglass wing tip tanks not only add to the attractive lines, they also reduce drag and bending loads while improving lateral stability. Optional auxiliary fuel tanks can be built into the wings for a total of 40.5 gal capacity. (Quality tip tanks are available from a private vendor for those who prefer the kit method.) Full tanks produce a range in excess of 900 miles with VFR reserves.

The tail surfaces use the same building techniques as the wings, and no portion of the aircraft is too large to be constructed in a single car garage. As a matter of fact, the Celerity is quite compact with its length and span of 23 feet.

The landing gear employ 5.00 x 5 tires mounted on a compression spring oleo suspension.

The retraction system uses a nine-pound hydraulic pump that is mounted under the seat to produce the 1000 + lb of pressure to raise the gear with their metal/fiberglass doors. Since builders of retractable-geared aircraft often complain of the difficulty of fabricating metal parts, Mirage Aircraft makes available an easily installed version in kit form. The gear is not available on a plans-built basis.

In addition to the Rattray-supplied tip tanks, a full raw materials package is available from Wicks Aircraft for approximately $4,400, for those who don't wish to chase around searching for "bargains."

Actually, Two Celerity Models

The prototype was completed in May 1985 by Burton and his friends Bruce Boylan and Dave Melby, and plans were made available in 1986. To subscribe to the Celerity newsletter, contact Dave and Brenda Brand at 7 Brookmount Road, Toronto, Ontario, M4L 3M9, Canada.

In order to qualify for the stricter Canadian Department of Transport limitations, the designer had to increase the wing span to reduce the wing loading slightly. As a result, there are effectively two Celerity models, the standard and the long wing.

The prototype Celerity, N5104X, lists an empty weight of 1169 lb and a gross of 1815, for a useful load of 646. While the wings have not been statically tested, Larry quotes the limit loads of +6 and -3 Gs. These factors sound suitable for aerobatics; however, the designer cautions against these gyrations, due to the extended propeller shaft used in this installation for improved streamlining. Wild turns would transfer very high loads from the 74" diameter Hartzell constant speed propeller to the shaft and engine. While the prototype is powered by a 160 hp Lycoming O-320, Larry recommends engines up to 180 hp for more amazing performance.

Walkaround, Sitdown, Startup

Removal of 14 cam locks exposes the entire engine compartment, to allow observers to view the exquisite award-winning installation. Oil level can be checked through a filler/access door on the cowling.

After a "giant step" onto the wing, it was a cinch to step over the cabin sill and snuggle into the cabin. The seat was very comfortable and adjustable with cushions. Future plans will have a mechanical adjustment for the back of the seat.

After start-up, we kept the rpm below 1400 so as not to overstress the open canopy on its unique scissors assembly. (A unique slider option eliminates this restriction.) Ventilation was excellent in this configuration. The fuel selector gave a choice of left tip main, right tip main, both auxiliary tanks, or off. We selected a tip tank, released the toe brakes and taxied to the active in the drunken zig-zag typical of tailwheel aircraft. Visibility over the nose was average for a taildragger. However, the vibration and sound levels were quite low, thanks to the absorbing qualities of wood and foam. Maneuverability was excellent with the fully castering tiny tailwheel (future kit planes will have the larger six-inch tailwheel) and a rudder that was effective even at the low speeds and power settings typical during taxiing.

Ham-Handed Pilots, Lighten Up!

With the pre-takeoff check complete, it was time to sample the brisk acceleration. Directional control was very good, with the aid of the self-centering tailwheel locking in its detent and the very effective tail surfaces. It was actually possible to lift the tail with full power and no forward speed. The rudder allowed precise control of yaw from the beginning of the short takeoff roll.

Eight hundred feet and 60 mph later we were off. Accelerating to the best angle-of-climb speed of 90 indicated gave a 1300-fpm rate of climb. After clearing the simulated takeoff obstacle, we lowered the nose to the 110 mph best rate-of-climb speed to yield 1700 fpm. Visibility was very good in all directions (except downward into the wing and directly overhead due to the canopy sunshade), and the vibration and sound levels were surprisingly minimal. This is partially due to the fact that Mr. Burton dynamically balanced the propeller with the engine.

The control feel was well balanced in all axes, making the Celerity a delight to fly. Ham-handed aviators will have to lighten up their grip to fly this hot rod.

Climbing to a safe altitude for stalls resulted in a CHT of 425 degrees F (25 below the red line) and an oil temperature of 185-190. Later, during cruise power operations, we found the oil stabilized in the same range and the CHT settled at 375 degrees in the summer warmth. At 10,000 feet, Larry normally operates at 21" of manifold pressure and 2300 rpm, for a true airspeed of 190 mph on 6.5 gallons per hour. This equates to over 29 miles per gallon! For those who like to boogie at and beyond the big two-zero-zero, power settings of 24 square will bring you right up to 200, and 25 square will have you scorching along at 210 mph.

During our high speed cruising, the elevator remained very light at all airspeeds, while the ailerons loaded up significantly. Increased control resistance with increasing speed is a good trait for cross-country flying to avoid over-controlling and subsequent airframe overstress. Appreciating this, Larry is modifying the elevator system on the second prototype—as well as on his future kits—to increase the aerodynamic loading.

Neither Frise-type nor differential ailerons are needed on the Celerity, as it exhibits excellent rudder and aileron separation, with no adverse yaw tendency. Cross-country pilots can rest their feet on the floor during the climb, cruise, and descent profiles. Although she has a fighter-like feel, nonetheless the Celerity demonstrates reasonable hands-off stability for those cross-country flights, as long as the elevator is trimmed accurately.

Similar to the V-tail Beechcraft Bonanza, there is some tendency to yaw about the vertical axis in turbulent air, although the amplitude is small and easily dampened with rudder. And even at speeds in excess of 200 mph, the cabin remained very quiet and vibration free.

Larry has set the red line V_{ne} at 200 mph and the gear and flap extension speeds at 100 mph. In preparation for stall envelope testing, we selected these drag devices down, and noted there was very little trim change during extension.

Plan Ahead

Because the aircraft is so clean aerodynamically, and the gear and flap extension limits are 100 mph, it will be difficult to slow down the Celerity in a high speed steep descent. Therefore, pilots will have to plan their approach profile at a considerable distance from destination. (Good piloting technique dictates, in any case, that pilots should plan well ahead of their present position.)

The flaps are selectable in 15-degree increments, with 45 being the maximum. The flap handle is located between the seats, hinged at the back and pulled upwards towards the throttle for deployment. Pilots are cautioned that interference could occur during throttle reduction with the flap handle selected up (flaps down). This installation has become quite common in homebuilts and could be modified somewhat by individual builders, for instance by shortening the flap handle, thus reducing the possible interference, but also lessening the mechanical advantage.

All stalls occurred with no appreciable warning. The power-off landing configuration stall occurred at 55 mph with a moderately fast dropping of the right wing. The ailerons excited into a quick flutter often called aileron snatch. While this is no problem, it is an interesting and uncommon phenomenon. Pilots who try to recover too quickly from the Celerity stall will notice a tendency towards a secondary stall. This is common on high performance aircraft with relatively high wing loadings, that are being forced to do something quicker than they want to. Suffice it to say that pilots hoping for a lengthy life span would find it imprudent to stall close to the ground.

The clean configuration stall, accompanied by the aileron snatch, occurred at 60 mph. Standard recovery techniques of opposite rudder and relaxing of back pressure, then application of power, resulted in altitude losses of approximately 200 feet.

Slow speed handling was flown at 70 mph. At this velocity, the controls were delightfully light and reasonably responsive. Large deflections generated attitude excursions of the aerobatic variety. Alternatively, one could patrol at this speed on a fuel consumption that would likely approach three gph.

Attempting sideslips at various speeds showed that the rudder's power was adequate only for generating small slip angles. This proved to be no problem, as the power-off/flaps-down descent angle was steep enough for any approach, thanks to the wing loading of 20 lb/sq ft on the standard, or short wing, version. The Canadian, or long wing, version would have a shallower approach gradient and more of a float in the ground effect.

Returning to the pattern, we indicated 100 mph on base leg and 85 on final approach. Speeds below 85 on final result in somewhat mushy control feel and could generate sink rates that would be difficult to arrest in the landing flare. The approach gradient is easily controlled with flap deployment; 45 degrees and power to idle results in a steep descent of more than 1500 fpm.

Landings in a seven-knot crosswind were easily and smoothly accomplished, thanks to the ground cushion effect of the low wing. Larry has consistently demonstrated landings with an 18-knot gusty crosswind component. Numerous touch-and-goes uncovered no untoward characteristics, considering that this is not an airplane for low-time pilots who have not had either a type checkout on the Celerity or other high performance retractables. The after-landing rolls had no surprises, and the braking and directional control were excellent.

Popping the canopy open for abundant ventilation, we taxied past many admiring gazes on our way to the display area.

Conclusions

The Celerity is carving a well established niche in the marketplace as a low-cost, high-performance, side-by-side composite. Unlike that of many of its competitors, the construction utilizes well proven, strong, and easily worked wood for the load-bearing structure. This allows first-time builders to be fully confident of the integrity of their project.

This form of fabrication also produces a quieter and smoother platform than many metal and "plastic" projects. And Larry's clients are delighted with the quality of the plans, building manual, and the level of his support. With the exception of the few minor characteristics noted in the flight evaluation, the Celerity would be easy for intermediate pilots to fly after a conversion to high performance retractables. Besides, what other 200 mph two-place aircraft can you build for $20,000?

Specifications

Mirage Celerity

PRICE	Kit approx $10,000, plans $195
BUILDING TIME	3000 hrs
NUMBER OF SEATS	2 side by side
ENGINE TYPE	Lycoming O-320
RATED HORSEPOWER	160
EMPTY WEIGHT	1169 lb
GROSS WEIGHT	1825 lb
WING AREA	90 sq ft
TAKEOFF DISTANCE	800 ft
LANDING DISTANCE	1000 ft
CRUISE SPEED	190 mph
TOP SPEED	220 mph
FUEL CAPACITY	40 gal
RANGE	1000 sm
REMARKS	Info kit $7.50
	Materials packages available

Performance figures supplied by factory.

Murphy's Renegade Spirit

Loads of Fun with a Lightweight Biplane

The recent advertising of my Baby Great Lakes aerobatic biplane, and the subsequent flood of inquiries, demonstrates the tremendous desire of numerous pilots to own one of these four-winged freedom machines. For those who missed out on acquiring my diminutive dervish, Murphy Aviation of Chilliwack, British Columbia has great news.

Murphy has improved an already popular design with the addition of the 64 hp liquid-cooled Rotax 582 engine, and has received a deluge of orders. I flew the new Renegade when offered the opportunity to be the first to exercise — or exorcise? — the new Spirit.

The air-cooled engine cowling has been replaced with a round cowling that looks like it must house a big, hungry radial engine. Most people who see the Renegade Spirit think it is a restored antique aircraft. You should see their surprise when they learn it can qualify as an ultralight in Canada. With an extra fuel tank and fire extinguisher, the empty weight reaches the realm of homebuilts. Its very low wing-loading makes it very forgiving and easy for a beginner to fly.

If It's So Light, Why Is It So Strong?

When you consider that the aircraft is very strongly built to an ultimate structural limit of +10 and -6 Gs, it is amazing that the airframe can be so light. As a matter of fact, the 3" tube that comprises the main wing spar has been tested to failure, at which time it sustained 18 Gs before deformation!

The secret of the Spirit's strength is the patented, extruded aluminum gusset system used to join the aircraft tubular members together. There is no need to worry about the integrity of this aircraft, since it matches or exceeds factory-built FAR 23 standards.

While the factory doesn't push the Renegade as a fully aerobatic sportster, due to liability considerations, Murphy advised me that during the flight test program, the Renegade accomplished the following maneuvers with ease and predictability: loops, rolls, snap rolls, hammerheads, whip stalls, spins, and wingovers. After watching the prototype under construction, my initial doubts about an ultralight-come-homebuilt being strong enough for aggressive flying were swept aside.

Top Quality Materials

Renegade's designer and company owner Daryl Murphy took me for a tour of the factory, pointing out the Spirit's features. From the pre-assembled 6061 T6 aluminum fuselage to the final cover of Stits Polyester Fabric, all components were of top quality materials. Aluminum extrusions and panels are all aircraft quality (to minimize corrosion and maximize strength), and the control rods are all push-pull to increase the pilot's feel and the aircraft's maneuverability. Also, redundant flying wires are used so that the structure is not compromised by the unlikely but possible failure of one wire. This flying machine is built to last.

None of the low-quality coverings common on all too many ultralight derivatives could be found on the Renegade. Poor coverings can lose more than half their strength in less than two years of exposure to the sun.

Additionally, the Renegade kit comes with the difficult stress-bearing portions largely assembled by the factory on their precise jigs. The fuselage is essentially complete, needing only sub-assemblies such as controls and seats to be secured. Once the controls and fabric work are complete, the wings are ready to attach to the fuselage.

This is not to say the kit can be built overnight. The builders had built three other air-cooled models of the Renegade, and this liquid-cooled prototype required 260 man/woman-hours to complete. Much of the time is devoted to prepping and painting, with 88 of the hours used in the fabric covering alone.

The big news is the addition of the Rotax 582. Hopefully, this engine will bring greater longevity and reliability to two-strokers. Its closer tolerances, and the even cooling of this liquid-cooled lightweight, promise considerably improved performance — a promise that was more than met in the flight test. The engine, complete with muffler and radiator systems, is only 100-115 lb on the Spirit. The gear box with 2.58:1 reduction ensures that the propeller converts the 64 hp into usable thrust.

The classic lines of the Spirit foretell aerodynamically proven concepts combined with modern advances. The use of the NACA 23012 airfoil results in both forgiving stalls and light flying control pressures. The biplane configuration allows a short wing span of 21 feet with a full 153 feet of wing area that produces a low wing loading of 5.5 lb/sq ft.

Sweeping the upper wing 10 degrees aft gives a very racy look while the three degrees of dihedral on the lower wings provides good lateral stability for cross-country jaunts. The positive stagger configuration also allows a wide center of gravity range while further increasing stability.

As I mentioned earlier, the round radial cowling gives the impression of a powerful engine lurking underneath, ready to roar to life. However, removing the cowling for a preflight inspection reveals a compact, fuel-efficient two-cylinder in-line powerplant that is more than enough to propel this multi-plane aloft, on approximately four gallons of regular gas per hour There is plenty of space to house the exhaust and cooling systems, and still leave lots of elbow-room to work on all parts of the engine.

With a gross weight on the latest model of 850 lb, a useful load of over 420 lb was left for fuel and flyers in the prototype.

During the pre-flight walkaround inspection, I was surprised to find that the aircraft had four ailerons (a factory option). This was a preview of the very snappy roll response that I was about to discover.

As if the multiple ailerons weren't enough, the designer added not only differential but also Frise-type construction to these control surfaces. These modern technological answers to adverse yaw — a problem so common on old biplanes — makes the aircraft much more pleasing and easier to fly.

Light and Sprightly Flight

In hindsight, I can say that the most difficult part of flying this two-holer was climbing into the cockpit, especially up front where one has to circumnavigate the trailing edge of the upper wing.

Protecting my face from high speed six-legged aviators was a Lexan windscreen. This shatterproof space-age material has proven to be impervious to the sun's ultraviolet rays. Additionally, owner Jim Lindsay loaned me his leather helmet and goggles.

After a little prime and a flick of the prop, the engine purred to life. My next surprise was the smooth hum this engine produces — it will certainly be neighborly with its quiet sound level. This proved true at all power settings.

Head-Turner

As I taxied out, a lot of heads were turned towards this macho-looking bipe. The full-sized radial cowling plus solo flight from the rear cockpit required a zig-zag taxiing pattern for visibility amongst the spectators. Control was excellent through the sensitive rudder and steerable tailwheel.

After a brief runup, controls were exercised and takeoff power applied slowly to avoid a swing. Even with the gentle advance of the throttle, acceleration was very invigorating and the Spirit was off and flying before full power could be applied. Subsequent takeoffs proved it was a challenge to apply full power before the aircraft wanted to fly. The controls were very effective, with the rudder being quite sensitive.

A caution here, though: Don't try to fly this — or any other taildragger — without a checkout.

The climb-out was spectacular, to say the least, with the extra power and geared thrust of the 72 x 32 pitched prop. All of the ultralights in the fly-by circuit were left below and far behind.

Leveling at pattern altitude before reaching the end of the runway, it was time to check the cruise performance. The addition of the 582 engine and large diameter propeller has increased the speed consider-

With the optional four-aileron system, the Renegade offers snappy roll response.

ably. I awed the designer when I told him I was getting a consistent indicated airspeed of 95 mph! (True airspeed 100 mph.) This was subsequently confirmed against other factory aircraft in the pattern.

Now that's fast for a biplane with only 64 horsepower!

But I didn't need the airspeed indicator to tell me I was really humming. The fragrant aromas of the summer evening were flaring my nostrils and the airstream was massaging my face. Sensing all of these inputs made the gauges and airspeed indicator seem redundant.

The approach and landing were easy and delightful, the controls well balanced, and the engine responsive.

Later in the afternoon, my wife decided she wanted to be indoctrinated into open cockpit/biplane flight. Her presence reduced the rate of climb somewhat and the cruise speed by five mph, but other than that, the performance was still excellent. (We weighed over 350 lb. Together, I mean.)

If you've been waiting for a well-designed, well-built aerobatic two-place biplane that can carry a hefty load and still have a very respectable cruise speed, your kit has arrived.

How Do I Get One? Let Me Count the Ways

The aircraft is available in five different levels of kits to suit the finances and skill capabilities of most individuals. The assembly manual was revised and perfected with submissions from the first 50 builders. The basic kit includes all hard-to-make parts, bent tubes, and stamped components, while the Quick Build Kit includes all parts pre-manufactured with assembled fuselage, wings, and engine mount. Float and ski options are also obtainable.

With so much success and so many Spirits flying and under construction, and with some thanks to a major overseas market developing, the company's service, plans, and materials have developed very high standards of customer satisfaction.

After inspecting and flying this Renegade, I could easily understand why it has been named the Spirit. The phantasm of yesteryear has been captured and given the performance of today, resulting in refreshing Rotax high performance at a meager cost.

Perhaps the designer's advertising flyer says it best: "There is nothing that quite matches the feel of the biplane. Pilots have had a love affair with the craft since the early days of aviation. Today, those who fly the biplane gain a unique perspective. They experience both the nostalgia and romance of a time when the biplane ruled the skies, and the exhilaration of performance we've come to expect from the modern day biplane."

Murphy has introduced an all-metal monoplane called the Rebel. The semi-monocoque fuselage has room for three occupants, including even liedown space. The airframe kit is priced at approximately $13,000 and resembles, to many observers, a DeHavilland Beaver. Cruise with a Lycoming O-235 is predicted to be 100 mph, carrying a useful load of 575 lb.

Specifications

Murphy Renegade Spirit and Renegade II

The figures in parentheses are for the air-cooled Rotax 503 engine installation

PRICE	Kit $13,735 ($12,095) incl engine
	Plans $295
BUILDING TIME	400 hrs
NUMBER OF SEATS	2 tandem
ENGINE TYPE	Rotax 582 (Rotax 503)
RATED HORSEPOWER	64 (53)
EMPTY WEIGHT	390 lb (360 lb)
GROSS WEIGHT	850 lb
WING AREA	153 sq ft
TAKEOFF DISTANCE	100 ft (150 ft)
LANDING DISTANCE	200 ft
CRUISE SPEED	80 mph (75 mph)
TOP SPEED	100 mph (85 mph)
FUEL CAPACITY	8 gal
RANGE	250 sm
REMARKS	Info kit $10, video $20

Performance figures provided by the factory.

The Lancair Series

Slick, Sexy, Strong, and Sweet

This design has just about all the desirables. It's fast, sleek, comfortable, high-tech, efficient, popular, etc., etc., and so forth.

Production of the Lancair 235 has been discontinued in favor of the more popular 320 (although parts support for the 235 is still being provided). The refinements of the 320 include an extra foot in length, a larger tail, a one-inch wider cockpit, and flaps now hinged on the bottom allowing twice as much travel.

High Technology in Kit Form

The forty pieces of the kit are delivered approximately one-third finished when the package arrives at a builder's door. The use of epoxy-based composites for the components, which are oven-cured at high temperatures and pressures at High Tech Composites Inc., allows the Lancair structure to be lighter and stronger per pound than much of its competition.

The higher heat resistance of the oven-cured pre-preg composition allowed the company to paint their 320 prototype red. You can believe that this draws a crowd wherever she goes, as the other composites are generally all white, with minor amounts of colored trim to offset the sameness. Many composite aircraft using inferior composite forms of construction would have sagged in the sun with a similar paint scheme. Composite stress analysis guru Martin Hollmann conducted the testing on the Lancair structures to prove their strength.

With a length of 21 feet and a wingspan of 23.5, the Lancair is rather diminutive on the outside. As you might expect, the measly wing area of 76 sq ft results in a moderately high wing loading of 22 lb/sq ft and a ride in turbulence that is one of the smoothest — but then, we're getting ahead of ourselves.

For the most part, Lancair owners are delighted with the plane and its performance. Building time has averaged 1,200 hours for most builders. With the 49-percent-complete "FAST-BUILD" kit, designer/president Lance Neibauer feels that the construction time will be reduced by 500 to 700 hours — at a cost of $6,000 additional. For many builders, this will likely be the more attractive package, since time is money.

Let's Try the 320 on for Size

My opportunity to fly the 320 occurred at the 1988 Arlington Fly-In, after the airspeed calibration had been completed on the prototype.

Entry over the low wing and cabin sill was facilitated by stepping onto the seat and lowering oneself into the plush interior. The comfortable, 22-degree reclined seats of the Lancairs give the pilot the interesting sensation, as he fastens his seat belt, of strapping on the aircraft. The contoured seats partially surround the dual joy sticks in a wide cabin of 43".

While the baggage compartment behind the side-by-side seats isn't huge by any means, it would prove adequate for prudent packers on a week-long outing.

The canopy can be left open for taxiing to provide ventilation, as it pivots up and forward. The castering capability of the nosewheel makes the plane easy to taxi and turn, using differential braking. Shock absorption is adequate, but would likely be severely challenged on rough ground.

Shop foreman Don Goetz rapidly firewalled the throttle on our first takeoff, providing dynamic acceleration through the 70 mph rotations speed. Leaping into the air after a 600 foot run, we selected the electrical flaps and gear up, reducing the drag and allowing the 320 to surge ahead.

The plane is able to get airborne in 700-800 feet, depending on weight, and the rate of climb is in the 1500-2400 fpm range. With the nose set at an attitude that allowed us to avoid other traffic being caught and passed, we indicated 120 mph at 2000 fpm. Wow!

Speed Freaks Rejoice

Leveling off at lower altitudes provided true airspeeds of 200 and 220 mph at power settings of 65% and 75%. High altitude cruising would add at least 20 mph to each. Some of the reasons for the Lancair series' high speed capabilities can be found in the attention to detail when it comes to drag reduction. Features include flaps that reflex upwards seven degrees after retraction, fully enclosed landing gear, and a laminar flow airfoil.

Another reason the Lancairs preform so well on small horsepower is the excellent design work that has been accomplished to reduce cooling drag. Most aircraft give up too much airspeed due to overly large cowling openings; the Lancair folks have done their homework on this one.

Some may wonder about the cooling competence of those small circular inlets. Have no fear. The CHT came nowhere near red line during the evaluation. As a matter of fact, Don felt that the engine was running too cool initially, so he restricted the airflow. Normally, it's quite difficult to cool an engine that flies through such a large speed range.

A full power run, as close to sea level as humanly possible, produced 247 mph, a blur of waves, and some seagull aerobatics. The pitch is light throughout the flight envelope, with a positive static stability and convergent phugoid tendency—better than one might expect. Much of the competition has to resort to mechanical magic to accomplish this profile.

Rudder response and load-up with airspeed is perfect—thank you— and the ailerons follow this suit. In fact, they become so firm (perhaps stiff) at high speed, it is unlikely that one would be tempted to make large control displacements for all-out aerobatics. But then, this is all to the good, because the company doesn't bill the Lancairs as aerobatic, and the firm lateral axis is beneficial for the 320's forte, namely cross-country flight.

It's easy to leave one's feet on the floor, as the differential ailerons effectively eliminate adverse yaw. The heavier windshield installed on the prototype produced an absence of sound that was profound. Vibration was also minimal – close to non-existent, in fact. Considering that the powerplant is a Lycoming four-banger, this is quite an accomplishment for the composite structure.

How Slow Can You Go?

Well, there was no question that the top end was impressive, but how well behaved would the series be at the bottom end? Slowing this clean machine down is no easy task, since the gear speed is a low 140 mph and the flaps 100. To avoid super-cooling an engine, it's a good idea to zoom climb to rapidly reduce the IAS to extension speeds. An alternative method for speed reduction would be to initiate a few steep turns to rapidly bleed off the knots.

When this was done, slow flight was accomplished at 100 mph on a fuel flow of 2.5 gph. That's an amazing 40 mpg! The controls were delightfully light, and again, noise was essentially non-existent. Ditto vibration.

Stall characteristics are a mixture of good and so-so. A pre-stall buffet gave adequate warning, but the wing is prone to a wild drop if the ball isn't kept in the center. The clean stall came at 75 mph and the gear and flaps reduced the stall to 71. The load ratings are +9 and -4.5 ultimate Gs, with a +6 and -3 limit load.

With attention to detail, builders can accomplish an empty weight of 1000 lb, giving a useful load of 685 lb. With a standard fuel load of 43 gallons, the 320 offers a range of 1100 miles.

And Now a IV

The addition of the Lancair IV provides kit builders with a four-place aircraft capable of carrying about 1100 lb for 1450 miles at nearly 300 mph.

Conclusions

Initial problems of not enough fiberglass cloth in the Lancair kits, errors and incomplete details in the plans, nosewheel problems, the absence of a flight manual, and lengthy backorders have subsequently been remedied by the factory. These are the sort of growing pains common with aircraft that are in high demand. Customers and the company have worked diligently to overcome these snags, with the result that there are hundreds of Lancairs flying.

When one looks at all of the capabilities of the Lancair series, it's easy to surmise they are a best buy in the marketplace. Low costs and high performance are an unbeatable combination, and the waiting list is an indication that builders agree.

Specifications

Neico Lancair 320

PRICE	Standard kit $19,950
	FAST-BUILD kit $25,900
	Plans $325
BUILDING TIME	Std 1500-2000 hrs
	FAST-BUILD 1000-1300 hrs
NUMBER OF SEATS	2 side by side
ENGINE TYPE	Lycoming O-320
RATED HORSEPOWER	160
EMPTY WEIGHT	1000 lb
GROSS WEIGHT	1685 lb
WING AREA	76 sq ft
TAKEOFF DISTANCE	690 ft
LANDING DISTANCE	900 ft
CRUISE SPEED	230 mph
TOP SPEED	250 mph
FUEL CAPACITY	43 gal
RANGE	1100 sm
REMARKS	Info kit $15

Performance figures provided by the factory.

Specifications

Neico Lancair IV

KIT PRICE	$43,900, plans price TBA
BUILDING TIME	1500-1900 hrs
NUMBER OF SEATS	4
ENGINE TYPE	Continental TSIO 550A
RATED HORSEPOWER	350
EMPTY WEIGHT	1650 lb
GROSS WEIGHT	2775 lb
WING AREA	98 sq ft
TAKEOFF DISTANCE	900 ft
LANDING DISTANCE	1200 ft
CRUISE SPEED	296 mph
TOP SPEED	300 + mph
FUEL CAPACITY	79 gal
RANGE	1450 sm
REMARKS	Info kit and video in preparation

Performance figures provided by the factory.

Pereira's GP-4

Ultimate Wood

If there is an aircraft on the market that deserves more attention than it's getting, it's the GP-4. Super fast, highly maneuverable, economical to operate, cheap and easy to build, etc., etc.

You ask, "If it's so darn good, why aren't hundreds of them flying?" Wait for it, Schmedley. It's coming. A flood of recent plans sales and the first flights of owner-built aircraft have brought this all-wood plane to the attention of the aviation public.

It's not that the GP-4 hasn't been around for a while. She won the Oshkosh Grand Champion award at her 1984 debut. Like the Questair Venture, this plane was shaped to present minimum obstruction to the relative air in order to increase cruising speed. However, unlike the Venture, the GP-4 causes everyone to drool over its gorgeous, graceful lines.

Two years ago, when I flew the prototype, designer George Pereira wasn't sure he wanted to expose himself to the sue-happy mentality prevalent in the US. As a result, he wasn't really marketing the plans, just supporting the current builders — something he does very well, according to his clientele.

While George isn't an aeronautical engineer, he qualifies as one of the finest gentlemen I've met in the industry over the last 25 years. And there is no question that he has what it takes to design efficient, attractive, high performance aircraft. Unlike many of the sales-oriented people in the industry, Pereira is more likely to tell a customer why he *shouldn't* buy his plans.

So there you go, another reason why the "Four" hasn't proliferated as much as the design deserves.

The other reason there isn't a GP-4 in every garage is the fact that the plane is plans-built only, with some prefab parts and a wood materials kit available from Wicks Aircraft. With the current craze for kit-built cruisers, this terrific project has been momentarily overlooked. But this is one great aircraft, if high performance is your bag.

The GP-4 may be just the ticket, if you're looking for speed and range in a two-place plane—and enjoy working with wood!

Why Wood?

Twelve hundred builders of the Osprey Aircraft amphibians know George Pereira quite well, as do a hundred pilots of this well-proven, diminutive two-place composite-and-wood wonder. The GP-4 is George's fourth design, thus the name. His goals were speed, long range, two seats, and construction simplicity.

There is no question that he succeeded in the first three. While the design is very labor intensive, the actual wood-working tasks are not difficult, although perfection requires cabinetmaker-level skills. The only machining necessary on the Four is on the nose gear.

High-strength water-resistant epoxy glues have taken away much of the worry associated with wooden structures. Now, keeping rats, termites, and moisture away from this noble, naturally grown composite seems to be the only worry. And there are numerous benefits to wooden aircraft other than the relative quiet and freedom from vibration they afford. A small, flat workbench is all it takes, along with the normal woodworking tools, to fabricate a GP-4.

Mahogany formers are used to avoid the need for laminating layers of wood together for added strength. The airfoil is a NACA laminar flow from the 63 series family, wrapped around a one-piece spar with 1/8" to 1/2" pine plywood ribs. Leading edge "D" cell fuel tanks of polyurethane foam hold 18.5 gallons each of the flammable stuff for the 200 hp Lycoming IO-360-A1A engine.

The wing is finally covered with 3/32 mahogany, either side, at a bias, to provide additional strength for the torsional loads encountered in flight. Then for the ultimate in smooth finishes, you could do what George did and cover the entire aircraft in fiberglass cloth, and fill the

1.7-ounce weave with a micro balloon-epoxy resin finish. Much sanding and shaping would, of course, ensue.

A few fiberglass fairings, the engine cowling, and some metal work
in the gear and engine mount, and your very own GP-4 is just about
complete — after an investment of 2000 to 3000 hours. Well, it kept you
off the streets.

As I crawled all around the experimental during the pre-flight inspection, there wasn't an angle anyplace that didn't brag about a low
coefficient of drag. It was sleek everywhere.

Climb Aboard for a Rush!

Stepping up onto the wing and over the sill, one is immediately
impressed by the exotic white leather interior on the flashy red
prototype. Sliding the modified Thorpe T-18 canopy back on its
tracks, I stepped onto the seat, and lowered myself into the roomy,
comfortable seat (designed to accommodate folks up to 6'6" tall).

Strapping into the 40" wide cockpit, I was rapidly falling in love. A
large solid rod, sticking straight up, caught my attention. George explained it was the mechanical gear retraction device, similar to the
Johnson bar on older Mooneys. Great idea — nothing to fail when it
comes to gear movements. Those electrical/hydraulic systems on most
aircraft are frequent contributors to gear-up landings.

Behind the seats, a 10.5 sq ft luggage compartment will absorb up
to 100 lb with two 200 pounders aboard. In front of the seats, the dual
controls and short but wide instrument panel call out for attention.
Those with a fancy for full-blown IFR avionics may find space somewhat limited, since the panel size has been chopped to reduce the
aircraft's height and therefore its drag.

After starting the injected engine, I noted that the nosewheel steering and braking were excellent as we expedited our way to the runway
threshold. George, worried about the sensitivity of the controls, made
the first takeoff. The Four must have been as keen to fly as I was,
because she jumped off the runway at 65 mph in less than 500 feet after
robust acceleration.

The Hartzell constant speed propeller clawed its way skyward as
George reached over and gave the gear retraction bar a yank, locking
the system in the Up mode. The bar is pulled aft and stowed between
the co-pilot's seat and the center console, completely out of the way.
Even though there are springs installed to aid retraction, it is best to

accomplish this before exceeding 90, as the air loads on the gear doors increase with airspeed, resisting retraction.

Raising the last 20 degrees of the electric flaps, we scorched upwards at 2000 fpm, indicating 140 mph. A couple of minutes later we leveled at 5000 feet with 60 percent power and a true airspeed of 225. It was at this setting that George flew his then-new prototype to Oshkosh with an average fuel flow of 9.4 gph, to collect the Grand Champion and Outstanding New Design awards on the plane's first outing. For those in a rush (and who can afford the 12 gph consumption) 75% power produces at least 240 mph at altitude. Those boasting Scottish blood can pull the throttle back for 160 true and a flow of 6 gph (and 26.7 mpg).

As he passed control to me, George warned that the aircraft had neutral stability and was very responsive. Actually, the aircraft does have a modicum of positive stability in all axes, and yes, it was delightfully light on the controls at all speeds, with some loading up due to aerodynamic forces with increasing speed. After a few minutes, he remarked that I was the first person who didn't initially over-control the Four. (Modesty compelled me to admit that thousands of helicopter hours develops a light touch.) I suppose the Four must therefore be very sensitive for most airframe drivers.

Phugoid pitch tests showed little tendency to return to the trimmed state; however, the aircraft was responsive and tended not to wander from headings and altitudes in level, steady flight.

Not for the Unskilled

George cautions clients that this is not a project for the unskilled craftsman any more than it is for the unskilled pilot. It's not that the GP-4 has dangerous or unforgiving habits; it's just that one has to think ahead and anticipate happenings in an aircraft that covers so much ground so quickly. Given her sensitivity of controls and close to neutral stability, she would be a handful for beginners. But then, many of us like them even better when they're a handful.

Espying one of the last SR-71 super spy planes approaching the Beale AFB pattern, I nudged the throttle to the firewall and passed the world's unlimited speed record holder. Granted, he was slowed to pattern speed; nonetheless, there are few homebuilts — or factory aircraft either — that could accomplish this feat!

Mentally challenging the spy plane to a low speed dual, I retarded power and initiated a zoom climb to reduce speed to the gear and flap limit of 140. We won.

The electric trim handled the broad band of speeds very well. Slow flight at 80 mph showed that the plane was still fully responsive to the light control inputs. The full 38 degrees of flap with power off produces a mild pre-stall vibration, followed by a gentle nose pitch-down nearing 60 mph. There was no tendency to drop a wing. While held in the stall, the ailerons remained effective thanks so the wing washout of 1.5 degrees. So both the top end and bottom end were very impressive.

As we cruised back to the northern Sacramento airport, I noted how low the sound and vibration levels were, especially for a fast aircraft. Visibility was very good, with some restriction forward due to the canopy bow, and downward due to the wing.

At cruising speeds, the GP-4 was free of adverse yaw, allowing us to make turns with our feet on the floor. This, combined with the wing loading of 19.09, mean the Four would be an excellent cross-country aircraft.

Back in the pattern, 90 mph was used on final with a slightly high cross-the-fence speed of 75 to handle the crosswind. The streamlined design dictates that no higher speeds be used, as this sweetheart has little in the way of drag, and a long float will ensue. This is why she requires three or four times more runway to land than to get off.

Fast Conclusions

I admit I'm biased. I like the man and machine very much. This design has few flaws, and they're minuscule. If this plane, as a project for homebuilding, has a major drawback for many individuals, it is the building time required. However, for the real craftsman and skilled pilot who wants to fabricate his own plane, not just assemble a kit, the GP-4 deserves very serious consideration. The plane is very fast and efficient, making it relatively inexpensive to own and operate.

Excellent qualities of this product include customer support, plans, materials package, ground, and airborne handling. To quote the Toyota ad, "Who could ask for anything more?"

Specifications

Osprey Aircraft GP-4

PRICE	Plans $365, materials pkg $8,000
BUILDING TIME	2000-3000 hrs
NUMBER OF SEATS	2 side by side
ENGINE TYPE	Lycoming IO-360-A1A
RATED HORSEPOWER	200
EMPTY WEIGHT	1240 lb
GROSS WEIGHT	1950 lb
WING AREA	104 sq ft
TAKEOFF DISTANCE	300 ft
LANDING DISTANCE	1750 ft
CRUISE SPEED	160-240 mph
TOP SPEED	260 + mph
FUEL CAPACITY	54 gal
RANGE	1100-1495 sm
REMARKS	Info kit $12

Performance figures provided by the factory.

Mini Master

Twin Engine Security

Do you live in a mountainous area, perhaps fly over water or large cities frequently? Does one engine seem one too few under these conditions? Have you been attracted by the larger margin of safety offered by twin engine aircraft, but been turned off by the high costs and pilot proficiency requirements of asymmetric flight?

Well, PBAC—Powers Bashforth Aircraft Company—have a plane that could answer your dreams. Their two-place, twin engine, center-line thrust Mini Master will be available soon in a 49-percent-complete kit. With an airfoil similar to the Piper Seneca, the production series can carry 675 lb, and at 75% power will cruise at 115 mph at 7000 feet. Thrust is provided by a brace of Rotax 582 engines with their dual redundant ignition systems.

Who are Powers and Bashforth? Harry Powers set the ultralight altitude record of 23,946 feet with a B1-RD. Designer Bruce Bashforth feels that their experience with Boeing and Robertson gives them a more flexible attitude toward design with a solid experience base of how to do things right.

CLT = No Asymmetric Thrust

An obvious benefit of the center line twin is the lack of unbalanced (asymmetric) thrust after an engine failure. Other twins, with wing-mounted engines, can be very deadly if inexperienced pilots attempt to fly them on one engine below the single engine safety speed of 75 mph or so. What good is a second engine if the single engine handling characteristics are overly challenging and simply a means of carrying you to the accident site?

Designed with the aid of a computer, the Mini Master prototype was originally powered with Rotax 503s. However, these were replaced with liquid-cooled 532s when the air-cooled engines were unable to give suitable single engine performance.

To prove their calculations, the designers subjected the aircraft to stress analyses that even examined the wing torsional loads that could occur due to gusts and control deflections — a task that all too few companies undertake.

According to preliminary performance figures, the prototype has come within a few percent of the computer predictions with the 64 hp engines. With the exception of single engine climb performance, the prototype achieved the computer predictions.

The recent addition of the Rotax 582s, with their oil injection and dual ignition, along with a new canard wing, has allowed the team to exceed their original expectations for speed and load carrying capabilities.

One of the aerodynamic refinements used in the Minimaster is the "sheared" wing tips. Easily incorporated in the constant chord wing, they dramatically improve stability while adding to the wing's efficiency. The three-wing-aircraft concept has been touted by many aeronautical experts as optimum for efficiency — as evidenced by more of these designs appearing at aviation events.

In normally configured aircraft, the horizontal stabilizer produces a download of approximately 10% of the aircraft's weight — a load which must be overcome by additional lift produced by the wings (with additional drag as well). The three wing strategy overcomes the drawbacks of the other systems, although canards have some disadvantages of their own.

Utilizing a blend of the best materials in the aviation marketplace, the aircraft uses fiberglass for the complex curves of the cowlings, a steel tube fuselage frame for strength and proven crash survivability, and aluminum elsewhere for its durability and lightweight strength.

The sleek fuselage has undergone considerable modification as intakes have been added, moved, deleted, and redesigned in order to maximize cooling and minimize drag as various engines were tested in the bright red prototype. The fore- and aft-mounted Rotax 582 powerplants appear to provide more effective thrust than the single ignition 532s they replaced, with cooling courtesy of heater core radiators (Chrysler and Ford) mounted in scoops.

The propellers, driven through a 2.58 Rotax reduction drive, have also accomplished a metamorphosis to achieve acceptable single engine climb improvements. Other engine options will include the more powerful 79 hp Rotax 912 and the Limbach four-stroke, four-cylinder powerplants.

The 32'7" wing, with an area of 158 sq ft, has been designed for removal in less than 30 minutes for aircraft storage in an eight-foot-wide space. The all-aluminum, fully cantilevered construction uses a diagonal semi-tension field beam main spar with "hydroformed" ribs and stiffened skins to form a semi-laminar flow airfoil.

The welded fuselage frame uses E-4130 chromoly tube that is covered with aluminum skins and a shatterproof Lexan windshield. With two all-aluminum vertical stabilizers, separated by the horizontal stab and elevator, the Mini Master measures a relatively short 23'4" — just garage size.

Construction videos, a building manual, and full-size plans should lead beginning builders through the jigsaw puzzle of converting hundreds of dissimilar parts into an airborne chariot.

An Intimate Look

The Mini Master prototype, N8004Y, has been designated Model MM-100, as it could be the basis for a series if it proves successful in the marketplace. After making three flights, one each with the different engines (503s, 532s, and 582s), this evaluation pilot feels that the more powerful version will be very popular.

A complete walk-around inspection, including a look at the engine compartment, required the extraction of approximately 40 screws to remove cowlings. This exposes a roomy and professional installation, creating plenty of space for large powerplants in the future. Most of the steel tube fuselage construction is easily viewed from the cockpit, allowing the pilot to check the condition of the structure at a glance.

Small 4.00 x 5 tires and heel-actuated mechanical caliper brakes are attached to a tube gear strut that has recently been beefed up, even though the first version adequately handled the cross-country taxiing as we plowed through the grass field on the Arlington Airport. Nonetheless, the small circumference would dictate operations from paved strips or smooth fields to prolong the integrity of the landing gear.

Because the canopy hinges on the left, access to the spacious cabin was achieved with a retractable step and an easy climb over the low right sill to the comfortable side-by-side seating. Sporting lap belts with one shoulder strap each, these buckets feature a 4" fore and aft adjustment. Coupled with considerable overhead room, it seems the cockpit would be roomy and suitable for any occupant—short of a gorilla. A large hopper-like area located aft would hold a considerable amount of baggage with a maximum weight of 60 lb or more, depending on gross. Bruce says, "The cockpit is larger than a C-150's in every direction."

After I voiced concern about the single, spindly canopy latch, Harry advised me that there had been no problem during the flight testing program, and that in fact the Mini Master can be flown with the plexiglass unlatched, as the relative airflow keeps it closed. This subsequently proved to be true during a third flight that was flown completely with the latch left undone.

Ample Panel Real Estate

The very large panel has plenty of room for an IFR instrument grouping and a very large glove box. Additionally, the prototype contained a voltmeter and ammeter for the dual electrical charging system to allow the design team to assess the charging capabilities of the Rotax engines. Central console-mounted throttles and twin yokes and rudder pedals allowed us to pass control back and forth during the flight test.

The aluminum wing carries 48 gallons integrally, giving a 115 mph cruise at sea level for 598 miles with no reserve. Obviously, cruising at higher airspeeds at altitude would extend the range 15 percent or so. Because most light aircraft using Rotax powerplants do not have accurate fuel consumption data, and since the lightly loaded propeller disks have not been operated at higher altitude during flight testing/evaluation, accurate consumption data have not been collected.

Rotax fuel flow charts lack accuracy for the broad range of propellers they are used with, according to Powers and other designers.

After adding bodies and two hours of fuel to the 755 lb empty weight, we taxied at 1375 pounds (175 under gross in the 582-powered variant). The designed maximum specified weight keeps the limit load factor to the FAR 23 Utility Category of +4.4 and -1.75 Gs.

Where's the Ceiling?

One of the major considerations in the selection of a gross weight for a twin-engined aircraft is the single engine service ceiling. The designers are optimizing the engines and propellers for an 8000-foot single engine service ceiling, and were still making minor prop changes after my last flight. The two-engine service ceiling is given as 20,000 feet, although the company says that the carburetors, lacking mixture control, won't work well at that altitude.

Start-Up Time

The twin-cylinder electric-start Rotax engines shimmied to life with the aid of their chokes, and settled down to a reasonably smooth, surprisingly quiet idle above 2000 rpm.

Visibility was excellent during taxiing, and the maneuverability very good with the castering nosewheel and differential braking. Because the low idle rpm of the Rotaxes produce too much thrust to taxi at a reasonably safe speed without the constant use of brakes, we used only the rear engine till it warmed up its coolant. Then we started the front 532 and shut the ignition off to the rear until we began the pre-takeoff checks. Due to the thermal mass of the liquid, the aft engine remained in the green operating range.

Waggling the controls proved them fairly free of static friction with the exception of the ailerons which had some drag. For added safety, a motorcycle battery powers a boost pump that is used for takeoffs, to provide a backup for the gravity feed/vacuum pump system.

With the pre-takeoff checks complete and a 15 mph wind on the nose, fire-walling the throttles gave a lift-off at 60 mph in less than 500 feet. Significant back pressure is necessary to make the nosewheel break ground, followed by a check forward after liftoff to avoid over-rotating.

With 128 hp tugging the Mini Master skyward, the obstacle-clearing rate of climb exceeded 1300 fpm at 70 mph indicated. Converting to the best rate of climb speed of 82 mph yields about the same rate, but better visibility for crowded airport environs.

While the sound level had increased to moderately high, vibration was still rather low, with no hint of the synchrophasing noise/vibration that is common on the Cessna Super Skymaster tandem twin. This problem arises in the factory aircraft when the engines are not synchronized to the same speed, and a sympathetic surging occurs. As a matter of fact, the Mini Master engines were run as much as a thousand rpm out of sync, with no audible noise or vibration.

During takeoff and climbout, the required rudder forces were reasonably low and directional control was excellent. Setting up for a cruise climb of 100 mph yielded a climb rate of 900 fpm on full throttles and a coolant temperature near the bottom of the limit in the 60 degree weather. Cooling radiator and intake proportions with the reduced inlet size allow full-power single-engine operation in temperatures of 85 degrees, according to PBAC testing.

Visibility was very good—albeit with a little restriction caused by the snout and the new canard. Control feel was adequately solid, making the Mini Master suitable for cross-country flying, but not onerous enough that the plane couldn't easily be thrown around the skies, short of aerobatics.

By blipping the MAC electrical trim system (one of the best ever designed for light aircraft), I was able to bring the Mini Master to 96 mph indicated, with the two-strokers brought back to 6000 rpm.

Harry and Bruce have used a number of propellers in the optimization process, and hope to achieve another 10 mph at all power settings in the future. Differing airflows over each prop has necessitated entirely different diameters and pitches on both props.

Feet on the Floor

The controls were delightfully balanced, and the absence of adverse yaw—thanks to 50 percent differential ailerons—meant that the pilot's feet could rest on the floor during turns in cruise flight. Because static pitch stability was also good, the Mini Master is a very stable platform for cross-country flights.

While the buzz of the Rotax engines was noticeable, it seemed low enough in amplitude to be of no concern to pilot comfort. To facilitate engine changes, the prototype had no firewall insulation, so good headsets and an intercom were used to reduce the noise. Owners will undoubtedly want to add a few pounds of noise-deadening material for the major benefit it provides.

Even though the wing loading was in the light range at 9.8 lbs/sq ft, the MM-100 handled the light turbulence around the Arlington, Washington airport in a most acceptable manner. While we didn't dive the aircraft to its V_{ne} of 155 mph in this early stage of its development, the builders advised me that they have dived to 130 mph without problems.

Because aerobatics are not recommended for the Mini Master, none was flown. However, we did shut down each engine in turn to determine that the twin was capable of maintaining level flight on one fan. Full power on the rear engine produced a 400 fpm climb, while the front was able to generate 300 fpm. With continued propeller refinement, Powers and Bashforth hope to improve this considerably. Much of their research and development work is aimed at obtaining superior single engine operation.

Slow Down

While maximized for high speed cruise, the Mini Master also has very desirable low speed handling. With those two big propellers creating tremendous amounts of disk drag with engines idled, the twin can slow down very quickly. Prior to the installation of the canard and drooping flaperons, we had conducted slow speed handling tests in this flapless aircraft at 60 mph and found that the stability and maneuverability were very good. Likewise, the gentle power-off stall at 56 mph was preceded by light buffeting and followed by a modest 700 fpm glide when held in the stalled condition. Running the engines below their power band at 4000 rpm resulted in a 53 mph stall with a descent of 300 fpm.

With no tendency to drop a wing, and a low rate of descent, the Mini Master, as tested, is certainly very forgiving. The twin could even be hand flown with aileron inputs while stabilized in the stall. Spin testing was not performed, as the design team has not yet conducted this portion of the flight envelope. When the drooping flaperons are connected for flight evaluation later in the program, the designers expect the stall to be in the mid forties!

While large sideslip angles are possible for crosswind landings, the rate of descent does not change appreciably under these conditions.

Nonetheless, reduction of power and the high disk drag can produce steep approach gradients for landing over obstacles.

Knowing this, when we returned to the pattern, we carried 80 mph on final, simply to keep up to the approach speeds of other aircraft. We were able to fly a large variety of glide path angles through varied power settings.

Using 70 mph across the threshold resulted in gentle landings in the ground cushion at approximately 50 mph. Braking action was only marginally adequate, due to a set of ultralight-type brakes. Harry advises that better quality brakes will be installed on the prototype and included in kit shipments.

The couple of dozen builders who have ordered the kit will be receiving the improved canard-equipped version at no extra cost.

Conclusions

Having flown all three prototype versions of the Mini Master over the years of the twin's development, I have gained considerable respect for Powers and Bashforth, and feel that the added dependability of the 582s with their dual ignition brings the MM-100 to a maturity that will make it a very attractive project for safety-minded homebuilders. Although the company recommends the 912 installation, this scribe believes that the added weight and much higher cost is counterproductive. Moreover, the prototype has not yet been flown with the 79 hp engines.

Those of us who cited low bank accounts and the potential hazards of asymmetric thrust as reasons for not switching to a multi can now overcome both drawbacks with this engineless airframe kit priced at $11,500. Invest a similar amount for 582 powerplants, props and instruments and most builders should be able to fly their new twin for $20,000 or so. Not much to pay for a twin's added safety, is it?

Note: I have included performance estimates for the Rotax 912 engine, assuming the installation of a kit-supplied variable pitch propeller from LECTRO-PROP. Incidentally, Rotax recently announced that a turbo version of this four-stroker will be marketed.

Specifications

Powers Bashforth Mini Master MM 100

Specs for Rotax 912 engine in parentheses

PRICE	Kit $11,500, plans $250
BUILDING TIME	500-1000 hrs
NUMBER OF SEATS	2 side by side
ENGINE TYPE	Two Rotax 582s (912s)
RATED HORSEPOWER	64 (79)
EMPTY WEIGHT	975 lb (1075)
GROSS WEIGHT	1550 lb (1800)
USEFUL LOAD	575 lb (725)
POWER OFF STALL	45 mph (48)
RATE OF CLIMB	1300 fpm (1550)
S/E ROC	350 fpm (425)
CRUISE SPEED	115 mph (130)
TOP SPEED	134 mph (145)
RANGE	595 to 950 sm (740 to 1200)

Performance figures provided by the factory.

Prowler

Ultimate Metal

The Prowler not only feels and flies like a piston-powered fighter, it also has the appearance of having been designed for the attack/aggressor role. From its sleek, streamlined spinner to the retractable tailwheel, this combatant looks ready for an aerial free-for-all — and indeed it is.

Testifying to the quality of George Morse's work is the impressive list of major awards collected to date: Outstanding Workmanship (Oshkosh), Homebuilt Special Award (Watsonville), Best Original Design (San Diego) and First Place/Most Original Design (Merced).

Before we start it up and put it through a combat sequence, let's
have a look at what makes this machine unique.

An Airborne Oldsmobile

Whether or not you are used to flying the Spitfire or Mustang, you
are in for a surprise when you lift the Prowler's bonnet to check the oil.
Nestled into the custom-designed cowling is an engine that has reliably
powered millions of automobiles around the globe—and is now helping to explore the frontiers of aviation.

The Prowler powerplant is the 266 cubic-inch-displacement Auto
Aviation V-8 conversion that would be easy to confuse with the 215 cid
aluminum version holding down the front of your Oldsmobile. However, it is very much modified for the task of pulling the Prowler
through the airways.

A choice of valves and compression ratios allows 200-230 honest
and reliable horsepower—or more. If you are unsure of the reliability,
ask the millions of car owners and racers who drive behind this V-8,
and then ask why you aren't using the other 400+ hp the engine is
capable of.

George has shoe-horned the immaculate engine into as sleek a
cowling as possible to minimize aerodynamic drag, while still allowing
good access for servicing. With all accessories and the gear reduction,
the V-8 measures approximately 43" long by 21" wide by 24" tall.

He has accomplished this by fabricating an accessories drive system that is operated off the back of the engine—where it can be readily
approached for maintenance. This Morse-designed system has eleven
drives, including two distributors; pumps for fuel, oil, hydraulic,
vacuum, and coolant circulation; plus the 55 amp alternator.

Incidentally, George Morse has been building and flying these engines for over 15 years, proving their reliability. Having served as parts
manager for an Oldsmobile dealer, George has learned what combinations of blocks and off-the-shelf engine components can be combined for optimum performance. If that isn't enough for you, then
kindly remember that it was automotive companies that made the
engines for the Prowler's parents—you remember, the Spitfire and
Mustang.

The Cooling System is Somewhat Unusual

This hybrid warrior uses 11 quarts of a 50/50 blend of ethylene glycol and water that is pumped from each side of the engine to Spitfire-like radiators in each wing. These "radiators" turn out to be GM Cadillac air conditioner evaporators that are mounted under the wings, with individual thermostatic controls that come from — can you believe it — a Volkswagen. He did admit he wasn't delighted with these units and plans some changes in this area. (My guess would be to a GM part).

In George's particular installation, a Buick 300 crankshaft produces 225 hp at a conservative 4350 engine rpm. Another unit flaunting the designer's workmanship is the gearbox mounted up front under the kidney-shaped coolant expansion tank. This 1.67:1 gear reduction uses a circulatory oil bath to lubricate Muncie helical gears that were liberated from a transmission to drive the Cessna 206 Model propeller/spinner. Horsepower is a measure of work done, but it's the engine torque multiplied by the gear ratio that provides the energy to the propeller. In the case of the Prowler, it is a strongly propulsive 405 lb of thrust that fire her through the troposphere at a low 2400 prop rpm.

A Bendix pressure carburetor, Model PSH-5BD, supplies the atomized fuel to the cylinder, while the dual electrical system modules supply the spark to the single plug. Future installations will have complete redundancy and Vertex super magnetos as a possible option.

You may want to know what the weight penalty of an auto conversion will be. Because cast iron weighs 2 2/3 more than aluminum, extensive use of the lighter metal has significantly reduced this GM product's mass. The Prowler powerplant has been trimmed to a competitive 420-lb package, including all normal accessories. When one considers all the cooling baffles and the firewall-forward equipment on the air-cooled engines, not to mention the extra fuel carried to feed their habit, these liquid-cooled engines begin to look better. Even the major air-cooled aviation engine manufacturers are now developing liquid-cooled engines: witness the main powerplant for the record-setting around-the-world Voyager.

For those of you who might be looking for a pusher powerplant for your amphibian or whatever, George states, "This engine can be used as a pusher because the propeller shaft bearings are identical and thrust may be applied in either direction without any changes in the engine." Additionally, he points out that radiators can be placed wherever design and thermal cooling will permit. The glycol pump will circulate coolant over long distances (at 15 psi). Increasing the distance from engine to radiator will allow heat loss in lines that is compensated by a smaller radiator requirement, according to the designer.

Looking to the future, the prototype was designed with oil and fuel systems that will allow inverted flight operations. This capability has also allowed airshow performer Wayne Handley to grind the Prowler through its paces from +6 to -3 Gs during practices for numerous air shows. Attendees were enthralled with this spectre from the past and its Merlin-like sounds and flights of fancy. The Prowler has been mistakenly identified as just about every single engine fighter the Allies flew in WW II.

Power Reinforcements Are on the Way

While this is being written, a second prototype, incorporating numerous improvements, is flying. It is powered by a Chevrolet engine with the Rodeck block that is commonly used in racing cars.

This conversion is estimated to be easily capable of 350 hp and approximately 700 lb of thrust. This represents an increase of 56 percent in Prowler-pulling ponies and 73 percent greater thrust at the prop. This powerplant will require the three-blade prop system from an aircraft such as the pressurized Cessna 210 to absorb the Chevy's power. By the time the flurry of checks settles, this engine will be rather expensive with its many refinements — but still half the price of a new Lycoming or Continental capable of producing approximately the same thrust.

Prowler Perfect

After the gorgeous engine installation is inspected and admired, the wings are the next portion of the airframe one encounters. From any view, these double-tapered semi-elliptical airfoils once again whisper "piston powered fighter." Based on the NACA 64A212 and 64A210 airfoils, this 25'4" span utilizes a three-degree washout to provide moderated stall characteristics.

George has designed the wing in three sections with the root portion spanning only eight feet for road towing purposes. The leading edge, "D," or nose sections, could be sealed to provide up to 60 gallons of fuel. Additionally, a header tank forward of the instrument panel provides direct flow to the engine fuel pump and adds 15 gallons to the

Prowler's capacity. This is the tank that provides the aircraft's inverted flying capability.

As this is not a certified aircraft engine complete with nameplate, one can use the fuel of choice. Nonetheless, it is likely that the lower compression versions could use the commonly available 92 octane car gas, while the harder working engines would prefer avgas 100 to preclude burping and detonating. The aviation fuel would burn cleaner and provide greater quantities of lead to protect the valve seats, but at a much greater cost per hour.

The push-rod activated differential ailerons and the flaps are so well constructed that the slipstream would be hard pressed to create drag where they intersect the wing.

The main gear, mostly fabricated from Morse-made parts, takes a wide stance on the pavement and is rugged enough to live on grass strips. Raked forward at a cocky angle, the Prowler looks as though it is ready to be catapulted into action. Few aircraft look so good on the ground.

The prototype has a rather unusual retraction system that requires a considerable pilot checkout and would therefore be subject to errors. However, he promises that it will be changed on production models, thus removing our need to dwell on the topic. In a nutshell, the doors and main gear legs must be operated separately and in the correct sequence so as not to crush the doors.

The windshield is backed by a strong member that doubles as a roll bar. The one-piece canopy comes from Bee Gee and is hinged on the right, providing easy access to the fore and aft seats. Apparently, production kits will come with a sliding canopy a la the P-51. Currently, the system is secured by two over-center arms with secondary fasteners for backup safety. Builders might want to fashion some form of sunshade between themselves and the plexiglass for warm weather wanderings.

Taking one giant step up to the trailing edge of the wing and another over the cockpit sill allowed me to lower 200 lb of pleasantly portly human ectoplasm into the rear seat. Some airframe drivers might find the accommodations a little tight, especially in the front cockpit, if they are over six feet tall or rotund — or both. It should be noted that George has accounted for this with plans to stretch the cockpit area in the second prototype and then in the kits.

To give considerable detail about the interior layout might be wasting your time, as it will largely be changed in the kit aircraft. There is certainly adequate room for builders to customize the cockpit with VFR panels. Finding adequate space for IFR avionics would be more challenging without considerable innovation—but that's what homebuilding is all about.

The second prototype will be flown solo from the front seat, improving visibility of the front-mounted instrument panel. The cockpit features dual controls, with a standard "T" layout of flight instruments and switches. There are no real surprises—until one turns the key and wakes up George's Auto Aviation handiwork.

As Easy as Starting a Car

With cranking power supplied by a 28 amp hour gel-cell battery, the V-8 immediately settled into a steady and reassuring purr that would be equivalent to a turbine at ground idle. Another turbine-like aspect was the slow-turning prop speed—about 400 rpm. A combination of the gearbox reduction and the naturally low idle rpm of a big "8" resulted in the prop turning at half the speed we are used to in our fuel-cooled Lycoming and Continental engines.

Missing was the vibration that helped keep pilots awake with aircraft engines as we know them. (Surely, there couldn't be very much horsepower reined in under the hood with such a quiet idle and no shake, rattle, or roll.)

With the pre-taxi check complete, it was a simple matter of releasing the brakes and starting my zig-zag to the departure end of the runway. No, it's not that the Prowler is difficult to taxi straight; it's the slightly reduced visibility caused by that big snout that requires the clearing turns to avoid obstacles. Even at low speed, the rudder has enough leverage to make the binders unnecessary for clearing turns as long as you keep the engine rpm up enough to induce adequate air flow over the tail.

It Keeps Its Cool

A major problem associated with many liquid-cooled conversions has been their tendency to overheat and boil the coolant during ground operations—or worse still, boil in flight. During the drive out to the far end of the airport, the temperature gauge remained at a stable 145 degrees F.

Unfortunately, my personal coolant temperature was approaching a boil with the greenhouse effect of the winter sun. Builders will want to fabricate a device to hold the canopy partially open in the slipstream for ground-bound operations.

The run-up was simplicity itself. The three-position magneto switch allows *left only,* *both,* or *off* when selecting the distributor ignition system. The right distributor with its retarded points is checked during the startup when it alone is automatically selected during cranking.

What is really impressive about this electronic ignition is the fact that there is no noticeable mag drop, and thus no loss in power, when only one distributor is selected. This must be some sort of tribute to the effectiveness of electronic ignition compared to the heavy, failure-prone magneto design that found its first use on the Model T Ford. Makes one wonder whether automotive engines will always have to bring us the significant advances in aviation.

Typically car-like, there was no need to check a carburetor heat control.

The gear shift equivalent — propeller pitch control — was exercised, and courage was summoned to fly my first WW II fighter-like aircraft. Waving the controls around to check for freedom and correct movement showed that there was a considerable amount of friction in the system. (Later, it was explained that the lengthy hinges and friction-producing bushings used in the ailerons and elevator will be replaced with ball bearings in the kit version.)

Up, Up in the Air

Following George's suggestions, the tail was allowed to raise itself during a flapless takeoff. Expecting a tendency for the Prowler to seek the weeds alongside the runway if large power and thus P-factor were used, I advanced the throttle gingerly. To my great surprise, there never was any great amount of yaw, but the acceleration was still very brisk. (Many pilots make the mistake of advancing aircraft rpm too quickly thus decreasing the propeller efficiency and increasing the likelihood of a bad swing.) The tail raised itself when it was good and ready, at approximately 55 mph, and liftoff was accomplished at 80 indicated. No difficulty there at all.

A rather steep deck angle ensued in order to keep the airspeed at the 120 mph maximum for gear retraction. She must have been in a rush to get to altitude for upper-air work, because the rate of climb approached 2000 fpm! With a power loading at this weight of 6.8 lb per horsepower, it wasn't surprising that she was reaching for the stars.

Lowering the nose for improved visibility in the pattern area gave 140 mph indicated and a climb rate of 1200 fpm. Racing out of the airport control area (and out of radio contact with George, as it turned out), we found ourselves in clear smooth air at 4500 feet just a few minutes after take-off.

Another problem that is to be rectified in the kit aircraft, the electric trim, made its shortcomings evident early in the flight. First of all, it is far too slow, and secondly, it doesn't have enough travel.

Well and Truly Smitten

But I must admit, with me and this airplane it was love at first flight. Perhaps the muscular, liquid-cooled behemoth under the hood, perhaps the sexy elliptical wings flanking me, maybe the tiger in my tank was the cause. Whatever it was made me tighten the harness, check for loose articles (other than myself) and throw caution to the wind. It was time for aerobatics! It wasn't a feeling of supreme confidence on my part that enticed me, but rather an awareness that this aircraft felt a fervor for full-fledged flight.

The control balance was so delightful that it tempted me to explore some of the edges of the flight envelope. (And I did. But let's not burden the already overworked FAA with details they don't really want to know.) Suffice it to say that I felt confident and comfortable in the Prowler and she rewarded me with outstanding responses to the gentle control inputs.

The moderate control pressures used to overcome the aforementioned stick forces are probably desirable for most pilots during cross-country flights, to help reduce over-controlling. The Prowler was reasonably stable in all axes, and while not an optimum IFR aircraft, it would be more than adequate for occasional instrument operations, when suitably equipped. But then, who would want to go punching straight-line holes in the clouds in a recreational aircraft that is perfectly optimized for cavorting?

However, if you've an inclination to fly straight and level for more than a minute or so, expect an indicated cruising airspeed in the 195-200 mph range at 3000 feet. Using 23 inches and 2300 rpm for this speed will result in a fuel flow of approximately 8.5 gph, according to George. At higher and therefore more efficient altitudes, one could expect true airspeeds in the 215 mph range, depending on the weight and workmanship on your particular aircraft.

At any rate, this all results in better than 20 mpg. Try that in your Oldsmobile at a cruise speed of 200 mph. (For that matter, try to cruise at 200.)

A Little Surprise

Electrically lowering the flaps at speeds below 150 indicated (and trimming the weight out of the nose caused by the moderate pitch-down), and then lowering the gear at 120, caused fairly rapid deceleration. This high drag can be very desirable when one must make a rapid descent. As a matter of fact, a rapid and very steep descent was exactly what the Prowler surprised me with when the airspeed dropped below 55 mph. She very quickly pointed at a spot below us. A moment later, she changed her mind and snapped into an autorotative turn to the right.

Not wanting to be the first to conduct spin testing in the Prowler, I immediately centered the joy stick and used opposite rudder to arrest this unplanned deviation. Whew! What caused that? Perhaps the ball wasn't centered. Let's try that again, ensuring that the ball is centered. And again she snapped!

Alas, it wasn't me. The spin culprit was the offset vertical fin that needs adjustment in later models. (George had neglected to warn me of this characteristic.)

Relieved that it wasn't my inept flying causing the rotation, I employed a trace of left rudder in the next stalls (with a right skid ball resulting), to keep the nose from yawing. However, no combinations of power or drag devices stopped that abrupt nose drop after the slight warning burble at approximately 60 mph. Apparently, this may be correctable with a change in the horizontal stabilizer's angle of incidence.

To put this all into perspective, the Prowler always recovered correctly and quickly, leaving me no doubt that she would recover from any spin that one might enter while she was within her weight and CG limits. Nonetheless, this is not the sort of aircraft one wants to stall on final approach.

But then, there are few that could be stalled during takeoff or landing without dire consequences.

Incidentally, the slow flight characteristics, short of the stall, were predictable and required only gentle stick forces. Worthy of note was the moderate amount of power needed to overcome the drag of the flaps, gear and wings at the lower end of the speed range. This drag, coupled with the rather high wing loading, at the 2150 lb gross weight of 19.25 lbs/sq ft, allows steep approaches and good glide path control for landings.

However, the same wing loading dictates a need to avoid low speed approaches with high rates of descent to avoid that sinking feeling on the round-out.

Back to Earth

Having determined all of this, I reluctantly decided it was time to take this fighter back to the ground crew for fuel and ammo. It was tempting to scorch down the active into a fighter break.

However, saner judgment, and the fear of incurring the wrath of the instructors and students droning laboriously around the pattern, held me at bay.

The first approach taught me that this machine should be wheel-landed rather than three pointed, in order to avoid instrument panel landings. A student pilot who took up residence on the runway forced me to carry power and slow down to allow enough time for him/her to clear the active. Unfortunately, this resulted in such a nose-high attitude that a go-around was necessary as I lost sight of the Cessna ahead. My reward was the surge of power as the prop beat the air into submission at its 2600 rated rpm, and the Prowler surged ahead.

The next approach was flown with full flaps and 80 mph on the clock once again. With a gentle and partial round-out, the Prowler kissed the asphalt and tracked perfectly down the center line with nary a hint of swing in the 5-10 mph crosswind.

Afterwards, it was difficult to answer George's questions about my impressions of the flight, because of the wide, silly grin on my face.

It would also be difficult to give any reasons that would stop you from getting into line for a kit—unless the package price of nearly $60,000 deters you. But remember, the kit also includes the engine, propeller, basic instruments, and other standard equipment—including battery, strobe, and navigation lights, aerobatic/inverted oil/fuel systems. Only the avionics options need to be selected by the builder.

For readers in Great Britain or Australia, or those who would like a new aluminum block 225, it is still in production in the two countries, and therefore readily available for builders to convert.

Assuming the production kit solves the mentioned deficiencies of trim, control friction, gear retraction selector, tail incidence re-rigging and front seat room, this is one heck of a lot of airplane—and it's all metal! Compare it to real warbirds at $300,000 + with their incredibly high operating costs. Considering that almost everything will be included in this 49-percent-complete kit, the price is quite reasonable for the high performance package that results.

Conclusions

Many have dreamed of a powerful, reliable, and efficient auto conversion, but it took George Morse to make it a practical reality with his Prowler installation. If you want warbird looks and somewhat similar handling, you'll be pleased to know that the Prowler package promises to fulfill your dreams at minimum cost. If the reaction of individuals around its home base is any indication, the Prowler will turn heads and draw compliments wherever you go.

Specifications

Prowler

Specs in parentheses are for the Rodeck V-8 conversion

KIT PRICE	$59,950 incl engine and prop
BUILDING TIME	1000 hrs
NUMBER OF SEATS	2 tandem
ENGINE TYPE	Buick V/8 conversion
RATED HORSEPOWER	225 (350)
EMPTY WEIGHT	1400 lb (1450)
GROSS WEIGHT	2150 lb (2650)
WING AREA	104 sq ft
TAKEOFF DISTANCE	800 ft
LANDING DISTANCE	1000 ft
CRUISE SPEED	200 mph
TOP SPEED	225 mph
FUEL CAPACITY	60 gal
RANGE	1200 sm
REMARKS	Info kit $12.50

Performance figures provided by the factory.

Questair Venture and Spirit

Simply Superb

After setting eight speed and time-to-altitude records in 1988, the Venture has continued to wow the crowds. Unfortunately, at this writing, Questair is undergoing a bankruptcy proceeding, but there is considerable hope that the company will work its way out of its financial difficulties — perhaps even by the time you read these words. Of course, you will want to get an update on Questair's situation if you are considering the purchase of one of their kits.

Beauty In the Eye of the Beholder

In a world where form follows function, the somewhat egg-shaped plane this team has developed reduces drag in so many ways, using nothing more than accepted practices, that they have produced the fastest of the current crop of homebuilts. In my opinion, the Venture is stunningly attractive, although maybe I'll make an exception of the gimpy looking landing gear. This aircraft is shaped to provide high efficiency, performance, and comfort. This, to me, is beauty!

In addition, the designers have put together a package that not only meets or exceeds FAR 23 parameters for factory aircraft, but also exceeds the handling and performance of the factory aircraft the regulations were designed for.

Questair's primary criteria were: comfort uncommon in today's aircraft, a stable IFR platform with elegant flying qualities cruising in the 275 mph range, a durable product with known structural integrity and "what the customer wants most — value." (They have, shall we say, eggceeded these goals without, umm, scrambling any other important requirements.)

If you become an owner, you will be very proud of the Venture's record-setting accomplishments. Although you shouldn't expect to match the speed record accomplishments of the factory (unless you turn up their propeller governor to produce more power, the way the record team did), the fact is, she will likely be the fastest piston-powered aircraft on the ramp.

Advanced Kit Materials with Aluminum

Construction is essentially all aluminum, and is estimated in the 2000-2500 hour range for kit completion. According to Questair, "All skilled labor jobs are done in the factory, so you do no welding, forming, braking or stretching with aluminum." Ribs, fuselage frames and skins are hydro-formed into final shapes, leaving the builder only edge preparation and assembly.

The company uses the new 6013 aluminum with a skin thickness of 0.032 inch. This alloy combines the strength of the 2000 series with the shaping and welding capabilities of the 6000 series.

After forming, the metal is heat treated in ovens at 350 degrees for four hours, to increase the strength to the T6 rating. Structures that would be difficult to form, such as the cockpit/canopy interface, arrive at your door, complete and ready to accept the new canopy with its increased headroom.

One of Questair's newsletters lists approximately 30 tools and items required to build the Venture, plus the need for a 25' x 23' x 9' room. The estimated cost for all of the tools is $1,000-1,500, depending on the current condition of your equipment inventory. Prospective builders might like to start practicing their rivet bucking, in anticipation of the kit arrival.

Designed for Personal Ease

The 46.5" cockpit is exceedingly wide for an experimental and the comfort level is very high. Access is easy, thanks to a large canopy that hinges at the leading edge and pivots up and out of the way on a gas strut. This strut can be locked in a position that holds the canopy open somewhat for ventilation on the ground. No worry about its departure during flight, as it is secured with four locking mechanisms.

Side-by-side seating with a center console ensures plenty of room for the broadest pilots. The seats are very deep and set low in the aircraft. This precludes good visibility over the instrument panel and engine cowling, but it is excellent for head-in-the-cockpit flying, such as IFR operations — something the Venture excels at.

The Continental IO-550-G engine produces its 280 hp at only 2500 rpm. For reliability, the system has been derated from 305-315 hp at 2750-2850 rpm. The hot, fuel injected engine started easily and the vibration and the sound levels remained very, very low.

On the Move

Since visibility was somewhat restricted by the nose, even in this tricycle geared configuration, we made gentle turns while taxiing to avoid spectators. The nosewheel is fully castering, allowing very sharp turns with differential braking—except that the nosewheel is steerable through the same brake pedals, as it has a double-sided piston that allows pressure on either side. Rather than enter on a lengthy dissertation on this topic, let me just say that, from this pilot's point of view, the system feels perfectly normal.

The same is true of the control stick/yoke. This rather unusual device, shaped like an "L" laying on its side, protrudes out of the bottom corner of the panel on either side, and is grasped by the pilot while he rests his arm on the elbow rest. Initially, this seemed quite peculiar. However, in flight, its operation was quite normal and its unique arrangement was not detrimental in any way. As a matter of fact, the design not only makes the cockpit easier to enter and less cluttered, it also eliminates the blind spots behind conventional con-

Some people joke about the Venture's egg shape, but it sure makes for a spacious, comfortable interior!

trols that prevent the pilot from seeing various instruments unless he tilts his head.

With the very close-set gear and high center of gravity, you wouldn't want to turn any corners at high speed. (During initial tests, someone did, and scraped a wing tip.)

The strength and durability of the prototype was examined when a special valve for the fuel system was left off for special tests. The dead stick, rough field landing that ensued proved it was difficult to scramble this egg.

Sunny Side Up

A firm ride on tiny 4.00 x 5 tires suggests you will want to stay on paved runways. Engineering specialist Doug Griswold tells me the prop has a mere two-inch ground clearance on level ground when the nose gear tire and oleo are flat. But to be fair, many tricycles would have to replace their divots and pay greens fees if both of these deflations occurred at the same time.

Getting the Venture into its element, we whipped the Egg's 280 horses into a frenzy that flung our 2000 lbs down the runway to the gasps of the Arlington Airshow crowd. After a few seconds, 1100 feet of runway, and 85 mph of airspeed, we departed the runway and rocketed skyward at 2500 fpm with 175 KIAS on the clock. The gear and flaps were retracted, slowly, at the flick of a switch. Peering over the broad IFR panel, it looked as though other aircraft in the busy traffic pattern were backing up at high speed to get a look at us.

The firm but responsive controls continued to load up with airspeed, contributing to the solid feel that is desirable for IFR flight. (The control sensitivity and effective perceived control surface loads are builder-adjustable by the use of variable spring rates in the trim system.) While the response was still sports-car-like for a given amount of control movement, the input forces were more similar to a heavy twin rather than a record setting debutante.

The side controller felt like a combination joystick/yoke in travel, with heavy springs dampening movements in all axes. Trim switches for all axes use a two-speed system that was too slow in the pitch axis for my taste, and will be replaced with a faster system on kits. Since that trim system can be the choice of the builder, I would suggest the "Chinese hat" style of trim switch mounted on the top of the control stick. Of course, a builder opting for this system will have some design work in store for himself.

Artificial Feel

Pilots should note that they are actually trimming an artificial-feel system by loading the spring systems in each axis. This negates the possibility of major stick loads in the event of a runaway electrical trim system, and eliminates the complexity and drag of tabs on trailing edges of control surfaces.

To the many of you who might ask if this short-coupled aircraft is yaw-twitchy around its vertical axis, the answer is a double no. Firstly, when we measure the moment arm to the rudder, we find the aircraft is not short-coupled at all, but rather better than average, and secondly, the Venture exhibited very positive directional stability.

Full span, 100% mass-balanced ailerons, on a very high aspect ratio wing, provided a snappy roll rate. Although the company doesn't push the fact, test pilot Rich Gritter claims the Venture is suitable for "sport or gentleman's aerobatics." The design loads are + 5 and -2.5 G at gross weight and + 6 and -3 for solo flight at weights below 1620 pounds dry, to quote the company brochure.

After some aerial ballet, we leveled at 4000 feet, where our true, corrected airspeed was 235 mph at 23 square. Company testing has produced a 275 mph cruise at 12,000 feet with a fuel flow of 13 gph. With continued optimization, Questair hopes to achieve a cruise of 300 mph. A typical power setting in the 65-75% power range at 7500 feet would provide 265-275 mph cruise.

In Flight

The cross-country comfort is unrivaled by any homebuilt I've flown to date. Couple this factor with low sound, minimal vibration through the rudder bar, and very good stability, and you'll understand why we should shortly see numerous Eggs hurtling between cities. The high redline speed of 346 indicated provides plenty of top end margin, as the Venture has been dived to 560 mph true!

To test the low end of the envelope, we extended the gear and 16 degrees of drooped aileron — actually flaperon — at the limit speed of 196 mph so that drag would assist us in a rapid deceleration. The effect was similar to driving a car into a dense hedge, or using a jet's speed brakes. This will be an excellent technique for pilots to use in descending from altitude without supercooling their engine — a major problem with those high performance planes that have low gear and flap limit speeds.

The L-shaped yoke provides an unobstructed view of the instrument panel.

Extension of these devices did, however, produce a moderate nose-up trim change initially and then a strong nose-down load. (That's why a faster trim system is necessary.)

Surprisingly, the stall characteristics were very tame, thanks to slots and a drooped leading edge that was added to the wings. The actual stall was preceded by adequate buffeting, followed by a gentle nose pitchdown at a measly 70 mph. In the stalled condition, the aircraft was so forgiving, it could be flown with aileron inputs. This is extremely impressive in an aircraft with such superlative top-end achievements.

The clean, power-off stall is in the 75-80 mph range with plenty of pre-stall warning, transmitted through the control stick 10 or so miles per hour in advance of the gentle, slow, pitchdown.

Slow speed handling was equally impressive, with control authority more like a training aircraft than a trend setter. Perhaps it should be marketed as a high speed glider, since it produced 105 mph forward speed, with a shallow descent of only 600 fpm. This aircraft does everything but STOL operations!

Returning to the circuit with our 27.6 lb/ft wing loading made me aware that I shouldn't set up too high a rate of descent at low airspeed, lest nothing be left to flare with at the threshold. However, subsequent experimentation in slow traffic that was cutting us off on final showed that this wasn't as much of a problem as I expected. Carrying 140 mph downwind so as not to pass all the pattern traffic, and 100 mph across the hash marks in a 20 mph crosswind, resulted in smooth landings every time.

Excellent brakes make the Venture suitable for 2000-foot fields when flown with precision — although 3000 feet would likely be a more suitable length for pilots who are not current or up to the plane's capabilities.

The small snags I noted in my evaluation flight are the type that are easily overcome by individual builders. Don't be like many pilots who select their aircraft by appearances only – unless you can perceive the beauty of the Venture. For it is truly an exceptional performer with excellent handling qualities.

The serious IFR pilot will be unable to find a comparable factory-built plane to rival this high speed yet forgiving experimental. Reasonable short field capabilities, considering the performance, and a semi-aerobatic bent make the Venture attractive to just about any pilot who wants to show those factory products a thing or two.

Note that it was Questair's practice in the past to include a new engine, prop, and governor as part of the Venture kit package. The company is no longer doing this; the price shown in our spec box is for the airframe only.

For the budget-minded, Questair now offers the Spirit. This design uses the same airframe as the Venture, except that it has a fixed tricycle gear. The Spirit is offered as a barebones airframe kit that does not include as many components as are supplied in the Venture kit. An optional package includes an electrical system, wheels, brakes, engine mount, oil cooler system, exhaust, induction system, and heater, to name a few.

The fixed-gear Spirit is a budget version of the Venture.

Specifications

Questair Venture

KIT PRICE	$42,000
BUILDING TIME	2000 hrs
NUMBER OF SEATS	2 side by side
ENGINE TYPE	Teledyne-Continental IO-550-G
RATED HORSEPOWER	280
EMPTY WEIGHT	1240 lb
GROSS WEIGHT	2000 lb
WING AREA	72.5 sq ft
TAKEOFF DISTANCE	1000 ft over a 50' obstacle
LANDING DISTANCE	1600 ft over a 50' obstacle
CRUISE SPEED	276 mph
TOP SPEED	312 mph
FUEL CAPACITY	56 gal (up to 85 optional)
RANGE	1150 sm

Questair Spirit

KIT PRICE	$24,900 (airframe only)
BUILDING TIME	1800 to 2200 hrs
NUMBER OF SEATS	2 side by side
ENGINE TYPE	Lycoming O-360
RATED HORSEPOWER	180
EMPTY WEIGHT	990 lb
GROSS WEIGHT	1700 lb
WING AREA	72.5 sq ft
CRUISE SPEED	213 mph
TOP SPEED	219 mph
FUEL CAPACITY	56 gal
RANGE	1324 sm

Performance figures provided by the factory.

RotorWay Exec and Exec 90

These Wings Go 'Round

If you haven't had the ultimate thrill of attempting to fly a helicopter, you may not understand the fascination of thousands of aviators for these fling wing creatures. Yes, it's true that helicopters are more challenging to fly. However, once one gets the hang of it, the movements and control pressures become quite natural.

The attraction for many owners is the helicopter's ability to land in almost any location that provides rotor blade clearance and maneuverability that exceeds the capabilities of all but the slowest of fixed wing aircraft. Another facet is the inspiring feeling of freedom one feels, to be able to fly like a bird, hover, and land in one's own back yard, using the garage as a hangar.

But there is a downside. For one thing, the helicopter license is quite costly to obtain (short of learning on your own helicopter). And that's just for starters. Helicopters are expensive to operate. They burn more fuel to fly one pound of payload one mile — about twice as much

A helicopter, such as this RotorWay Exec, can provide more flying freedom than a fixed wing bird, but operating costs are considerably higher.

as a fixed wing aircraft. Maintenance costs can be quite high — and are a requirement for your continued health. On the Exec, for example, the rotor hub universal bearings should be disassembled and inspected every 100 hours, and they should be replaced at the factory every 200 hours, along with other critical bearings, bolts, and pins. Also, because the Exec will be "manufactured" by you, there is no warranty on the engine, etc.

(Incidentally, if you're considering the helicopter option, pay particular attention to center of gravity and payload considerations. Rotary wing aircraft use brute power to lift their cargo, often restricting the amount they can carry. Also, a loaded helicopter, although it can lift vertically into a three-foot hover, still may require hundreds of feet to accelerate to a speed where it will be able to climb over obstacles.)

Many individuals build helicopters only to find they can't afford to maintain or operate them. Nonetheless, for those who can afford the optimum flying experience, nothing compares to the pleasures of helicopter flight.

A Case History

Ian Vantreight, General Manager of Vantreight Farms, knows about agricultural uses of helicopters. And after years of paying high-cost commercial aerial applicators, Ian bought an Exec kit.

He and two farm equipment mechanics completed it five months later. They say that they had no trouble putting the pieces together with a very high level of workmanship after a time investment estimated at 1200 man-hours. However, Ian feels that an experienced builder could do the job in half that time. He says that the plans and photos are excellent and easily followed: "One logical step followed another until it was time to turn the project over to the painters."

Because RotorWay has their own foundry, they are able to construct materials and forgings to the close tolerances necessary for the highly loaded and stressed components inherent in helicopter operations.

How This Homebuilt Paid for Itself

The project cost Vantreight Farms $48,000 by the time all the required equipment was installed. In less than two years, they'll be ahead of what they'd have paid an aerial spray company to do the work for them. After that, they will have only the operating costs of approximately $30-50 per hour. The purchase price will have been written off in the savings.

Fling-Wing Flight Evaluation

Because the Exec is built so low to the ground, it is easy to inspect all components and remove the tiedowns and pitot cover. To pre-oil the main rotor chain drive, thus increasing service life, you tilt the Exec tail down and rotate the blades in a forward direction in the oil bath.

One can't rotate the blades backwards due to the one-way clutch that prevents the rotor system driving the powerplant after an engine failure. If autorotating blades were forced to overcome the engine's compression, the blades would lose much of their inertia, thus jeopardizing the likelihood of success in the engine-out landing flare.

Squeezing into the cockpit is the norm with two people aboard; RotorWay had to keep the cabin area small to reduce weight, cost, and drag. With a 1320-lb takeoff gross and a maximum cabin limit of 380 lb, the Exec is at its maximum legal weight with full fuel and two 190-lb pudgy pilots.

Prospective purchasers should be aware that there is currently no baggage compartment or provision for storage of any payload. Our spray gear was all externally mounted on the skid gear cross tubes.

Watch Those Appendages

In the semi-supine seating, with the dual controls installed, it is necessary for the passenger to constantly keep legs, arms, and feet reined in, so as not to interfere with the pilot's control movements. And if, as a builder, you're inclined to customize your Exec, be sure when installing switches and pilot-adjustable controls that they're reachable with your seat belt secured; the laid-back position you'll be in requires that you have the arms of a gorilla to reach the instrument panel.

Visibility is excellent in most directions and better than in most helicopters, which usually have structural members creating numerous blind spots. The Exec can be flown in an unrestricted manner with the doors off, resulting in a 360-degree field of vision when leaning out the doorway, which is normal rotary wing procedure. Most other helicopters have reduced allowable airspeeds when the doors are off.

Starting procedures are standard for the most part. One difference requires a few degrees of collective to be held up during rotor rotation to avoid damage to the rotor head. Presumably this is to prevent lower droop stop pounding, as the blades are not set with a positive angle of attack sufficient to allow them to cone high enough. As a result, collective pitch is held on during all ground operations. (Of course, the collective can — and should — be fully lowered for all autorotations.)

Even though a clutch system is installed, the rotors turn as soon as the engine is started. After the engine is running smoothly, the clutch is fully engaged with a lever, and the engine/rotor systems run at high idle until the engine temperatures and pressures come into the green. Stick force is rather light on the collective and would likely be held with the knee by pilots experienced on type, while their hands scurry around the cockpit with maps, etc.

Quiet Inside and Out

Throughout all ground operations, the helicopter was so quiet that we found the intercom unnecessary. Moreover, the exterior sound level is so low, even at takeoff, that it is unlikely any neighbor would complain. This is the quietest rotary-winged device I've barely heard.

And vibration was essentially absent. Now, that's impressive for a helicopter.

One feels very close to the ground in the Exec; belly clearance is marginally adequate on level ground without protruding obstacles. This problem can be rectified by mounting a pair of Full Lotus flexible floats. This rugged installation has proven very successful on builder John Hugill's Exec, which is flown in the border areas around the San Juan and Gulf Islands.

Hovering characteristics are much improved with the later elastomeric rotor head compared to RotorWay's old system. Requiring almost full power to lift off to a low hover, one quickly finds the Exec is very light, and has controls that are sensitive compared to heavier, piston helicopters.

Throttle correlation is the best I've felt on a piston helicopter, and the transition through translation is smooth without settling. Often, very significant vibration and sinking occur in other types of helicopters on acceleration from hover to approximately 15 mph.

Climbout at 60 mph produced a steep climb in the 1000-1400 fpm range, depending on all-up weight.

While RotorWay does not restrict the use of full power for cruise, we considered 75 percent to be more reasonable, to prolong engine life. This gave an indicated airspeed of 85 mph for a true airspeed of 90 on approximately seven gph. Since the fuel minimum octane requirement is 92, we were able to use Chevron Unleaded Supreme. This saves approximately $10 per hour in operating costs, and eliminates the need to visit congested, controlled airports for fuel.

The internal noise level at cruise was acceptable, but we put on the headsets for discussion between seats and for hearing protection. Any helicopter pilot should wear high quality noise-suppressing headsets, to avoid long term ear damage from the high frequency/high decibel uproar common in cockpits.

The Exec's light controls provide excellent response and maneuverability. At the same time, the Exec exhibits a high degree of stability in the vertical and lateral axis, showing no tendency to sashay in yaw as many rotary wing craft do.

However, she is very sensitive in the longitudinal axis. This could lead some pilots to over-control in cruise, causing a nose-up-and-down bobbing cycle even in smooth air; this would be aggravated in turbulent air. At speeds below 70 indicated, the "hunting" tendency is absent.

Practicing autorotations (with power recoveries) at max gross weight and high density altitude generated a 1500 fpm rate of descent at 60 mph indicated. For a light chopper, the Exec had a good margin of energy stored in the rotor system for touchdown. Apparently, these very good engine-out parameters are a result of the newer asymmetrical blades. This is the only piston helicopter to use this type of high lift blade.

Confined area operations were made easy due to the small size of the Exec and the low stick trim forces of about two pounds. For a reasonably proficient rotary wing pilot, it was possible to fly the aircraft quite well after less than 15 minutes of stick time.

The Bad News and the Good News

For readers interested in older Scorpion models, RotorWay has issued a notice grounding all pre-1975 Scorpions because of rotor system deficiencies. Owners now have an expensive static display. While this doesn't seem to be the epitome in company support, readers will be delighted to know that the recent financial collapse of B.J. Shramm's operation has a positive ending. The mismanaged firm has been purchased by a gentleman named Netherwood, previously the British distributor, and as of May 1990, the company has marketed an improved version of the helicopter known as the Exec 90.

Abandoned are the Elete and four-place RotorWay products, as the company puts all its efforts into the improvement of an already well proven design. Most of the popular optional equipment has been included in the April 1991 price upgrade of $42,500. The kit now contains: stainless steel exhaust, multiple switches on cyclic grip, sodium filled exhaust valve on the improved RW 162 engine, dual controls, a carburetor air temperature gauge, eyebrow windows, a high temperature cooling fan, and dual electronic ignition.

An important improvement in the Exec has to do with weight and balance requirements when changing from two-person flight to solo. Previously, the battery had to be shifted from one location to another and up to 70 lb of ballast was placed on the right seat for solo flight. (This could be a real nuisance if you were dropping a passenger off somewhere and continuing alone.) Now, a 25 lb weight is moved from behind the engine to the right front skid for solo operations.

Other improvements include: thicker skins on the tailboom and tail rotor blades, a heavy duty version of the elastomeric rotor system (increasing the TBO to 500 hours), and a higher skid gear. All of these advancements are very important to helicopter handling.

The company has also reduced the performance claims to more conservative levels — generally correspnding to those observed during my dozens of operational flights.

Conclusions

The Exec 90, with all its improvements, will likely continue to be the market leader in the rotary wing homebuilt arena.

With a low price for a complete, high performance kit, it's no wonder there have been no challengers to the dominance of Rotor-Way in the marketplace. When one considers that the kit comes complete with engine, instruments, rotor system and construction video, one marvels that so much helicopter can be purchased for so little money. Add the highest kit quality imaginable, improved factory support, and a package that builders say is rather easy to assemble, and you have a tempting project.

Specifications

RotorWay Exec 90

KIT PRICE	$42,500 incl improved engine
BUILDING TIME	500 hrs
NUMBER OF SEATS	2 side by side
ENGINE TYPE	RotorWay RW-152
RATED HORSEPOWER	140
EMPTY WEIGHT	925 lb
GROSS WEIGHT	1425 lb
ROTOR DIAMETER	25 ft
CRUISE SPEED	95 mph
TOP SPEED	115 mph
FUEL CAPACITY	17 gal
RANGE	180 sm
REMARKS	Info kit $10

Performance figures provided by the factory.

The Glasairs

They Outperform the Specifications

Sales have grown in a spectacular fashion from the beginning when the Stoddard-Hamilton folks built and flew their prototype speedster off the old pig farm strip. Since then, the company has become the number one composite kit supplier, and has set up a major production facility at the Arlington Municipal Airport in the state of Washington.

Major reasons for their success are customer support and very high quality kit components, not to mention high levels of aircraft performance. Interviewing dozens of owners and observing the condition of their aircraft revealed not only their pride, but also the durability of the design.

The kits follow the 49-percent-complete rule, and are shipped with all parts machined and one of the best construction manuals in the business.

Both the Glasair II-S and III series use the same vinylester composite construction system, with the spar laminated into the lower wing at the factory. Fuselage halves come with fitting joints and the gullwing canopy sides already fitted to the frames. Attention to detail is very high throughout the kit, in an effort to make the task as easy as possible for the builder – and still remain within the 49 percent rule. All metal parts, fittings, nuts and bolts are prepackaged and readily identifiable. Quality is top notch.

GLASAIR III

When the time came to evaluate the Glasair series, it seemed that starting at the top and working down might be very anticlimactic. However, tomorrow might not come – and I wanted to fly this one today! The Glasair III is 16" longer than the II-S, with most of the stretch in the engine compartment and tailcone to ensure plenty of powerplant space and increased stability for cross-country flight.

With 300 horses up front, the III is the brute of the series.

The instrument panel was loaded — and so was the engine nacelle. The latter was apparent when those 540 cubic inches sparked to life transferring those energy pulses into the large paddle-bladed constant speed prop. A three-blade propeller was not used, as it is less efficient, heavier, and more costly than its two-blade counterpart. Nonetheless, with two blades, prop clearance is a lengthy 10 inches, suitable for off-pavement operations.

While the vibrations smoothed somewhat at high idle, I was always aware of the brute power available under the cowling, thanks to the moderate sound level. The fuel system has an eight-gallon header tank in the forward fuselage and 53 gallons located in "D" cell tanks on the wing's leading edge. All fuel level indicators are mechanical direct reading gauges to increase reliability and improve accuracy.

Let's Fly

With all pre-flight checks complete it was time to unleash the 300 horses. They must have been thoroughbreds; acceleration was ex-hilarating. Ninety mph rushed up, then with light back pressure, rota-tion occurred and the "Three" rocketed skyward. With the gear up and the 20 degrees of flap manually retracted, the aircraft thrusted itself and me upwards at 200 mph and 1500 fpm. While much higher climb rates are possible, I chose to sacrifice rate of climb for visibility.

Leveling off at 2000 feet to avoid low stratus and setting up a con-servative 24 square power setting resulted in an indicated airspeed of

260 mph. According to the sales literature, we shouldn't be going this fast. Indeed, each of the Glasairs that I would later fly out-performed the specifications.

Control forces at these high speeds were moderate and the aircraft's stability plentiful, making the III a solid IFR platform. I can't tell you from experience that this cross-country aircraft was surprisingly aerobatic, as we didn't have enough of a ceiling to legally perform all of those maneuvers. Suffice it to say that various performers have put on first class air shows around North America with this aircraft. The generous G limits of +9 and -6 (ultimate loads) ensure that pilots have a very large margin of safety.

Surprisingly, at the high cruise speed, the sound level was notably low. The semi-reclined seats were very comfortable — so much so, that it seemed possible for a pilot to outlast the Glasair's six hours of cruise endurance.

At the bottom end of the scale, the power-off full flap stall speed was under 70 mph with the standard wing and flaps (the company claims 80). For the optional extended wings and new slotted flaps, the company claims a stall of 67 mph. The strong buffeting that preceded the stall was only a few mph before the actual nose-down pitch. However, when we played with the stall by using just enough power to fly on the ragged edge, the aircraft had no unforgiving characteristics and was quite manageable, with no tendency to drop a wing. No amount of horsing the aircraft around could expose a dark side.

Returning to the pattern, it was time to consider the fact that the jet-like performance and smooth ride in turbulence was largely due to the relatively high wing loading of almost 30 lb/sq ft. (For comparison, a King Air C90A is 32.8 and a Cessna 172 a floating 13.8.) As a result, 110 mph was carried on final approach, slowing to 90 mph over the threshold. (Flight with extended wing and slotted flaps would be flown

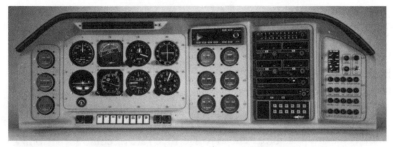

The factory offers an instrument panel with handy removable sections. Note that the sections on the right side are canted for good visibility.

at speeds 10 to 15 mph slower.) The reward was a gentle landing in the ground cushion at 80 mph.

A note to prospective pilots: Carry power on the approach and keep the glide path reasonably shallow, as the power-off sink rate is 1500 fpm and calls for a great deal of skill to judge a gentle round-out. While an experienced pilot could operate this aircraft out of a 2000 foot strip, 3000 feet would be more realistic and less harrowing.

Control forces and response during all slow speed flight were light but not overly sensitive.

Flying the Longer Wing

Later the same day, the wing tip extensions were attached. The longer wing reduces the 140 degrees-per-second roll rate and is not approved for aerobatics. However, from there on it's all gravy. It is possible to plumb the extended wing tips to hold an additional 11 gallons of fuel. The takeoff run is reduced and the rate of climb improves by 350 fpm. Surprisingly, the economy cruise speed is increased at least 7 mph. My suggestion for those considering the Glasair III is to purchase the optional 10 square feet of wing area.

When you are planning a day of aerobatics, simply invest 10 minutes and exchange wing tips. With 72 gallons, including the optional fuel, there is still enough useful load to carry two standard pilots and 65 lb of possessions 1512 miles at 250 mph at 55% power. Conversely, you can scorch along the airways at 285 mph for approximately 1100 miles at 75% power.

Yes, it is very easy to be impressed by this all-around avion athlete. Two options worth considering are electric trim and electric flaps; the latter avoids interference caused by the manual flap handle when reaching for the throttle.

Glasair includes an article with their information package that details the piloting abilities required to safely fly their various aircraft. The section referring to this model sums up the way I feel about the plane: "... the Glasair III is in a similar performance category as many WW II fighters, and can be thought of as a lightweight P-51 Mustang."

While the aircraft is easier to fly than a Mustang, pilots considering this very-high-strutting steed should have considerable experience or invest in a number of hours in other fast, advanced aircraft.

The base price is $33,500 for the 49-percent-complete kit. Hundreds of purchasers have lined up for this package — the ultimate compliment and testimony to the popularity and market acceptance of the Glasair III.

And now, the optional turbocharged version allows cruising speeds up to 313 mph at 24,000 feet. While the extra weight, complexity, maintenance, and fuel flow may not attract everyone, for those who want the capability of maximizing cruise speeds, this high performance variant provides fast climb rates and the ability to fly above most weather. This is the reigning king of two-place fantastic plastic planes.

GLASAIR II-S RG

At two-thirds the price of the Glasair III, this slightly smaller aircraft is an excellent value. It offers delightful control response — automatic aerobatics: think about it and you've done it — and high speed cross-country cruising. With a conservative power setting of 55% and extended wing fuel tanks, it will produce a true airspeed of more than 200 mph over 1593 miles of countryside. A sea level top speed of nearly 260 mph and a solo rate of climb of 2700 fpm result in exhilarating rides.

While considerably more sensitive (less stable) than its big brother, nonetheless, the RG is — with a modicum of pilot training — a high performance platform that would satisfy most jet jockey tastes.

In the busy traffic area, we climbed out at 130 mph indicating 1400 fpm. Leveling off at 2000 feet, a fuel-sipping setting of 23" MP and 2300 rpm gave 210 mph true airspeed. Loops were entered with a 3 G pull-up and rolls were quick and light.

After a considerable play period, it was time to check out the low speed spectrum. Gear down at 130 and the flaps at 110 led us to a gentle stall at a speed — 60 mph — that was off the bottom of the dial. (The factory conservatively claims 63 mph for the standard kit and 50 mph with extended wings and slotted flaps.)

The landings, though pitch sensitive, were gently cushioned by the low wing in ground effect. The recent stretching of the Glasair II-S series (that's why the "-S" designation), reduces the sensitivity and makes the aircraft more stable for cross-county jaunts.

GLASAIR II-S FT (FIXED TRICYCLE)

If you're seeking champagne at beer prices, fill your glasses here. This plane could be for you — 'cause it has it all. The 180 hp version can top 238 mph, and cruise 1475 miles at 185 mph. For those with astronaut blood in their veins, the 2750 fpm rate of climb will leave the Spam Cans struggling behind to catch up. You will also leave them at the gas pumps as this sleek speedster delivers 25 mpg. (A Cessna 182RG gives less than 15 mpg at this speed.)

At the bottom end, the forgiving landing-configuration stall comes at 60 mph on the standard version, and a very low 49 with slotted flaps.

For a homebuilt, the useful load of over 900 lb is very high, making it unlikely one would over-gross this plane. Using the optional wingtip tank extensions permits a 100-lb-higher gross still. What amazes me most about the FT is that it is as easy to fly as most trainers, and priced under $18,000 for the airframe kit.

GLASAIR II-S TD (TAIL DRAGGER)

Cruising at nearly 240 mph and similar in performance to the FT, this speedster looks racy just sitting on the ground. Retired airline pilot/builder Jim Cline was delighted with his cross-country machine. Cruise economy at 23 mpg was of paramount importance to Jim. With the tachometer indicating 2400 rpm on his polished and ported engine, he gets 196 mph TAS at 7500 feet. With landing and takeoff distances quoted as 350 and 500 feet, one would believe this plane could land any place that is designated an airport.

Conclusions

Having revolutionized homebuilding with their fast-build kits in the early 1980's, Stoddard-Hamilton continues to provide unparalleled service, and parts of unquestionable quality. The development of a stretched fuselage, slotted flaps, and wing extensions keeps this series in the forefront of high performance homebuilt aircraft. Dozens of builders interviewed over the years can find nothing wrong with the company and its products, suggesting that Stoddard-Hamilton sets the standard other companies hope to achieve.

Specifications

Stoddard-Hamilton Glasair III

Specs for turbo version in parentheses
short wing/extended wing

PRICE	Kit $33,500, plans $200
BUILDING TIME	1800 hrs
NUMBER OF SEATS	2 side by side
ENGINE TYPE	Lycoming IO-540 (TIO-540)
RATED HORSEPOWER	300 (300)
EMPTY WEIGHT	1625 lb (1650)
GROSS WEIGHT	2400/2500 lb
WING AREA	81/91 sq ft
TAKEOFF DISTANCE	800 ft
LANDING DISTANCE	1000 ft
CRUISE SPEED	282 mph (313)
TOP SPEED	295 mph (327)
FUEL CAPACITY	61/72 gal
RANGE	1281/1512 sm

Stoddard-Hamilton Glasair II-S RG

PRICE	Kit $24,500, plans $200
BUILDING TIME	1600 hrs
NUMBER OF SEATS	2 side by side
ENGINE TYPE	Various Lycomings
RATED HORSEPOWER	150-200
EMPTY WEIGHT	1100 lb
GROSS WEIGHT	2000/2100 lb
WING AREA	81/91.5 sq ft
TAKEOFF DISTANCE	380 ft
LANDING DISTANCE	400 ft
CRUISE SPEED	235 mph
TOP SPEED	250 mph
FUEL CAPACITY	48/59 gal
RANGE	1296/1573 sm

Performance figures supplied by the factory.

Specifications

Stoddard-Hamilton Glasair II-S FT

PRICE	Kit $17,500, plans $200
BUILDING TIME	1200 hrs
NUMBER OF SEATS	2 side by side
ENGINE TYPE	Various Lycomings
RATED HORSEPOWER	150-200
EMPTY WEIGHT	950 lb
GROSS WEIGHT	1800 lb
WING AREA	81/91.5 sq ft
TAKEOFF DISTANCE	350 ft
LANDING DISTANCE	350 ft
CRUISE SPEED	231 mph
TOP SPEED	238 mph
FUEL CAPACITY	48/59 gal
RANGE	1200/1475 sm

Stoddard-Hamilton Glasair II-S TD

PRICE	Kit $16,900, plans $200
BUILDING TIME	1200 hrs
NUMBER OF SEATS	2 side by side
ENGINE TYPE	Lycoming O-360
RATED HORSEPOWER	150-200
EMPTY WEIGHT	925 lb
GROSS WEIGHT	1900/2000 lb
WING AREA	81/91.5 sq ft
TAKEOFF DISTANCE	350 ft
LANDING DISTANCE	500 ft
CRUISE SPEED	241 mph
TOP SPEED	242 mph
FUEL CAPACITY	48/59 gal
RANGE	1200/1475 sm
REMARKS	Info kit $20, video $25, both $40

Performance figures supplied by the factory.

Super Emeraude

One Man's Dream

Renowned propeller maker Colin Walker perused the selection of wooden aircraft and concluded that the CP 328 Super Emeraude was obviously the homebuilt for him. One of the late Claude Piel's designs, the Super Emeraude utilizes all-wood construction and elliptical wings. Piel's products — more than 30 aircraft — are extremely popular in Europe and especially in his native France. In fact, the Cap 10 is still produced by the factory there. Other popular designs available from the distributor, D. Trivisonno, include Zephir, Beryl, Saphir, and Super Diamant, with seating from single place to four.

Colin began construction in September of 1970 and finished a decade later, after investing $5,000. He advises builders to take their time and do the job right the first time.

Model plane builders will feel right at home with the creative process, since the fuselage construction will appear very similar to the normal truss-type structure employing gussets and bulkheads. Colin, who is a retired cabinet maker, found the most difficult portion of the construction was making the canopy. "That is," he said, "if you don't count finding the money in the household budget for aircraft materials."

With 300 flying hours on his award-winning Emeraude, Colin claims that the most-loved aspect is the easy handling. Operating off grass runways, he typically uses only 650 feet with 10 degrees of flap to get airborne at gross weight. Solo short field departures consume only 500 feet! While the 1000 lb empty weight is considerably higher than other Super Emeraudes, the small Lycoming O-290D of 115-125 hp is more than adequate thrust for Colin's homemade 70 x 56 pitch propeller.

Looking for Faults—and Finding None

Easy-opening cowling halves made engine inspection easy — a very important consideration when it comes to safety. We also peered into the wheel fairings to find 6.00 x 6 tires mounted on oil/spring oleo struts.

Stepping over the cockpit sill, I discovered a spacious 42" wide, 44" long cabin. Located behind the seats, the baggage area is rather large, with a 110 lb limit. Good shoulder harnesses and seats with foam cushions ensured secure comfort. The canopy slides on tracks, providing excellent ventilation, and latches positively with two fasteners.

The side-by-side seating results in a broad instrument panel with plenty of room for IFR expansion. Colin's headsets and homemade intercom provide excellent communications and sound suppression. In fact, it proved better than any of the commercial units I've used. Leave it to homebuilders when one wants an advance over existing equipment.

The fuel system uses a main fuselage tank of 22 gallons (nine-gallon wing tanks are optional) for a maximum total of 40 gallons. This should easily provide a still-air range of over 1000 miles with reserves.

Average finished empty weights vary from 750 to 1000 lb, with the gross set at 1540. A builder completing a Super Emeraude in the average weight range at 875 lb would be able to load full long-range fuel, two 170-lb occupants, and 85 lb of whatever.

Peace, Performance and Pulchritude

After startup, the noise level was conversationally quiet and the idle very smooth, both likely due to the dampening effect of wood construction. The steerable tail wheel and good visibility over the nose took the chore out of taxiing. Shock absorption and braking were very good and there was no appreciable static friction in the controls.

While takeoff acceleration was energetic for 115 installed hp, directional control was as easy as a tricycle-geared aircraft. This would be an easy plane in which pilots used to a "training tire" could convert over to taildragger gear. The rudder effectiveness was very good but not overly sensitive, and we were airborne in 800 ft — and in only 500 to 650 ft in subsequent efforts, using short-field techniques. The rate of climb was 1000 fpm dual and 1200 solo. Now that's performance with a capital P for a small engine.

Control feel was delightful in all axes. Setting up for cruise at 24 square produced a true airspeed of 145 mph on 6 gph. Top speed would be well over 160.

As befits a good design, the controls load up with airspeed, making the Emeraude a pleasure for cross-country flying or for limited aerobatics. Pitch stability was very good and the trim system uses a flap-like handle for rapid yet sensitive trimming. This is the best manual system I've used. Maneuverability was sprightly and the roll rate approached 180 degrees/second. The designer recommends that only basic aerobatics be flown and has set the red line at 185 mph.

At the low end of the speed spectrum, full flaps of 40 degrees can be selected below 80 mph with almost no pitch change, thanks to a mechanical connection between flaps and the right trim tab that automatically trims the aircraft. Docile slow-speed handling led to almost no warning approaching the stall. The power-off clean stall occurred at 50 indicated, with moderate nose-down pitch and left wing drop. With a normal recovery, 200 ft of altitude were lost. The full-flap stall at approach power gave no warning and a very steep nose pitch-down at 40 mph. Some wing drop also occurred at the stall.

While the Emeraude generally is very easy to fly, it is not the sort of plane one wants to stall inadvertently. Out of curiosity, we set up a power-off descent that resulted in 800 fpm down at 80 mph — not a bad glider.

With the low stall speeds, we flew base leg at 80 mph and final at 65. Crossing the threshold at 55 with 40 degrees (full flap) allowed us to have a steep gradient over the trees and still retain enough inertia for flares into smooth landings. The shock-oleo system helped admirably in some cases, as I wanted to land on the numbers—or as close as possible on the short runway with its power lines and trees near the threshold. Undoubtedly, this is one of the easier taildraggers to fly.

The Ultimate Compromise?

Excellent visibility and virtually vibration-free operation in a rather quiet cabin environment made me yearn to have this economical aircraft.The Super Emeraude does everything so well, it's perhaps the ultimate compromise for wooden aircraft in the mid-speed range. This is truly an all-around performer, with its capabilities in the areas of short-field operations, cross-country comfort, and aerobatics.

While it may not score a 10 out of 10 in any one category, nonetheless it scores 8+ in almost everything. When one totals the ratings, this aircraft places very highly. Ease of construction, low cost, high performance, forgiving characteristics (other than no real stall warning), and a sporty feel produce an aircraft that is suitable for most types of flying. As plans-built wood-and-fabric flying machines go, this is a "best buy."

Specifications

Trivisonno C.P. 328 Super Emeraude

PLANS PRICE	$160
BUILDING TIME	Approx 2000 hrs
NUMBER OF SEATS	2 side by side
ENGINE TYPE	Varied
RATED HORSEPOWER	Specs based on 100 hp
EMPTY WEIGHT	850 lb
GROSS WEIGHT	1500 lb
WING AREA	117 sq ft
TAKEOFF DISTANCE	600 ft
LANDING DISTANCE	740 ft
CRUISE SPEED	120 mph
Vne	172 mph
FUEL CAPACITY	32 gal
RANGE	600 sm
REMARKS	Info kit $6

Performance figures supplied by the factory.

Van's RV Series

Champagne on a Beer Budget?

Designer and graduate engineer Dick VanGrunsven is batting a thousand with his tried and true RV series: the RV-3, RV-4, RV-6 and new tricycle geared version of the latter, the RV-6A.

Sales of these plans and kits total more than 3000 units since the company's beginning in 1980, and sales show no signs of slowing down. This series is suitable for first-time builders and low-time flyers, as the aircraft have no dangerous flight characteristics and they offer high speed, short field, and aerobatic capabilities to boot!

Yes indeed, with kit prices starting at $5,700 for a package that's 20 to 25 percent complete, builders can have high quality champagne – at lite beer prices.

Crafts & Common Construction

The differences between the materials and construction of the models are so small, we will describe them as one.

While plans are available separately (except for the RV-6), most builders opt for the four-package kit comprised of wings, fuselage, empennage, and finishing kit (canopy, engine, landing gear, wheels, brakes, spinner, and fairings). The excellent plans consist of 44 drawings, many of full scale parts, on 24" x 36" sheets. Included is a large construction manual with building tips and an excellent newsletter, *The RVator.*

All kits utilize aluminum skins with semi-monocoque construction techniques. Adding punch – so to speak – to the RV-6 kit's allure, Dick now allows pop rivets in most of the structure. This well proven, rugged type of construction remains very attractive to builders. (See the chapter on selecting a homebuilt aircraft design to discover why.)

The integral engine mount/landing gear of 4139 chromoly steel is available pre-welded from the factory – a real bonus for many customers. A constant chord, low aspect ratio wing with the well proven NACA 23015 airfoil makes construction simple—not to mention providing safe flying characteristics. More on this later.

Dick has concentrated on making his designs a pleasure to fly. He feels that most builders keep their Van's aircraft longer and fly them on the average 2-3 times more than most homebuilt designs, because the series is such a joy to handle.

THE RV-6 AND 6A

Designed as a concession to the many customers who wanted side-by-side seating, the Six series is a development of the very popular tandem two-place RV-4—although few parts are interchangeable. The RV-6A is a further product revision for pilots who want tricycle gear as well. For this evaluation, we will fly the conventionally configured RV-6, as it should be slightly more challenging for prospective builders to fly than the RV-6A with its "training wheel."

The very large, somewhat flexible canopy is hinged forward of the instrument panel and pivots upwards so as not to obstruct entry. This configuration makes ventilation during taxiing and inadvertent opening in flight less likely to create problems. Strong, well designed latches hold the system closed for flight.

The RV-6 offers comfortable side-by-side seating.

The beautiful blue prototype was easy to enter, after a big step over the flaps up to the wing, then over the sill into the spacious side-by-side seating. The interior cabin width is 40.5", with plenty of headroom and legroom for tall occupants.

The aft baggage compartment is an improvement over the smaller RV-4 stowage area, and measures approximately 43" x 22" with a volume of 15 cu ft. With due attention to the CG limits, the maximum load is given as 60 lb. If you prefer center line seating, a la the RV-4, you may end up a convert, like me, when you try the comfort, increased seating space, luggage space, and the IFR-sized panel available on the Six.

Taxiing was typical taildragger. Excellent maneuvering with a fully castering tailwheel and differential braking, combined with zig zag turns, ensured that we weren't about to trim the taxiway lights on our way out to the Arlington, Washington show line.

For takeoff, all we had to do was select one notch of flap, since the gear was down and welded and the propeller was a fixed pitch 68 x 69 Pacesetter.

With this general purpose pitch setting and a static rpm of only 2250, it was surprising to find that the aircraft accelerated aggressively to break ground, on its own, in 600 feet at 60 mph. Building to 110 indicated produced a reading of 1300 fpm on the VSI. Not bad for 160 hp and a fixed pitch prop! (An obstacle clearing climb of 1500 fpm is possible at 75 indicated.)

Suitable for a Low-Time Pilot

All controls were perfectly light without being overly sensitive. This combination would be suitable for a low-time pilot — after a type check. Numerous low-time pilots in my neighborhood have built RV series aircraft and have had no problems with the reliable airframes and powerplants. In fact, many of them have been tempted into the world of aerobatics, and seem to be doing quite well.

Cruise speeds on the prototype, which needed some aerodynamic refinements, were in the 165-185 range, with builders reporting speeds up to 195 at 75 percent power. Quick calculations show a very efficient 30 mpg.

The V_{ne} for the RV-6 is a fairly low 210 indicated. The prototype has shown itself to be free of flutter at this speed. Considering that the aircraft is capable of cruising within 15 mph of this red line, owners will have to be careful to monitor their airspeed, especially during turbulence penetration.

In the slow speed department, the controls were equally well harmonized, as was the Six's behavior. Flap extension is via a Johnson-type bar that pulls up and aft for the 30 degrees of extension. Not very pretty, but fully serviceable — even during an electrical failure. (How I love those mechanical devices.)

Power-off flapless stalls are in the mid-fifties, and flap-extended stalls, with a smidgen of power, are below 50. That's terrific for an aircraft that can top 200 mph, especially when you consider the stalls and recovery as very tame. Modest pre-stall buffeting precedes a moderate nose drop. Relaxing the back pressure ends the stalled condition. Simply said, simply done.

Landings were equally easy with an approach speed of 75, reduced to 60 at the threshold, producing perfect touchdowns with the tail down in the three-point attitude. I'm all for landing at the minimum speed (except in crosswinds), to reduce wear and tear on the tires and brakes. Additionally, this technique reduces the likelihood of a significant skip-bounce since the plane is near its stalling speed and has less inertia.

In the case of the new trike, the RV-6A, Dick will be using a castering nose gear on the kits. Otherwise, expect performance and construction to be equivalent to the conventional Six. And that's nothing to sneer at when you consider this monoplane can fly four times faster than its stalling speed — in level flight.

THE RV-4

Flying the RV-4 was such a thrill, I felt I needed one. After all, the in-line seating and the aft sliding canopy on owner Joe Meyer's plane made the Four somewhat of a Mustang look-alike. (Normally, the kit is built with a side-hinging canopy.) In the air, the flying characteristics whispered, "Interceptor/Pursuit/Fighter" while we cavorted with the clouds — maintaining, of course, the legal distance from them.

At any rate, for those who just have to sit on the centerline and don't mind giving up some baggage capacity and back seat comfort, the slightly improved performance of the RV-4 could be for you. If you're riding in the back seat, watch out for the flap lever up-and-down movement. It will require your left foot to dance about to avoid a conflict during extension and retraction. The rear area is large enough for smaller passengers, but at 28" wide and with 24" between the seats, larger specimens of humanity will feel somewhat cramped during a cross-country flight.

Minor vibration and moderate sound levels are the order of the day. A small weight sacrifice, in the form of some extra sound insulation, would be a good investment over the long term.

Handling is very crisp and quite light, with the roll rate in the region of 140 degrees per second. Having also flown the 180 hp version belonging to Larry Berg, with its improved vertical penetration, made me realize the RV-4 is a very fine aerobatics trainer that even well-qualified aerobatic pilots can delight in. (Don't expect to make it to the world championships, but *do* expect some really exciting flying if wild gyrations are your bag. Perhaps with all the Fours and Sixes about, a class for competitions could be formed.)

The series seems to be free of adverse yaw and can be flown, for the most part, with feet on the floor — although I believe that God gave us feet to coordinate turns with. (I suppose that tradition is disappearing as quickly as smog-free air.)

Visibility is excellent in all models, with the exception of the rear seat of the Four, where the sills and the back of the front seat are view-restrictive.

Other than the above, there is very little difference from the RV-6 that warrants mention. See the performance charts for the details.

A Series of Conclusions

Or should one say, conclusions on a series? At any rate, the RVs are immensely popular because they do everything so well. These vice-less aircraft cruise very fast, stall at exceptionally low speeds, and perform well on short, unimproved fields.

When you look at the low prices for the kits, and realize that the RV-3 could be built for less than $15,000 and the two-place versions for less than $20,000, it's obvious you can have champagne for beer prices.

Perhaps the best indication of the RV-4's and RV-6's value in the market place is the difficulty of finding one for sale. And when you find an ad, you discover the owner wants $35,000-$40,000 for his plane. Homebuilts sell for a premium over the builder's costs only when there is a strong market demand for that type.

So if you want a maximum aircraft at a minimum price, you would do well to consider building one of the Van's Aircraft series.

Specifications

Van's RV-3

PRICE	Kit $5,700, plans $125
BUILDING TIME	1300 hrs
NUMBER OF SEAT	Single place
ENGINE TYPE	Lycoming O-320
RATED HORSEPOWER	150 (range 100-160)
EMPTY WEIGHT	750 lb
GROSS WEIGHT	1100 lb
WING AREA	90 sq ft
TAKEOFF DISTANCE	250 ft
LANDING DISTANCE	300 ft
CRUISE SPEED	200 mph
TOP SPEED	212 mph
FUEL CAPACITY	24 gal
RANGE	600 sm
REMARKS	Info kit $8

Van's RV-4

PRICE	Kit $7,875, plans $165
BUILDING TIME	1800 hrs
NUMBER OF SEATS	2 tandem
ENGINE TYPE	Lycoming O-320
RATED HORSEPOWER	150 (range 150-180)
EMPTY WEIGHT	905 lb
GROSS WEIGHT	1500 lb
WING AREA	110 sq ft
TAKEOFF DISTANCE	450 ft
LANDING DISTANCE	425 ft
CRUISE SPEED	186 mph
TOP SPEED	202 mph
FUEL CAPACITY	32 gal
RANGE	650 sm
REMARKS	Info kit $8

Performance figures provided by the factory.

Van's RV-6

PRICE	Partial kit $8,450
BUILDING TIME	1800 hrs
NUMBER OF SEATS	2 side by side
ENGINE TYPE	Lycoming O-320
RATED HORSEPOWER	160 (range 150-180)
EMPTY WEIGHT	950 lb
GROSS WEIGHT	1600 lb
WING AREA	110 sq ft
TAKEOFF DISTANCE	525 ft
LANDING DISTANCE	500 ft
CRUISE SPEED	192 mph
TOP SPEED	202 mph
FUEL CAPACITY	38
RANGE	775 sm
REMARKS	Info kit $8

Van's RV-6A

PRICE	Partial kit $8,900
BUILDING TIME	1800 hrs
NUMBER OF SEATS	2 side by side
ENGINE TYPE	Lycoming O-320
RATED HORSEPOWER	160
EMPTY WEIGHT	995 lb
GROSS WEIGHT	1600 lb
WING AREA	110 sq ft
TAKEOFF DISTANCE	600 ft
LANDING DISTANCE	600 ft
CRUISE SPEED	189 mph
TOP SPEED	190 mph
FUEL CAPACITY	38
RANGE	760 sm
REMARKS	Info kit $8

Performance figures provided by the factory.

The Zenairs

Quite a Family

Only recently, I discovered an amazing aviation company that manufactures exquisitely engineered, durable, aircraft kits. The fact that Chris Heintz has been producing his popular planes for over 17 years must indicate that I am the slowest-witted observer on the block. It's not that I haven't flown the entire fleet, nor that I was unaware of this rather amazing aeronautical engineer's past. Rather, I was not cognizant of his dedication to consumer satisfaction nor the quality of service and design innovation that flows from his 11,000 square foot factory located in central Canada's bushplane country.

After a few days with Chris's family (actually, *two* families: sons and aircraft fleet), I readily saw that Zenair is well established to be a world leader in aircraft production with the advent of recreational categories worldwide. To maximize market penetration, Heintz has ensured that his recent aircraft offerings will fit the homebuilt/experimental category, the new Canadian ultralight regulations, and primary and recreational aircraft categories. This has also resulted in significant sales overseas, especially in Europe, helping to balance North America's deficit with an infusion of foreign income.

Between the 49-percent-complete and the 85-percent-complete kits, purchasers have the opportunity of selecting the category of their choice. Alternatively, the company can assemble an 85 percent kit to provide a ready-to-fly aerial chariot for pilots with no time to build.

All Zenair kits utilize stressed, single curvature metal skins riveted to structural members. Aircraft quality Avdel avex blind rivets are employed because they are easy to use, corrosion resistant, and robust, and the stem secures and seals the rivet in its hole. Also provided are select 6061 aluminum alloy skins, pre-formed spars, and bulkheads. Rivet holes are pre-drilled and lightening holes are cut and deburred to provide components that are ready to assemble. Compare this with most other manufacturers' offerings!

Heintz over-designs the structure so that the long term affects of metal fatigue will leave the aircraft with a large enough margin of safety such that structural failure will never be a problem. Four hundred flying aircraft have proven his concepts.

THE CH300

Bill Tee and his young wife, Sharon, allowed me the pleasure of sharing the airspace with their Zenair one spring.

Under the severe clear sunburning skies, Bill's flawlessly built all-aluminum three-seater made the Spam Cans around the airport look hastily assembled.

Mind you, this Piper Cherokee look-alike *should* look great, because Bill Tee invested a decade in the fabrication, making sure everything was perfect on one part before moving on to the next. You don't wonder that the light plane manufacturers are giving up when you look at the quality and performance of aircraft built by EAA and RAAC members.

Bill wanted his aircraft to be able to land almost anywhere, so consulting with Chris Heintz, the designer, he made a few modifications to the basic airframe. Perhaps the main change is his use of 4340 steel bar to fabricate the main landing gear. These bars are sharply tapered backwards; combined with a trailing arm-wheel attachment, they make for a tremendous amount of shock absorption on rough strips. Bill has left off the wheel pants, resulting in a lower cruise speed but greater utility.

As Bill has done a lot of the design work on fuel systems for De-Havilland (now a Boeing company), he also devised a somewhat novel route for the engine's fuel. The 80/87 is pumped from the right tank to the left tank, where it is picked up by the Lycoming O-320. What if the transfer pump fails? Well, that is what the emergency cross-feed valve is for; it allows fuel to go directly from the right tank to the engine-driven pump. This system features a simple on/off fuel valve, and, as a side benefit, allows the pilot to control the lateral CG.

Aside from the trim system, which uses discarded parts from an Austin Mini and DeHavilland Twin Otter (with rudder pedals and brake cylinders from a CF-100 all-weather fighter), the aircraft can be said to conform to plans.

The plane is very strong, with a gross weight of 1850 lb, and is stressed for an ultimate load factor of 5.7 Gs both positive and negative, in accordance with FAR 23A.

Painted by a Pro

The CH300 is all metal, and Bill's was painted by a professional. Many builders use professional painters because, like welding, painting is a specialty skill. Those who have applied $600 worth of paint to their project, only to have the finish sag, peel, or flake, will understand. Additionally, many finishes are toxic; still others require special spray equipment.

The easiest access to the cockpit is by making an imprint of your shoe in the seat cushion and sliding into the side-by-side seating. The back bench seat could hold two persons, baggage, or whatever, with the total not to exceed 210 lb. This makes the CH 300 an excellent 2 + 2 design.

After arranging one's bulk, it becomes obvious that the cockpit has but one joystick and two throttles. The stick is located between the pilots, and the throttles are located on the outboard cabin walls. Bill offered me the left seat — thanks for the confidence. However, I declined, as he had already mentioned that his springy gear modification made landings very challenging initially. As a result, I ended up in the right seat with a stick to the left of my left knee and a throttle on my right. As it's hard to teach an old dog new tricks, it would take some getting used to.

This design reduces weight and clutter on the cabin floor, and results in less likelihood of a front-seat passenger fouling the controls.

Engines with horsepower ratings from 125 to 180 are suitable for this aircraft, and the factory even mentions that the water-cooled Ford Javelin is acceptable.

Let's Fly

Startup procedures were normal for the Lycoming O-320 we were flying. The aircraft taxis very well and has a tight turning radius for confined areas. The visibility over the nose in this taildragger was as good as any tricycle I can remember. This negated the requirement to zig-zag while taxiing. (You can also opt for a tri-gear version of the Zenair.) The effect of every bump and stone on the ground was dampened by the very soft suspension; however, it wasn't difficult to have a series of ruts result in a considerable up and down bobbing motion. Bill isn't sure whether he wants to stiffen up the gear legs until he has tried them on rough fields. They are certainly strong enough and are stressed for high landing impact loads.

After completing all pre-flight checks, we found ourselves lined up for departure in a light and variable wind condition. Takeoff acceleration was swift, with liftoff occurring at 40 mph indicated after a roll of only 600 feet — and this wasn't using the short field technique! Although Bill questions his airspeed indicator, the short takeoff distance shows that the aircraft's high-lift wing — a modified NACA 64A515 with Hoerner wing tips on its 26'6" span — is capable of considerable load lifting.

Bill isn't happy with his propeller, but its climb and cruise performance appeared perfectly adequate to me as we indicated an average rate of climb of 900 fpm at 70 mph. Trading ROC for airspeed and visibility, we departed at 80 mph and an ROC of 700 fpm.

145 mph is Possible

Our cruise tests were done at 3000 feet where the OAT was 54 degrees Fahrenheit. The economical and quiet power setting of 2250 rpm resulted in an indicated 100 mph. A more realistic setting of 2500 rpm yielded 125 mph, and the full-rated rpm of 2700 gave an indicated 135 mph. There is no doubt in my mind that this aircraft could deliver a solid 145 mph or more TAS in cruise at optimum altitude. (Chris Heintz assures me that the addition of Zenair wheel pants yields an increase of 8% TAS). This would result in a range with this engine of approximately 530 miles with the standard fuel tanks totaling 34 gallons.

The best glide speed of 70 resulted in a gentle descent of only 700 fpm.

Next, we explored the realm of slow flight and stalls. (As Bill's airspeed indicator seemed to be under-reading in the lower end of the flight envelope, we will use the numbers from the kit manufacturer's brochure.) The power-off full-flap stall occurred at 53 indicated and the characteristics were very gentle. We tried numerous configurations of stalls and had no surprises. Slow flight was accomplished at around 60 mph, and even steep turns showed no dangerous tendencies.

Control forces are firm in cruising flight, giving the Zenair the stable feel of a heavier plane than it is. That's not to say that a little force and the desire can't turn this machine into a sprightly performer. As an all-around aircraft, it will fit many roles and fill them well.

The National Association of Sport Aircraft Designers (no longer functioning) rated the Zenith aircraft as follows: Completeness of drawings: Superior; Clarity of Drawings and Manuals: Superior; Complexity of Construction: Low; Complexity of Piloting: Medium. Actually, as far as piloting skill is concerned, I think the aircraft is very forgiving and can be easily flown by relatively low-time pilots.

There are lots of options that builders may wish to consider: floats, removable wings, skis, a glider-towing package, and double the normal fuel capacity, to name a few. Zenair has had the package deal down pat for years with your choice of an airframe material package or a 45 percent pre-manufactured kit. The former has some preliminary work completed, while the latter has many of the parts cut and formed, resulting in a time saving of approximately 50 percent.

If you are looking for a well-designed, solid, easy-to-build aircraft consider the Zenair CH 300 in your selection process, but be prepared to wait two to two and a half months for kit delivery.

THE STOL CH701

If you've got a short, rough field with obstacles on the approaches, I've got an aircraft for you. It's Chris Heintz's answer to ultralight short-field performance.

The CH 701 is intended to excel at Short Take Off and Landing operations (STOL). This it does — admirably! Other desirable concepts include crashworthiness, weather resistance, superior low speed handling, adaptability to skis and floats, plus a durable structure able to take the abusive treatment provided by off-airport strips. Chris designed the aircraft to FAR 23 and beefed up the structure to +6 and -3 Gs to ensure a long life for the builder's investment. Contrary to standard homebuilt/ultralight company practices, Zenair has not only proof-loaded the wings, but also the empennage and other members of the structure. Additionally, the wings have been tested for gust and torsional loads, while the gear and engine mount have proven themselves for heavy landing loads. This detailed stress examination provides a large safety margin.

Knowing that most accidents are survivable when impact speeds are below 50 mph, Heintz uses high lift airfoils to ensure that stall speeds are low. The 3.1 lift coefficient on the STOL allows the wing to hang in there to a slow 25 mph. Extra occupant protection is built into the cabin area with a crashworthy chromoly steel structure. This acts as a barrier, protecting pilots from trees and rocks that might fling themselves at the plane.

Initially, observers concluded Heintz's use of a central Y-shaped control stick was designed to save weight, simplify construction, and increase usable legroom. While it accomplished these goals, the main purpose was safety. Realizing that the last thing flyers need is a pole directly in front of them, ready to impale them on impact, Chris placed the control stick between pilot seats and the throttle in the outboard, upper portion of the instrument panel—where they are unlikely to meet with a human's soft tissue during sudden decelerations.

Heintz is very much aware that many low time pilots are attracted to high speed planes. He also pointed out that most sport builders generally fly within 50 miles of their base and they spend more time driving to and from the airport than they do flying.

This is why his designs utilize large tires, high lift wings, and a rugged, utilitarian shock absorption system that enables the aircraft to land or take off from minimal clearings. This allows pilots to fly more often, as they can base their planes close by at almost anything that resembles a takeoff area. For instance, the author flies the Zenair prototype out of a one-way, tree-surrounded, narrow, 500-foot-long horse pasture on Vancouver Island, with plenty of room to spare — and this with the air-cooled 503 engine. The only operational problem in this environment is avoiding the deposits the horses make.

STOL performance combined with amphibious floats adds up to a very versatile airplane.

Construction and Building Details

The shocks found on unprepared fields are absorbed by 16"
diameter wheels, coupled with a progressive rate monoleaf aluminum
spring suspension on the main gear and a standard bungee on the
steerable nose wheel.

For simplicity of construction, the leading edge slats are fixed —
that is, bolted onto the wing's leading edge. Steel engine mounts and
cockpit structure are pre-welded so that builders need suffer no clothing burns associated with acetylene welding. A step-by-step photo
guide and construction manual ensure hundreds of hours aren't taken
up with the reading of plans or rebuilding parts that were assembled
incorrectly.

A Zenair Skyhook

Early morning passage of a cold front left clear skies and steady
winds in the 25 mph range. Bundled up against the freezing temperatures, Qamar Aziz and I stretched gunwale to gunwale (40 inches)
across the STOL. The Zenair instructor/demo pilot was well over six
feet tall, and with my bulk added in, we pretty much filled the CH 701.
The large hat rack has three times as much volume as the early
prototypes and could swallow enough baggage for a week away — with
diligent packing.

While we flew both of the liquid-cooled Rotax versions — the 582
two-stroke and the 912 four-stroke — the following details will apply to
the latter. Details of 582 performance will be specified in the performance chart.

During the walk-around inspection, one must confirm that the
aileron push-pull tubes' quick release connections are secure. This
mechanical device allows the wings to be folded or removed without
altering the ailerons' rigging.

The upper cowling was easily removed (this is unfortunately not
the case on many homebuilts) with four Dzus fasteners, allowing us to
check the oil level on the four-cylinder engine. With both air and liquid
cooling, the 912 has a myriad of tubes, hoses, and wires to inspect.
Zenair says that the installation weighs 40 lb more than the 582, while
providing an additional 15 hp.

Because the four-stroker didn't want to awaken in the sub-zero
temperatures after cold-soaking outdoors overnight, we were delayed
an hour or so till she warmed up in the hangar.

Purrr

Once started, the 912 ran smoothly, partially due to Zenair's coni-cal engine mount that mutes vibration. (Even the two-stroke, two-cylinder 582 was surprisingly smooth.) The company adds springs to the throttle push rods to ensure that the engine will go to full power if the linkages fail. This tends to result in self-application of power unless the pilot keeps constant aft pressure on the throttle.

Rather than fight it, I surrendered to the STOL's desire to taxi and headed for the active. A choice of mechanical or hydraulic brakes provides okay or excellent braking, respectively, and ground steering is very precise with the large diameter, steerable nose wheel. (The STOL is also available with taildragger gear, but few builders seem to select this no-cost option.)

After checking the dual ignition capacitance discharge system with its integrated magneto generator, along with other items on the pre-takeoff checklist, we headed into the teeth of the 25 mph wind. By the time full throttle was applied, we were pointed skyward in an absurd nose-high attitude. Since we needed an angle of attack in excess of 30 degrees to stall (15-18 degrees is typical), you can image that our elevator-like ascent was spectacular to ground bound observers — and that was without using the drooping flaps that double as full span ailerons.

Delightfully light and balanced controls make stick forces a joy at all airspeeds up the 110 mph red line. Unlike many aircraft, these forces don't load up excessively at cruising speed. Visibility, comfort, and sound level with inexpensive headsets scored well on the tally sheet.

Leveling off at cruise power, I could see why Questair Venture pilots aren't in the market for the CH 701. The STOL specializes in going somewhere slow — or is it nowhere fast? But then, Heintz created the plane for the pleasure of flying. If you do want to go on an occasional major cross country trip, take an airliner. This is not to say that the CH 701 isn't suitable for distant travel. The STOL is a very stable, comfortable, reasonably quiet flying carpet, albeit at 80 mph. For those who aren't in a rush, this airborne aluminum viewing plat-form will transport you across the countryside without giving you jet lag.

In the low-speed handling department, the STOL excels. Aerodynamicist that he is, Heintz has combined all of the desirable features possible: light but not overly sensitive controls, adequate response and feedback thanks to direct linkages, and plenty of control authority. While others make modifications to their aircraft to improve faults, Chris designs it right the first time.

Stalls are straightforward and straight ahead. With a slight buffet preceding the gentle nose-down rotation, pilots would be hard pressed not to notice the stall in the 24-27 mph range.

In the strong wind, with such an easy-to-fly plane, Aziz and I spent a lot of time flying on the edges of the flight spectrum, concluding with patterns that were little more than hovering turns over the button of the runway. Sideslips are easily generated with lots of rudder authority, allowing Zenair staff to land in cross winds that have exceeded 30 knots on numerous occasions!

Because the STOL is so much fun to fly, my normal single short evaluation flight became several lengthy ones. At no time did the CH 701 show any tendencies that would be unsafe for low time weekend pilots.

One STOL and One Car in Every Garage

Some folks feel that the STOL is rather homely, like the Gooney Bird and Cessna 150. If this is true, the STOL is in really good company, because these designs were extremely successful as utility aircraft. What they share is rugged aluminum construction, a capability to do their job, and freedom from flying vices.

Flights with both 912 and 582 engines proved that there was little to choose between the powerplants in terms of performance. However, for those who demand a four-stroke and are prepared to invest an extra $4000-5000, the 912 is an attractive option. Personally, I'd prefer to bank the difference and go for the twin ignition 582, an engine that has had a successful growth from the popular 532 series.

THE ZODIAC CH600 and 601

Perhaps the world became aware of this aircraft during World Expo 86 in Vancouver, Canada, when local members of the Recreational Aircraft Association of Canada assembled a Zodiac in a week!

This side-by-side, all-aluminum monoplane was designed to be a safe, easy-to-build, easy-to-maintain homebuilt that could be powered by a reliable, inexpensive Volkswagen engine.

Now, with the advent of lighter, more powerful engines in the marketplace, perhaps a different powerplant would be more suitable,

A typical comment on the 600: "The plane is both cheap training and pleasant sport flying."

such as the Rotax 912 currently installed on the prototype. It significantly improves on the quoted performance for the VW and Rotax 532. Many builders may balk at the price of the 912: three times the other powerplant alternatives. However, keep in mind that the engine is of such high relative quality, the company plans to certify certain versions.

A new lightweight version of the Zodiac, designated the CH 601, will open new markets for the company. Essentially, the new 601 will be an 80-lb-lighter version of the CH 600, with significant improvements and many options now included as standard equipment. Enlarged floor space of 11 sq ft, plus lockers in the thick and beefy wing, provide generous baggage room. Purchasers will have the choice of converting wing lockers into additional fuel tanks as well.

Electric trim, dual carbs, liquid-cooling system, cabin heat, instruments, and an adjustable three-blade propeller will all be included in the kit. Chris calls the 601 "an ultralight that is a real plane." Because the empty weight will be in the 470-530 lb range (depending on engine), it will not qualify as an ultralight in the US. However, Canada's new ultralight rules seem as if they were designed for the CH 601, it fits so well.

For those who want the extra speed generally associated with the homebuilt category, Heintz advises that a new version of the Zodiac, with a speed wing incorporating tapered outboard panels, will have a cruising speed of 150 mph, landing speed of 60, and 80 hp in the snout.

Lotsa Plane for Less Than $10,000

Since the basic construction of the various versions is essentially the same, let's look at the CH 600 design and then fly it as a baseline for performance. Most builders will choose the lighter CH 601 with the less weighty Rotax 582, and the performance will be roughly equivalent between the CH 600 with 80 hp and the CH 601 with 65 hp.

Zodiacs are available with tricycle or taildragger landing gear, and sprouting a low, thick, Hershey Bar wing that is stressed for 6 or more Gs at gross weight. The 27-foot span wings can be easily removed, leaving a fuselage with wing stubs that are only 7.5 feet wide.

Access to the very comfortable and roomy 41" wide cabin (44" optional width) is via an ingenious canopy that hinges and opens wide to either side. (One has to give full marks to Heintz's design genius.) Visibility, except straight down, is totally unimpeded.

While VW engines have been typical powerplants since the Zodiac's introduction in 1984, they are quickly giving way to the much improved Rotax engines. Zenair easily mounts the Rotax 582 or 912 engines within the sleek cowlings and provides easy access via four Dzus fasteners for pre-flight inspections. The radiators are mounted below the firewall in the direct airflow, to maximize cooling for the hottest of operating environments.

The 16-gal fuel tank has its filler located just ahead of the canopy, just behind the fiberglass cowling. Almost all the rest of the aircraft is high quality aluminum alloy, guaranteeing long life and low maintenance costs, thanks to its durability and weather resistance.

Builders of this kit have found the quality to be first class and the building manual and instructions perfect for first-time builders. Having flown a number of Zodiacs and interviewed their owners, I hear typical comments such as, "The plane is both cheap training and pleasant sport flying." Builder and aircraft mechanic Paul Muller claimed, "Most aircraft are unnecessarily complicated, expensive, and seldom achieve their design goal. I never wanted to own the fastest, flashiest, most expensive or sophisticated aircraft on the patch. I wanted but one thing—the nicest aircraft to fly!" He chose the Zodiac.

Another builder selected the CH 600 for its low noise level and freedom from complexities such as flaps, fuel pump, and mixture controls.

For all its simplicity, this two-place boasts a speed ratio of more than 4 to 1 (cruise speed divided by stall speed). Few aircraft achieve this efficiency, even with the use of retractable gear and high lift devices!

Simple Construction = High Completion Rates

Many builders don't finish their projects because they are overwhelmed by difficulty of construction and the large amount of completion they must perform.

Knowing this, Zenair packages 45-percent- and 85-percent-complete kits. Attention to small details ensures that the Zodiac can be easily completed within the 600 hours claimed for the homebuilt kit version (the 85-percent kit requires about 150 hours).

For instance, the ribs are not only shaped, but the lightening holes are made, beveled, and smoothed to a finished state. Flanges are shaped, bent, and crimped so that no further work is required by the builder other than assembly to the spar.

Look at other kit manufacturers and compare their attention to detail; typically, one can double or even treble the time claimed by salesmen for project completion. The owners of some of the 700 flying Zenair planes I've had a chance to interview tell me that the company time estimates are valid and the support is unsurpassed.

Inexpensive, Fun Flying

After piloting a Volkswagen-powered Zodiac around New Zealand's north island on a flying tour, my conclusions were very positive — although a little more power and a more efficient propeller were on my wish list. Zenair's Rotax 912-powered prototype adds 20 horsepower and a geared prop that likely increases the effective thrust by more than 40 percent.

Firewalling the throttle proved that this four-cylinder, four-stroke powerplant has the VW beat, hands down. (But then, at more than $9,000, it should.) Takeoff acceleration is impressive. Less than 300 feet of Huronia's paved airstrip were required to get us airborne in the 15 mph winter wind. In sub-zero temperatures, the rate of climb was timed in excess of 1200 fpm, and the controls proved sympathetic to my wishes on an airframe that is stable enough for major cross country tours.

Almost full span ailerons yield an impressive roll rate and the elevator and anti-servo combination give light and responsive action in the pitch axis through the T-bar control stick.

Slow speed handling is precise and was safely accomplished at airspeeds below 60 mph. Although the stall had almost no perceptible warning buffet, the extreme nose high attitude generated by the thick, high lift wing would make the most inattentive pilot realize that the 44 mph stall was imminent. When the break did occur, it was more like a gentle mush, and a rather low rate of descent ensued.

Final approaches of 60 mph are perfectly safe, and the ground cushion caused by the low wing makes smooth landings commonplace.

Really, one would be hard pressed to find something to complain about in this recreational all 'round performer.

CH 600 Series Conclusions

With sons Matthew and Sebastien following their father's footsteps in production and sales, Zenair is almost assured of continuing its leadership role in light aircraft design and manufacturing. Because the new CH 601 variant is tailor-made to the growing demand for recreational aircraft categories around the world, the Zodiac series should become a successful sales leader for this Canadian company.

Exquisite handling, combined with a complete absence of bad characteristics, make the Zodiac delightful and safe to fly. Simple systems make the plane a good trainer and also minimize expenses. With performance that is equivalent to or better than the Cessna 150 series, the Zodiac costs much less to buy and operate, while providing superior flying characteristics. When you consider that they are both built to the same regulations, the homebuilt is an even better value.

Specifications

Zenair CH 300

KIT PRICE	$15,350
PLANS PRICE	$300
BUILDING TIME	800 hrs
NUMBER OF SEATS	3 to 4
ENGINE TYPE	Lycoming O-320, O-360, or automotive conversion
RATED HORSEPOWER	180 for specs
EMPTY WEIGHT	1140 lb
GROSS WEIGHT	1850 lb
WING AREA	130 sq ft
TAKEOFF DISTANCE	650 ft
LANDING DISTANCE	650 ft
CRUISE SPEED	153 mph
TOP SPEED	170 mph
FUEL CAPACITY	34 gal
RANGE	480 sm
REMARKS	Info kit $20

Performance figures are those of the factory.

Specifications

Zenair STOL CH701

Specs for Rotax 582 engine are in parentheses

PRICE	49% kit $16,945 incl Rotax 582
	85% kit $20,985
	Factory-assembled $24,520
BUILDING TIME	350 hrs
NUMBER OF SEATS	2 side by side
ENGINE TYPE	Rotax 912 (582)
RATED HORSEPOWER	75 (65)
EMPTY WEIGHT	500 lb (480 lb)
GROSS WEIGHT	960 lb
WING AREA	122 sq ft
TAKEOFF DISTANCE	90 ft (125 ft)
LANDING DISTANCE	150 ft
CRUISE SPEED	80 mph (75 mph)
TOP SPEED	90 mph (83 mph)
FUEL CAPACITY	11 gal (6.5 gal wing tanks optional)
RANGE	250 sm (450 with wing tanks)

Performance figures are those of the factory.

Specifications

Zenair ZODIAC CH600

Specs for Rotax 582 are in parentheses.

PRICE	45% kit $15,720, plans $230
BUILDING TIME	400-600 hrs
NUMBER OF SEATS	2 side by side
ENGINE TYPE	Rotax 912 (Rotax 582)
RATED HORSEPOWER	80 (65)
EMPTY WEIGHT	520-540 lb (470-490 lb)
GROSS WEIGHT	1200 lb homebuilt
	1058 Canadian ultralight CH601
WING AREA	130 sq ft (future speed wing will differ)
TAKEOFF DISTANCE	400 ft (600 ft)
LANDING DISTANCE	600 ft all versions
CRUISE SPEED	115 mph (105 mph)
TOP SPEED	120 mph (115 mph)
FUEL CAPACITY	16 gal for all versions (more in optional wing locker tanks)
RANGE	420-550 sm for all versions
REMARKS	Info kit $20

Performance figures are those of the factory.

Section Four

Regulations, Paperwork, and Insurance

– 13 –

Following the Regs

Staying Legal in the US and Canada

In this chapter, we'll try to answer many of the questions that prospective homebuilders ask about their rights and the legal requirements involved in constructing an aircraft.

One question I'm asked often: "Is it safe?" Accident statistics show that homebuilders have a significantly lower accident rate than general aviation as a whole. (The highest accident rate per thousand hours of flying belongs to ultralights.)

Another question I'm asked is: "How did all this get started?" In our part of the world, the experimental aircraft movement began decades ago after WW II, when interested builders headed by Paul Poberezny obtained permission for citizens to build their own aircraft. From Poberezny's basement, the Experimental Aircraft Association had its humble beginnings, and subsequently grew into the major organization it is today.

In Canada, a cooperative effort between Arthur Empe of the Department of Transport and "civilian" Keith Hopkinson brought homebuilding rights to Canadians.

The Origin of the "51-Percent Rule"

Federal Aviation Regulation 21.191 (G) details the circumstances that permit a builder to qualify his aircraft under the experimental certificate by "operating an aircraft the major portion of which has been fabricated and assembled by persons who undertook the construction project solely for their own education or recreation." The "major portion" clause has given name to the "51-percent rule," and the "education and recreation" limitation precludes companies or individuals from building complete projects to sell to the public.

This means that manufacturers are restricted to offering kits that are no more than 49-percent complete. Kits that qualify under the

51-percent rule can be builder-assembled, as long as the government inspector deems that more than half the project was owner built. (This is why you see many manufacturers promoting their kits as "49 percent complete.")

This proviso also includes projects that have already been started by another individual. In the latter case, the builder or group of individuals must complete at least 51 percent of the work on a non-commercial non-production basis. As a builder, you can farm out some of the construction — welding and painting operations, for instance — to professionals, as long as the major portion of the effort is your own.

Getting Started

According to the FAA regulations, an applicant must contact the local FAA district office to obtain permission and to advise of the intent to build. After filling out form AB 83-1, he will become a registered builder. In Canada, after contacting the Department of Transport with the intention to build, it must be determined whether the particular aircraft meets the Canadian restrictions for wing loading, engine power and climb capability.

Both the FAA and Canadian DOT district offices have locally assembled handouts filled with information that is valuable to builders. They also have a list of aircraft that qualify under the 51-percent rule. With the crossover of many designs, you will often find that a given aircraft is light enough to qualify both as an ultralight and a homebuilt. As the builder, it's your choice. Remember, the US empty weight limit for ultralights is 254 lb and in Canada it's 430 lb. This does create some confusion in advertising. In Canada, both ultralights and homebuilts must be registered.

Materials used for construction must meet aviation quality specifications, and any kind of engine is permissible (short of liquid or solid fuel rockets in Canada).

When a project nears completion, an application for registration (Form 8050-1) with $5 is sent to the FAA Aircraft Registry, Department of Transportation, P.O. Box 25504, Oklahoma City, OK 73125. This should be mailed three months before project completion, along with complete data on your project, and Form 8050-88 "Affidavit of Ownership for Amateur Built Aircraft," to confirm your ownership. Keep the registration application's pink copy for your records.

Once the identification plate — a fireproof plate with building information inscribed — is attached to the aircraft and the registration painted on the project, an experimental certificate can be applied for. FAR 45.25 describes ID plate regulations and 45.25 has registration letter information.

North of the border, the project must be inspected by Canadian Department of Transport personnel, or their representatives, at various stages of the assembly before any portion is "closed," to ensure that correct procedures and construction standards are being met.

In both countries, when the project is complete, a final inspection is required that determines if the project can be signed off for test flying or if it requires further modifications. In the US, you will work with the FAA inspector to arrange the final — and only — inspection and the operating limitations. At this point, the inspector may want to see your construction log, kit purchase receipt, aircraft plans, and photos of the various stages of construction.

A restricted test flight program must be flown within 25 (sometimes 40) miles of an airport, designated as a base of operations, during which time passengers can not be carried. The use of an FAA-approved engine/propeller combination will usually result in the minimum restricted flight test limit of 25 hours being assigned by the inspector; otherwise, 40 hours will apply.

After the restricted time is flown off, a letter requesting the removal of restrictions and application for a Special Airworthiness Certificate is completed in the form of three-part application 8130-6.

At this point, a further visit from the FAA engineering branch may occur to ensure that log books and an operating manual with limitations, procedures, and the like, have been completed.

While this is not an in-depth look at all of the intricacies of the procedure, it does give you an idea of the paper train. With the help of EAA and FAA personnel, the registration process is easily accomplished.

Who Can Perform Annual Inspections?

As is the case with factory-built aircraft, yearly inspections must be accomplished. If you built the aircraft, you can carry out the inspections and sign off on the paperwork, provided you have requested a Repairman Certificate for your particular homebuilt. Apply at the local FAA office at the time that you show completion of the test period; one trip to the Feds with logs and records in hand should do it.

If someone else built the aircraft, an AI will be required for the inspection signature. Other paperwork requirements include registration, flight permit (in Canada), Special Airworthiness Certificate (in the US), radio station license, weight and balance reports, log books, and Operating Limitations in the US.

Also in the States, a builder has the option of registering his aircraft in numerous categories, with applicable restrictions in each, i.e.: homebuilt, exhibition, crew training, racing, or research and development. (For more information on operating limitations, see the chapter entitled "Buying a Completed Homebuilt.")

To be flown for aerobatics in Canada, the aircraft must have successfully undergone a type-evaluation for aerobatic flight — and few have qualified for this approval.

Pilot License Requirements

Pilots of homebuilts must have a current private pilot's license as a minimum. Pilots must, of course, meet all currency and proficiency requirements, with Americans needing a valid Biennial Flight Review. Naturally, to fly off the water, a seaplane endorsement is necessary. Similarly, multi-engine and rotary wing aircraft require their respective licenses. In Canada, a helicopter pilot must receive an endorsement for every type he wishes to fly.

In the US, a new type of "ticket," the recreational pilot license, will allow pilots to qualify for the freedom of flight with less training and expense. However, this "freedom" is significantly restricted as to the type of aircraft, number of passengers, distance of flight, etc.

Those of you who are interested in rotary winged flight will be delighted to know that numerous models are available. However, do not undertake one of these projects lightly, as they require very close tolerances. They are very difficult to fly compared to fixed wing aircraft and are exceedingly maintenance-intensive in order to keep them airworthy and safe. Don't let anyone tell you otherwise.

It is strongly recommended that builders begin a "Construction Log" to document details of materials, photos of assemblies, bills, and shipping documents. This not only provides interesting reading as a future reference, but also helps prove you built at least 51 percent of the kit when the government official comes for the final inspection.

Restrictions, Restrictions

By way of caution, Canadian readers should be advised that a partially completed project cannot legally be imported. Also, homebuilt aircraft are not allowed to fly across our mutual border without prior permission of the other country's transport department. Canadians need to contact the New York FAA office while Americans must write, FAX, or phone the Canadian DOT in Ottawa, Ontario.

While instrument flying in homebuilt aircraft is permitted in the US (with approval on the Operating Limitations), it is not approved in Canada — yet. However, aircraft suitably equipped can be flown at night during VFR conditions. Canada also requires each carbureted powerplant to be fitted with a carburetor heat system to avoid icing, and firewalls to be more substantial than called for in many plans.

Homebuilts are forbidden from carrying persons or property for compensation or hire, according to FAR Part 91.42. A newly completed homebuilt must be flown in a restricted area for a certain period of time, without passengers, until its performance is proven and it is shown that "the aircraft has no hazardous operating characteristics or design features." Normally, the limitation is 25-40 hours within 25 miles of a given airport. (Ultralights, gliders, dirigibles, and balloons require only 10 hours of restricted operation.) In Canada, the regulation is 25 hours of trouble-free operation within 25 miles of a designated airport.

And here's an FAA reg that few flyers are aware of: "Unless otherwise authorized by the Administrator in special operating limitations, no person may operate an aircraft that has an experimental certificate over a densely populated area, or in a congested airway." While this is the law, in practice this regulation is essentially overlooked — for the time being. Builders should ask the FAA inspector to waive this restriction when he issues the pink special airworthiness certificate after the flight testing has been completed.

Additionally, as the aircraft captain, you must "advise each person carried of the experimental nature of the aircraft," and when operating near tower controlled airports, "notify the control tower of the experimental" designation.

A Look at the Ultralight Regulations

Because there is a great deal of confusion in many minds concerning what is a homebuilt and what is an ultralight, the following is an abbreviated look at the US regulations that define and delineate the limitations of ultralights. Let's clear up a few misunderstandings and then take a look at FAR 103.

Many of the aircraft offered to the public can be built as ultralights or homebuilts because of overlaps in their capabilities. In the States, any aircraft that exceeds the weight, maximum airspeed, or other limitations of ultralights, cannot be an ultralight and therefore must be a homebuilt. However, the higher standards required for homebuilts in terms of material quality, the 51-percent rule, and other factors may preclude a given design from being licensable as a homebuilt. In some cases, with high quality ultralights, you will be able to choose whether you will build it as an ultralight or an experimental.

Before you buy a given product, check with your local EAA chapter and/or the FAA.

"Ultralight Vehicles" are defined by the FAA as vehicles that are to be used for manned operation in the air by a single occupant for recreational or sport purposes only.

Unpowered vehicles must not exceed an empty weight of 155 lb, and powered planes must not exceed 254 lb. The fuel load may not exceed five gallons, the maximum level calibrated flight speed must not exceed 55 knots (63 mph) and the stall speed must not exceed 24 knots (approximately 27 mph).

These vehicles can be inspected by their owners and "their component parts and equipment are not required to meet the airworthiness certification standards." Further, "operators of ultralight vehicles are not required to meet any aeronautical knowledge, age, or experience requirements to operate...." Scary, eh?

Nor do they need to carry identification or registration. (This is not the case in Canada.)

Additional restrictions limit ultralights to daytime VFR, operations away from congested areas or open air assembly of persons, and forbids them to enter controlled airspace or operate in restricted or prohibited airspace without prior authorization from ATC or the controlling agency, as appropriate.

Caution: Higher Weight Limit in Canada

Be careful if you are planning to buy an ultralight from Canada. The higher empty weight limit of 430 lb exceeds the American maximum. Also, if you are building an experimental, be sure the quality of the materials supplied, in a kit that can be built as either category, is high enough to be approved on your final inspection. Otherwise you may receive an expensive lesson in regulations.

More Legal Differences for Canadian Builders

Canadians should realize that not all homebuilts on the market can be flown in their country.

Legally excluded are those aircraft with flapless wings that exceed loadings of 17 lb/sq ft, and flapped aircraft wings exceeding 20.4 lb/sq ft. This rule is designed to provide relatively low stall and landing speeds to protect recreational flyers (and the public). It is expected that these limitations may be removed in the near future.

Some Designs Just Don't Fly in Canada

Don't count on the manufacturer who is selling you the kit or plans to be aware of and inform you that his product is not legal in Canada. And don't assume that because there's one under construction at your airport, it's approved. Numerous kits exceeding the wing loadings are currently being built in Canada; however, they will never fly legally under the current regulations. Don't get caught! The new Chapter 549 of Canada's Department of Transport Airworthiness Manual details the specifications and limitations that apply.

As for helicopters, the RotorWay Exec and late model Scorpions are currently the only approved designs in Canada, although others are being evaluated for future authorization.

It's the law in Canada—and good advice in any country—for builders to keep a construction log that shows all materials, costs, and photos of the fabrication. Not only will this help the inspector to determine that the aircraft is at least 51 percent constructed by the amateur and that he used aircraft quality materials, but it will be a testimonial to your workmanship for years to come.

Before beginning construction, you would be well advised to contact the local federal aviation authorities to advise them of your intentions. They can be very helpful with their years of experience. Since their mandate covers only inspection of projects, don't be surprised if inspectors don't offer construction tips—strictly speaking, they are not allowed to offer suggestions—but they are often remarkably helpful with advice.

One Canadian restriction bans flying under instrument meterological conditions regardless of aircraft equipment or pilot credentials. While this law is under review, it will likely be years before Canadian homebuilts will be able to fly IFR like their American brethren.

While it is illegal in Canada to use amateurbuilt aircraft for reward or hire (that is, commercially), you can use your plane for personal transportation on business trips, and if others ride with you, they can share fuel costs.

Canadians are restricted to homebuilt aircraft with a maximum gross weight of 3968 lb. (I am not aware of any designs that exceed 3800 lb.)

And to ensure obstacle clearance and adequate climb performance, a calculation must be performed to determine the minimum installed horsepower, and a climb test must prove a minimum climb rate of almost 400 fpm.

In Canada, farmers can spray their own crops. Additionally, with a suitable instructor, you can obtain your private pilot's license on your own homebuilt — thus saving a great deal of money — if you can find an instructor who will fly in your experimental aircraft! (Many won't.)

Major changes — advances — were incorporated into Canuck regulations for homebuilders in 1984. Some of these rule modifications are as follows: Certain helicopters are now approved, as are two-place gyro planes; the maximum seat limit has been raised from two to four; and the 50-hour flight test period (often called the no-passenger restriction) has been reduced to 25 trouble-free hours.

Carte Blanche for Composites

The list of approved composites has been terminated and official approbation has been given to all of these high tech aircraft. However, proving the structure with typical loads is necessary, using sand bags or whatever, since flaws in the composite wing spars, for example, could severely restrict your aircraft's capability to withstand vertical gusts.

Gyroplanes have had their allowable gross weight raised to 1125 lb while helicopter maximums are now 1540 lb or a disk loading not to exceed 4.1 lb/sq ft.

Also in the Canadian homebuilt category, manned free balloons and airships are allowed to levitate with up to four people aboard as long as their maximum displaced volume does not exceed 77,690 and 151,850 cu/ft respectively. Additionally, their empty mass must not exceed 1000 lb and 5511 lb respectively. (These changes haven't exactly crowded the skies with lighter-than-air bags.)

One of the differences in Canadian regulations that often catches the unwary is the requirement for a carburetor heat system on carbureted engines, to prevent icing. While it has been generally well proven that two-stroke engine installations do not suffer from carb ice, nonetheless, most Department of Transport inspectors will insist on a heat system.

Another variable in different regions is the need for a separate circuit breaker on each electrical service. Also, the Canadian regulations require improved firewall materials, such as stainless steel, to provide adequate protection for occupants. Check with your regional inspector or RAAC representative to be sure how the regulations are interpreted in your area.

Some four-place aircraft are reduced to two- or three-placers when the formula that considers the installed power is calculated. It would be wise to read the regulation in Chapter 549 completely before considering or committing to a kit purchase.

Much grinding of the wheels of progress is causing advances in regulations. For instance, high performance homebuilt aircraft with high wing loadings will probably be allowed shortly. The current thinking is that the applicant/pilot of such an aircraft would be required to have some additional flight testing that would result in a high performance endorsement on his license.

Canadian purchasers of American kits, plans, and materials should be aware of the good news: there is no duty. And now the bad news: the Federal Excise Tax has been raised to 13% on all goods. (So much for the Free Trade Agreement. Don't forget to add this slice to your costs.) Also, the recently enacted 7% GST (Goods and Services Tax) applies to all aircraft purchases.

Help from EAA and RAAC

While the load of limitations and regulations may seem onerous, thousands of builders have lived with them for decades with no more stress than some paperwork. Thanks to sport aviation groups such as the EAA and the Recreational Aircraft Association Canada (RAAC), these restrictions are steadily being lifted or reduced.

For further aid and information, the author strongly recommends that American citizens contact the EAA—and Canadians the RAAC—when you decide to enter the rewarding world of custom

aircraft. Your local EAA or RAAC chapter can assist you in the interpretation of the regulations. See Appendix C for the addresses and
phone numbers of the organizational headquarters. Also, no
Canadian builder should be without the concise and readable *Airworthiness Standards, Amateur-Built Aircraft*, Chapter 549, available from
the Queen's Printer or the Canadian Government Publishing Center,
Supply and Services Canada, Ottawa, Ontario, K1A 0S9.

Want another prime source of regulation information? Try the feds
themselves. After all, you are going to be working with them in the
future. However, be prepared for differing answers to similar questions on occasion, since the regulations are complex, interrelated, and
difficult to interpret. Nonetheless, almost all of the rules that will affect
you are well determined and accepted at this point and should pose no
problem when you follow the guidelines contained in this book.

There you have it. Let's hope that, by being forearmed with
knowledge of the requirements, you will be able to avoid difficulties
with both the authorities and your project.

– 14 –

Buying and Registering Your Aircraft

The Beginning of the Paperwork Trail

I hope that before reaching this point in a purchase transaction, you have perused the information in the earlier chapters relating to buying a used homebuilt, flight evaluations, the true costs of aircraft ownership, regulations, pilot skills, and selecting a homebuilt design. Studying these fact-filled sections will help to protect you from a purchase that could be unsuitable for many reasons.

Now let's follow the trail of the papers you'll need.

The recent sale of the author's BD-4 and Stinson 108 aircraft required a search for a bill of sale form that would be suitable in both Canada and the US for factory and homebuilt planes. The following sample has been used successfully in both countries.

A Generic Bill of Sale

The following form should be completed in triplicate to provide copies for the seller, the buyer, and the Feds.

Any additional information or conditions to the sale should be added and initialed by both parties on all copies. While the completion of the witness portion is not mandatory, it provides increased protection to both members of the transaction.

BILL OF SALE

Date_____

This document details the agreement for the sale of the Aircraft/Project described as_____, serial number _____,

Registered as _____, being sold by (seller)_____, of (town) _____, (country) _____,to (buyer) _____, of (town) _____, (country) _____.

The aircraft/project is being sold for a deposit of $_____ for a total price of $_____.

1) The buyer realizes that the aircraft/project has been designed and built by amateur(s) and possibly does not meet the workmanship standards for certified aircraft.

2) The seller does not warrant in any way the condition, safety, airworthiness, or suitability of the materials used in construction.

3) This document represents the entire agreement between the buyer and seller.

4) The buyer assumes responsibility for all taxes, duties or other fees that may arise from this sale.

5) This sale is being made on a "where is and as is" basis.

6) The buyer covenants that all future purchasers will be advised of and accept the contents of clauses 1, 2, 3, 4, and 5 of this agreement.

7) The seller is providing the aircraft/project free and clear of liens and encumbrances.

SELLER NAME _____

SELLER ADDRESS_____

_____

BUYER NAME_____

BUYER ADDRESS _____

_____

WITNESS _____

_____

WITNESS _____

_____

Once you have signed on the dotted line — welcome to the wonderful world of experimental flight! If you are like most other custom aircraft owners, you will wonder why everyone isn't flying these low-cost, high-performance products.

Registration, Taxes, and Your Talking Ticket

The topic of registration seems to create a considerable amount of consternation for new owners. In the USA, FAR 91.27 states a civil aircraft cannot be operated without a registration certificate issued to its owner. Similarly, in Canada, all aircraft must be registered and the completed form carried in the Journey Log Book.

Don't forget in your financial planning that, depending on the state or province you reside in, you may receive a tax notice requesting the applicable sales tax on the purchase price of the aircraft.

And if, like most aircraft nowadays, your steed possesses radio communications equipment, you will need a radio license from the FCC or from Communications Canada.

Log Books

The Canadian yearly Condition and Conformity Inspection has been changed as of April 1989 from a very basic certification to a full-blown 100-hour equivalent inspection. This can be very costly if deficiencies are discovered. Make sure that all entries in the Journey Log and Technical Log books are brought up to date by the seller, on the off chance that DOT might wish to inspect them.

And while you are looking over the books, ensure that a valid Weight and Balance record exists for the plane.

Armed with this completed paperwork, you should have no trouble licensing your new aircraft in either country.

– 15 –

Getting Covered

Insuring Your Aircraft, Yourself, and Your Family

Is your homebuilt project properly insured? Are your personal assets protected against loss and the lawsuit craze plaguing the continent? Did you know you can protect your pride and joy while it's still in the construction stage?

In this look at insurance for homebuilts, we will extract tips and warnings from the experts in this field, including the EAA, Eastern Aviation and Marine, and AVEMCO — the company that for many years was the official insurer for the Aircraft Owners and Pilots Association. Having severed that tie, AVEMCO now serves in that capacity for the Experimental Aircraft Association.

Let's Meet the Insurance Experts

Some of our expert advice came from Debbie Fitzmaurice, a senior underwriter with Eastern Aviation and Marine; from Jim Nelson, Vice President of Underwriting at AVEMCO; Mark Williams, an AVEMCO Sales/Underwriter and "the man who runs the operation;" and from AVEMCO Executive Vice President Chuck Hubbard, who says that "Some people can obtain insurance for any type of aircraft." AVEMCO's strength, Hubbard maintains, is that it "provides a stable marketplace — not necessarily the lowest price."

First, let's review the types of coverage that are available to you.

Coverage for Your Unfinished Bird

The coverage you will want to consider initially is often called builder's risk insurance. This protects your project against loss while it's being constructed.

Now, you may think that your homeowner's insurance takes care of that. Read your policy. Chances are you'll find that "airplanes and parts" are among the excluded items. Alternatively, it may not be mentioned, but nonetheless is not covered due to some other fine print clause. Having had a number of experimentals decorating my garage, barn, and yard for years has been a considerable risk because I was uncovered and unaware of this type of coverage.

Coverage for Your Finished Bird

Once your plane is ready to fly, you should obtain liability and hull coverage. The liability insurance is most important, because without it, a judgment arising from damage to property or injury to persons could be a financial catastrophe for you and possibly for innocent victims.

Chuck Hubbard points out that experimentals have fewer accidents per unit compared to factory aircraft. However, the rate per exposure is higher, meaning that for a given number of flying hours, the homebuilt accident rate is slightly higher than general aviation aircraft as a whole. This is probably because the homebuilts are flown less per year, perhaps with pilots who aren't as current, compared to production aircraft.

Liability coverage is expressed in terms of the following: a total limit for an accident; a limit for injury to each passenger (or sometimes each person, whether or not a passenger); and a limit for property damage. Thus, a $300,000/$100,000/$50,000 policy would pay up to $300,000 for a single accident, including a limit of $100,000 bodily injury per passenger (or person) and $50,000 for damage to the property of others.

A more comprehensive type of coverage is called "single limit" liability, and this is offered in two ways.

If you have what the industry calls a "smooth" or "level" single limit policy for, say, $300,000, there is no lower limit for bodily injury or property damage. In other words, every type of liability is insured up to the total of $300,000.

The other type of single limit policy has a sublimit that puts a lower cap on the amount that will be paid for bodily injury for each passenger, and, with at least one insurer, each person on the ground.

The liability insurance just described is no different than the coverage you would buy for a car or a production plane, except that the policy may address itself to FARs that are related to homebuilt

aircraft, such as flying off the area restrictions and passenger limitations.

However, the complexity of the regulations may leave you uncovered when you least expect it. For instance, flying passengers at no
charge during a fly-in, or even making a low pass there, may not be
insured, since it may require an FAA waiver. To be sure, check with
your agent.

Perhaps the major surprises are discovered when one attempts to
secure hull insurance. This covers the damage or loss of your aircraft,
and it can be very different from factory aircraft policies.

For instance, some carriers write a component parts endorsement
into the policy. This, in effect, divides the plane into sections and sets
limits on the amount that will be paid for each section. The endorsement might call for a limit of 15% for the fuselage, 10% for the wings,
8% for the radios, etc.

In that situation, if your total coverage is for $10,000, you will get no
more than $1,500 reimbursement for damage to the fuselage, even if
the cost to repair or replace it is higher.

And Coverage for Your Time

Then there's the matter of labor. You may be satisfied to insure
your plane for no more than the cost of materials, or you may prefer to
add an amount that will compensate you for your time in making
repairs. If the latter is the case, ask your agent or broker how a compensation figure is arrived at. Some companies will reimburse you for
your labor at a rate equal to 50% of the labor estimate of a commercial
repair shop. Others will allow homebuilders to make their own
repairs, and compensate them at a fixed rate — say, $7.50 an hour.

When asked what happens if an owner takes his plane to a maintenance facility, Debbie Fitzmaurice replied, "Then it would be just
like any other aircraft. We would get estimates." She added, "We
endorse with what we call an aerobatic flight restriction. That simply
repeats what the FAA says about aerobatic flight: there's no coverage
on your insured aircraft if you are engaged in aerobatic flight over
congested cities or towns, over an open air assembly of persons, within
a control zone, or below an altitude of 1500 feet AGL."

"Since affiliating with EAA," AVEMCO's Jim Nelson says, "We
are now offering what we call a construction/reconstruction endorsement that attaches to our standard non-commercial policy. When
somebody goes out and spends $11,000 for a kit, he wants to insure it

while he's putting it together. What this endorsement does is come up with the value of the kit in receipts or other proofs of purchase. We're insuring against fire, theft, and windstorm, and we do allow taxiing under this endorsement.

"We call it a construction/reconstruction endorsement, because it also works when you're rebuilding, for example, an old Cub. It basically covers the cost of the materials. It would not cover labor, tools, or jigs. And there is liability available for it, so if a builder is worried about kids falling off the wing of the Stearman he's rebuilding, there is a basic liability available, excluding occupants."

Once your project has been completed and prepared for flight, the time comes for insurance revisions. Nelson suggests, "Once the FAA comes out and issues you an airworthiness certificate with the fly-off and area restrictions, you call us and the coverage on that would stop, and we would rewrite it over to a non-commercial policy to cover flight."

When You Sell Your Project

After an aircraft has reached the point when it can be sold, whether flying or not, builders are subjected to another risk. According to Mark Williams, "It is not unheard of for the builder of a plane to be sued after a sale," because he is deemed to be the manufacturer. Hubbard suggests that it is nearly impossible to obtain the requisite coverage, and the likelihood of someone collecting a claim against you is very low since the plane was built for education and not for sale to the public in normal commerce. (Nevertheless, there is a risk involved, even if it's "only" the cost of defending yourself in court.)

Homebuilt vs Production Aircraft Premiums

Comparing the costs of insuring a homebuilt versus an equivalent production airplane can be very challenging because there are so many variables and a couple of extra considerations. Nelson claims, "It's hard to nail down a percentage, because for some of the really light and docile airplanes, such as the Wag-Aero Cuby, the rates aren't that much higher than for a production aircraft.

"On a higher-performance plane, like a Swearingen, the rates are going to be higher because of the value on it. We've talked with the folks up at EAA, and broken the airplanes down into six categories, determined by ease of construction, ease of flight, and ease of repair, with category One being best and Six being worst."

Most of the Sixes are ultralights, whereas Fives include the Pitts, Rand KR series, Cassutt racer, Starlight and Christen Eagle. Rutan designs go in the middle. In the best-risk category, we find Jodels, Christavia MK 1, Emeraudes, the Pietenpol Aircamper, and others.

Many aircraft, once they have proven themselves with a safe track record, end up in the low risk category. For instance, the rates for the Glasairs and Lancairs, Hubbard announced, have just been lowered.

Keeping Premiums Low

When asked how owners can keep costs down, Nelson replied, "There are some ways they can control their premiums. If they're in a part of the country where they're not flying all year 'round, such as the states in the northern tier that have rougher winters, they can change their hull coverage down to exclude flight and to exclude occupant coverage on the liability, when they stow it for the winter. That way, the aircraft is still protected against fire, theft, vandalism, and windstorms.

"Our ground risk coverage also provides taxiing coverage, so you can taxi, take it out to get the engine warm, run the oil through it. If you pickle the engine, we also have a pure storage quotation. When you get ready to haul it out in the spring, it's just a matter of doing an endorsement to put it right back into in-flight coverage.

"People could save almost half their insurance costs by doing that. Most of the time, a ground risk rate on a airplane could be almost 60 percent off what the full in-flight rate is."

Another tip offered by Nelson: "Take a look at the limits of liability. Look to see if you're carrying any unnecessary coverage. A lot of people have an open pilot warranty on their policy, and I know that nobody else besides the builder flies a lot of the homebuilts. So they should find out if their open pilot warranty is costing them anything, and delete it if it's not needed.

"The other thing is, before you buy or build a specific airplane, call and get the cost of the insurance." Some aircraft are not insurable at all!

Factors That Can Affect Your Premium

The main factors that determine premiums are the experience and age of the pilot. On homebuilts, coverage is written for named pilots only. Thus, total time in all aircraft and time in type of aircraft, such as retractable or taildragger, figures in the setting of the premium.

Pilots who have zero time in the make and model will often be told to obtain two to five hours of dual in order to obtain reduced rates — or coverage at all. Obviously, this is not possible for a single-seater, but if the same aircraft is made as a two-seat model, insurers will ask pilots if it's possible to get some dual time. For example, a Pitts Special is a one-seater, but there is also a two-seat Pitts.

If that's not possible, pilots might be asked to get ground-orientation training from somebody who is experienced in the aircraft, all in an effort to obtain reasonably priced coverage.

As for age, rates are higher for pilot under 20 and over 60.

Pointing out a real pitfall, Debbie Fitzmaurice warns, "Of course, the aircraft has to be certified for flight by the FAA." Mark Williams further cautions that many builders have violated FARs by installing a different engine or propeller or some other major modification that affects the aircraft performance — such as the changing of an exhaust system — without having a further inspection and approval by the FAA. This voids the insurance!

Why Is Homebuilt Insurance Costlier?

When asked why it is more expensive to insure a homebuilt than a comparable production airplane, Fitzmaurice answered: "There are, of course, lots of variables. You could have a highly qualified pilot flying a Cherokee 140, and a very unqualified one flying a Glasair. You might think the Glasair in that same configuration isn't any more difficult to fly, but you have to look at the pilot qualifications."

Let's look at rates for comparable pilots for the same coverage on a Cessna 150 and a fixed-gear model Glasair. The homebuilt's rate is just about double for liability, and about one third more for the hull coverage. One of the major reasons for the higher hull rate is the more restricted availability of parts. One can pick up a part for the Cessna almost anywhere. Additionally, it is very difficult to find an A&P who can accomplish repairs on composite materials.

Hubbard also advises that "mixed construction is a problem that raises rates." In other words, aircraft that entail a mixture of techniques, such as composite, wood, and tube and fabric will always cost more to repair.

Well, there's not much you can do about the fact that it will probably cost more to insure a homebuilt than a production plane. But by carefully examining the kind of flying you do, your seasonal use of the plane, whether or not you'll be the sole pilot, and other considerations, you can avoid paying for coverage you don't really need.

The Premium as a Percentage of Aircraft Value

Hubbard points out that the actual percentage rate for protection varies from 2% up to and beyond 10%, with an average in the 4% to 8% area. The more expensive an aircraft is, the lower the overall percentage, as a function of its value.

On this topic, I asked Williams to provide a quote for two levels of pilot skill on a Glasair III, including full liability of $1 Million, with $100,000 per person/passenger, and $300 deductible on the hangared aircraft.

Liability for a fully experienced, ATP pilot was $449 and for the low timer, $676. Inclusion of hull brought the total to $1817 and $4285 respectively.

The effect of pilot experience on the cost of coverage is obvious!

As far as the percentage for this full coverage is concerned for the ATP pilot, based on a value of $75,000 for the aircraft, his rate is only 2.4%, whereas the low time pilot is paying 5.7% for the same aircraft and coverage.

Risks are Higher for Partners

If you are not the sole owner of the plane, it is wise for the partnership to obtain extra coverage in the $2-3 million range, as lawsuit claims tend to run higher when the plaintiffs learn there is more than one person whose assets can be attacked. Also, because you are in a partnership, you are more likely to be sued because your incidence of exposure is higher.

Hubbard also mentioned that insurance could be purchased to protect visitors or your guests against your liability in a rented hangar.

Another tip to note is that the second or third million dollars of coverage costs far less to obtain than the first, making that extra in-

surance more attractive for those of us who need extra protection —
and these days, who doesn't? Under the "principle of vicarious
liability," claimants tend to sue everyone: pilot, copilot, manufacturer,
mechanic, FBO, and any warm bodies in the area of the incident. Extra
coverage can be very attractive under these circumstances.

Assuming One's Own Risk

In a strange quirk, many aircraft owners have no insurance, in the
belief that no one will sue them if there isn't a major profit in the
litigation. (Don't bet the farm on it!) In fact, many of the major kit
manufacturers carry no insurance for this reason. They feel that they
will just close the doors if someone goes after their assets.

To those of you who feel that you require no aviation liability insurance because you are covered under an umbrella or blanket policy,
I recommend a careful reading of your contract. It will likely disclose
that aviation-related activities are excluded.

Well, there you have it, insights into a complex business, where
builders bet they are going to have an accident and the insurance
company bets they won't.

The final tip: Discuss your needs thoroughly with your insurance
broker or agent. Shop around every time your insurance comes up for
renewal. Insurance rates fluctuate from company to company, and
from year to year. A little judicious telephone dialing — most of which
can be done on toll-free numbers — could bring you a substantial
saving.

– Appendix A –

Directory of
Manufacturers and Suppliers

How to Locate Your Dream Machine

The listings on the following pages will help you contact the company supplying kits, plans, or materials packages for the aircraft that interests you.

I have not attempted to list all of the many manufacturers and suppliers that are offering their wares, and the absence of an company from this list does not in any way suggest that it is inferior — although many poor aircraft designs and companies considered deficient in customer support have been intentionally excluded.

Remember, your best allies are local aircraft building chapters of the EAA or RAAC and your local airworthiness representative of the FAA or DOT.

Note that this appendix includes suppliers of aviation books and videos. For additional information on reading and viewing material, see Appendices B and C.

Aces High Light Aircraft
Cuby I, II
RR#1, London, Ontario
N6A 4B5, Canada
519-552-3020 or 472-7409

Acro Sport
Pober Pixie, Acro-Sport II,
Pober/Corben Junior Ace
P.O. Box 462
Hales Corners, WI 53130
414-529-2609

Aero Composites
Sea Hawker
RD 3
Somerset, PA 15501
814-445-8608

Air Command International
Commander Elite, Sport
1585 Aviation Center Pkwy
Bldg F #601
Daytona Beach, FL 32114
904-258-5010

Aircraft Designs
Various books by Martin
Hollmann
25380 Boots Rd.
Monterey, CA 93940
408-649-6212

Aircraft Spruce and Specialty
Plans, materials packages, books
P.O. Box 424
201 West Truslow Ave.
Fullerton, CA 92632
800-824-1930   714-870-7551
FAX 714-871-7289

Aviation Book Company
Various books
25133 Anza Dr., Unit E
Santa Clarita, CA 91355
800-423-2708   805-294-0101
FAX 805-294-0035

Aviation Publishers
Various books
P.O. Box 36
1000 College View Drive
Riverton, WY

Avid Aircraft
Avid Flyer series
P.O. Box 728
Caldwell, ID 83606
208-454-2600

Barnett Rotorcraft
J4B-2 Gyroplane
4307 Olivehurst Ave.
Olivehurst, CA 95961
916-742-7416

Tony Bingelis
Builder's books
8509 Greenflint Lane
Austin, TX 78759

Peter M. Bowers
Bowers Fly Baby
10458 16th Ave.
Seattle, WA 98168
206-242-2582

Ken Brock Mfg.
KB-2 Gyroplane, KB-3
11852 Western Ave.
Stanton, CA 90680
714-898-4366
FAX 714-894-0811

Buethe Enterprises
Barracuda
P.O. Box 486
Cathedral City, CA 92234
619-324-9455

Bushby Aircraft
Midget Mustang, Mustang II
674 Rte. 52
Minooka, IL 60447
815-467-2346

Butterfield Press
Various books
990 Winery Canyon Rd.
Templeton, CA 93465
800-648-6601, 805-434-1134
FAX 805-434-3185

Canadian Home Rotors
Excell 200
P.O. Box 104
Ear Falls, Ontario
P0V 1T0 Canada
807-222-2474

Canadian Manda Group
TAB books in Canada
P.O. Box 920
Station A, Toronto, Ontario
M8Z 5P9, Canada
416-251-1822
FAX 416-251-3679

Canadian Owners & Pilots Assn
Various discount books
P.O. Box 734
Ottawa, Ontario
K1P 5S4, Canada

CGS Aviation
CGS Hawk
P.O. Box 41007
Brecksville, OH 44141
216-632-1424

Christen Industries
Christen Eagle II
P.O. Box 547
Afton, WY 83110
307-886-3151

Circa Reproductions
Nieuport 11
8027 Argyll Rd.
Edmonton, Alberta
T6C 4A9 Canada
403-469-2692 or 477-0024

Cirrus Design
Cirrus VK30
S3440 A Highway 12
Baraboo, WI 53913
608-356-3460

Eric Clutton
Fred
913 Cedar Lane
Tullahoma, TN 37388

Cosy-Europe
Cosy Classic
Ahornstrasse 10
D-8901 Ried
West Germany
498 23 36 05 94

Denney Aerocraft Co.
Kitfox (similar to Avid)
100 N. King Rd.
Nampa, ID 83651
208-466-1711
FAX 208-466-7194

Earthstar Aircraft
Laughing Gull series
Star Rte., Box 313-KA
Santa Margarita, CA 93453
805-438-5235

Elmwood Aviation
Christavia MK1, MK4
RR#4 Elmwood Drive
Belleville, Ontario
K8N 4Z4, Canada
613-967-1853

Evans Aircraft
Volksplane 1 (VP-1)
P.O. Box 744
La Jolla, CA 92038

Experimental Aircraft Assn
Plans, Sport Aviation magazine
Wittman Field
Oshkosh, WI 54903-3086
800-322-2412
In WI: 800-236-4800

Falconar Aviation
Falconar-Jodel F-9
F-10, F-11D, F-12
19 Airport Rd.
Edmonton, Alberta
T5E 0W7 Canada
403-454-7272

Fisher Flying Products
FP-101, FP-202 Koala
P.O. Box 468
Edgeley, ND 58433
701-493-2286
FAX 701-493-2539

General Publishing Co.
Books
30 Lesmill Rd.
Toronto, Ontario
M3B 2T6, Canada

Great Plains Aircraft Supply
Books and videos
P.O. Box 1481
Palatine, IL 60078

Jurca Plans, c/o Ken Heit
Various 75% WW II fighters
1733 Kansas
Flint, MI 48506
313-232-5395

Kestrel Sport Aviation
Kit Hawk, Float Hawk
P.O. Box 1808
Brockville, Ontario
K6V 6K6, Canada
613-342-8366

Leading Edge Airfoils (LEAF)
Books and videos
331 South 14th St.
Colorado Springs, CO 80904
800-LEAFINC   303-632-4959

Loehle Aviation
5151 Mustang Replica
Shipmans Creek Rd.
Wartrace, TN 37183
615-857-3419
FAX 615-857-3908

Macair Industries
Merlin
P.O. Box 1000
Baldwin, Ontario
L0E 1A0, Canada
416-722-3411

Ed Marquart
Marquart MA-5 Charger
P.O. Box 3032
Riverside, CA 92519
714-683-9582

Jim Maupin
Woodstock, Windrose,
Carbon Dragon
Star Rte. 3, Box 4300-37
Tehachapi, CA 93561

Maxair Aircraft
Drifter series
3855 Highway 27 North
Lake Wales, FL 33853
813-676-0771

Mirage Aircraft
Celerity
3936 Austin St.
Klamath Falls, OR 97603
503-884-4011   612-674-7233

Mosler Airframes &
Powerplants
Dragonfly, Cygnet SF-2A,
Sonerai series, Monerai
140 Ashwook Rd.
Hendersonville, NC 28739
704-692-7713

Murphy Aviation
Renegade, Spirit
8880C Young Rd. South
Chilliwack, B.C.
V2P 4P5, Canada
604-792-5855
FAX 604-792-7006

Neico Aviation
Lancair 320, IV
403 South Ojai St.
Santa Paula, CA 93060
805-933-2747
FAX 805-933-2093

Barney Oldfield Aircraft Co.
Baby Lakes, Buddy
P.O. Box 228
Needham, MA 02192
617-444-5480

Osprey Aircraft
GP-4, Osprey Amphibian
3741 El Ricon Way
Sacramento, CA 95825
916-483-3004

Pazmany Aircraft
PL-2, PL-4A, various books
P.O. Box 80051
San Diego, CA 92138
619-224-7330

Don Peitenpol
Pietenpol Aircamper
1604 Meadow Circle S.E.
Rochester, MN 55904

Powers Bashforth Aircraft
Mini Master
4700 188th St. N.E., Ste. G
Arlington, WA 98223
206-435-4356

Prowler Aviation
Prowler
3707 Meadowview Drive
Redding, CA 96002
916-365-4524

Questair
Venture, Spirit
7700 Airline Rd.
Greensboro, NC 24719
919-668-7890

Rand-Robinson Engineering
KR-1, KR-2, KR-100
15641 Product La, A5
Huntington Beach, CA 92649
714-898-3811

Rans Co.
Chaos, Courier, Sakota, Coyote II
1104 E. Highway 40 Bypass
Hays, KS 67601
913-625-6346

Replica Plans
SE5A Replica
P.O. Box 346
Yarrow, B.C.
V0X 1A0 Canada
604-823-6428

RotorWay International
Exec90
300 S. 25th Ave.
Phoenix, AZ 85009
602-278-8899
FAX 602-278-7657

Sequoia Aircraft
F.8L Falco
2000 Tomlynn St.
P.O. Box 6861
Richmond, VA 23230
804-353-1713
FAX (804) 359-2618

Sorrell Aviation
Hiperbipe
16525 Tilley Rd. South
Tenino, WA 98589
206-364-2866

Spencer Aircraft
Spencer Air Car
P.O. Box 327
Kansas, IL 61933
217-948-5504 or 948-5505

Sport Aircraft
Thorpe S-18
44211 Yucca, Unit A
Lancaster, CA 93535
805-949-2312 or 945-2366

Stits Aircraft
Fabric covering video
P.O. Box 3084-Q
Riverside, CA 92519
714-684-4280

Stoddard-Hamilton Aircraft
Glasair series
18701 58th Ave N.E.
Arlington, WA 98223
206-435-8533
FAX 206-435-9525

Stolp Starduster
Mark II Skybolt
4301 Twining St.
Riverside, CA 95209
714-686-7943

TAB Books
Various books
Blue Ridge Summit, PA 17294
800-822-8138   717-794-2191

Molt Taylor
Mini-Imp, Coot-A
P.O. Box 1171
Longview, WA 98632
206-423-8260

Harry Thompson
Dormoy Bathtub
P.O. Box 423
Alexandria, MN 56308
612-763-6537

TRADE-A-PLANE
Used aircraft, parts publication
Crossville, TN 38557
615-484-5137

D. Trivisonno
Piel, Emeraude series, Zephir,
Beryl
Super Diamant, Saphir
10426 Parc Georges Blvd.
Montreal Nord, Quebec
H1H 4Y3, Canada
514-321-0826

Van's Aircraft
RV series
P.O. Box 160
North Plains, OR 97133
503-647-5117

Volmer Aircraft
Sportsman
P.O. Box 5222
Glendale, CA 91201
818-247-8718

War Aircraft Replica
Focke-Wolfe 190, F-4U Corsair,
P-47 Thunderbolt, Hawker Sea
Fury, P-51D Mustang
348 S. Eighth St.
Santa Paula, CA 93060
805-525-8212

White Lightning Aircraft
WLAC-1, Lightning Bug
Walterboro Airport, Box 497
Walterboro, SC 29488
803-538-3999

Wicks Aircraft Supply
Sidewinder, engines, materials,
kits
410 Pine St.
Highland, IL 62249
800-221-9425   618-654-6253
FAX 618-654-7447

S.J. Wittman
Wittman Tailwind
Red Oak Ct., Box 2672-3811
Oshkosh, WI 54903-1265
414-235-1265 (May to Nov)

Zenair
CH 701, CH 300, CH 600
Huronia Airport
Midland, Ontario
L4K 4K8, Canada
705-526-2871

– Appendix B –

Collecting Information

The Suppliers' Catalogs are often Gold Mines!

In their desire to serve the aviation public, the major parts suppliers provide very useful catalogs that are chock full of information that is most instructive for builders.

Aircraft Spruce & Specialty The tome offered by Aircraft Spruce & Specialty is perhaps the best example available. With a circulation of 30,000 or so, this yearly opus becomes available in July at the massive Oshkosh extravaganza when members of the AS&S staff man the booths at their large display. The catalog contains more useful information in 300 pages than a whole collection of books. It offers discounts, costs only $5, and that $5 is refunded on an order of $50 or more. These benefits make the catalog a "must have" for builders.

From the day Burt Rutan walked into AS&S with a request that the company stock a large supply of composite materials, these products have become the mainstay of sales. The catalog reflects the dedication to composites by listing the following: properties, usage, weights, strength, building techniques and compatibility with other substances. This first section of the catalogue begins with a selection of composite aircraft kits available from AS&S. The wood products section details the selection and cutting of quality spruce trees and discusses dimensions and characteristics of various types of woods.

Similarly, the Metals/Plastics chapter begins with an introduction to modern steel-making and the characteristics of various grades of aircraft steel tubing and bar stock, then delves into the production and grades of aluminum, finishing with "Everything in Plastics." This latter portion of the chapter provides tips on working with Plexiglas, plus the characteristics of Plexiglas, Lexan, acetate, Mylar, glass epoxy rod, etc. Everything you ever wanted to know about fasteners can likely be found in the section entitled "Hardware."

Subsequent chapters, following the same format, include: Airframe Parts, Landing Gear, Engine Accessories, Engine Parts,

Covering Supplies (Acetone to Zinc Chromate), Instruments, Electrical & Radio, Tools, and Pilot Supplies.

The entire catalog is so well illustrated that most items can be easily found through the use of the comprehensive index, followed by finding a picture of the object in the applicable section. In case that isn't adequate for some individuals, each article has an explanation as to its use. Very educational. As a matter of fact, many schools use the catalogue as a reference book.

The toll-free number, 800-824-1930, not only serves the US, but also Canada. (Overseas customers can call 714-870-7551.) With six order-taking lines, a busy signal is relatively unlikely. The order desk is staffed from 6 AM to 6 PM Monday through Friday and 9 AM till 3 PM on Saturdays. The toll-free number should be used only for placing orders, as other extensions are not accessible from this line.

For customer service and other inquires, phone 714-870-7315 or FAX (714) 871-7289. Aircraft Spruce is closed only on Sundays, Christmas and New Year's. The operation is located at 201 W. Truslow Avenue, Fullerton, California. The mailing address is Box 424, Fullerton, CA, 92632.

Wicks Aircraft   Providing similar products and services as AS&S, Wicks Aircraft is well known for their custom work with wood, such as spar laminating. A very detailed catalog costing $5 — refundable with a $35 order — is also an excellent investment for the builder. For those who wish to purchase plans and build from scratch, Wicks also provides packaged materials kits for numerous aircraft.

Their customer service and information number is 618-654-7447 and their address is 410 Pine Street, Highland, IL 62249. The toll free order line is 800-221-9425 from 7 AM to 5 PM CST, with rush orders shipped within 24 hours. They also have a panic capability for builders in "dire emergencies."

Wag-Aero   Well known for their prefabricated and aircraft surplus parts supply, especially for older certified aircraft, Wag-Aero is also known for their development of affordable Piper Cub-like aircraft. These include the four-place Sportsman 2 + 2 and the Sport Trainer J-3 replica with the bargain basement plans price of $65.

Their free catalog lists more than 9000 aircraft parts, and their toll-free phone number is 800-558-6868. For those seeking other customer service, call 414-763-9589 or write P.O. Box 181, Dept. KA, 1216 North Road, Lyons, WI 53105.

Alexander Aircraft Company   Their free catalog can be obtained from 90 Montgomery Drive, Griffin, GA 30223, or phone 404-228-3815. Their toll-free order line is 800-831-2949. FAX 404-229-2329.

Alpha Plastics Inc.   This company has been providing a free catalog and friendly service on their specialty — composite materials — for years. While they don't have a broad spectrum of other aircraft parts, their composite prices have earned them a place in this directory. Contact them at 8734 Daffodil St., Houston, TX 77063 or phone 713-780-0023.

Falconar Aviation Ltd.   This Canadian company is a major supplier of Hirth engines and the Hipec covering process. Dozens of aircraft plans and fabricated parts are available at 19 Airport Road, Edmonton, Alberta, T5G 0W7, Canada. The phone number is 403-454-7272.

Fullerton Air Parts   This company, founded by the late Flo Irwin (who also launched Aircraft Spruce), is headquartered at 4010 West Commonwealth Ave., Fullerton, CA 92633. Phone 714-525-8226.

J & M Aircraft Supply   For your free catalog, write P.O. Box 7586, Shreveport, LA 71137 or phone 312-222-5749. The toll-free order number is 800-551-8781.

Leading Edge Airfoils   For Rotax operators, this $6 catalog is a best buy. My choice for Rotax parts and service can be contacted at 331 South 14th Street, Colorado Springs, CO 80904. Phone 800-LEAFINC or 719-632-4959. FAX 719-632-2815.

Univair Aircraft Corporation   This $5 catalogue has many Stinson parts and other custom factory aircraft supplies. Write to 2500 Himalaya Road, Aurora, CO 80011 or phone 303-364-7661.

U.S. Industrial Tool & Supply Company   Billing themselves as the "primary supplier of tools for the aircraft mechanic," their free catalogue can be obtained from 15119 Cleat, Plymouth, MI 48170-6098. Phone 800-521-4800, FAX 313-455-3256.

A Word or Two of Advice

While this is not a complete listing of all aircraft parts suppliers, they are companies that I have had good success with or heard positive comments about from other builders. Many will accept Visa or

MasterCard charges to provide faster processing of your parts. Once you are on the mailing list, you will receive sales flyers from some of these companies, allowing you to take advantage of special orders and clearance/surplus items.

Shop around. Prices will vary as much as 50 percent for a given part, due to fluctuating market conditions. Other specials that are not advertised will often be available to those who visit the warehouses. Take your wife to involve her. Who knows – she may have some great ideas for your plane's interior, etc. Happy shopping!

For more details on companies offering aircraft kits, plans or supplies, see Appendix A.

– Appendix C –

Recommended Reading and Watching

More Help for Homebuilders

The following reviews are offered to help you obtain other reference materials to benefit you during and after construction of your project. While the list is by no means complete with all of the good materials currently available, it includes many of the best that could be helpful. For addresses and phone numbers, see the directory in Appendix A.

Books and Videos

Elements of Sport Airplane Design for the Homebuilder   Originally published in 1977, this book was reissued in a third edition in 1986, but that doesn't mean this reference is outdated. To the contrary, it is chock full of useful tips and thought-provoking insights into aircraft design and construction. In a book of only 105 pages, it would be very difficult to cover the myriad of considerations a designer must contemplate. To overcome this limitation, the author, P.E. Bird, uses a precise style of writing and numerous illustrations to minimize the words necessary to convey his ideas.

Essentially, the book follows the development of the Vogel Vixen, a sleek automotive-powered speedster designed by Fritz Wolfe. This aerobatic single-place monoplane used a welded steel tube fuselage covered with foam/dynel/epoxy and a wooden box-beam wing spar covered with fiberglass and epoxy.

This writer doesn't know what became of this design. However, regardless of the vintage date or success of the design, the rules of thumb that are plentiful through out the text will be extremely helpful to anyone conceiving a new aircraft or modifying an existing design. While the book isn't comprehensive enough to be the be-all and end-all of aircraft design, the chapters cover the basic requirements to be considered and thus give insights into the topic. And there are more than 25 pages of very useful charts and other technical data that make this Aviation Book Company offering, at $14.95, a good investment.

Helicopter Design & Data Manual   This primer is written as a down-to-earth explanation of helicopter aerodynamics. Stanley J. Dzik has used the summary format to squeeze a great deal of useful information into this compact 118-page publication. His primary purpose was to educate individuals who wish to design and construct their own helicopter. Portions of the book would also be beneficial to fledgling helicopter pilots. A technique he frequently uses is to explain a phenomenon in different words and from different directions to help the reader through difficult passages.

Profusely illustrated, he starts with preliminary rotary wing aerodynamics and five pages later progresses to advanced. However, at no time does the author move too quickly—he just doesn't waste time or words. Six pages of helicopter controls leads to Chapter 4, Design Sketch Section, showing diagrams of numerous existing helicopters and discussing their control and drive systems.

While the author does not state his background, a reasonable guess might be that he has invested some time in the field of rotor blades adhesive bonding. Mr. Dzik devotes Chapter 5 to this topic.

A "Helicopter Theory of Flight Review" rounds out the general theory of aerodynamics as applied to rotary wing flight. This is well done and could logically be an extension of the training new pilots receive. The last 15 pages, "Helicopter and Related Nomenclature," is a fine dictionary of rotary wing terms and expressions.

Available from the Aviation Book Company for $9.95.

Composite Aircraft Design   Author Martin Hollmann is a strong supporter and prolific designer of composite aircraft. When he discusses composite construction, the world listens.

This book is a very good broad-spectrum introduction to "what's happening" and "how to" in the design and assembly of aircraft, discussing materials such as fiberglass, graphite, Kevlar, foams, and epoxy, polyester or vinyl ester resins.

Hollman whizzes through fabrication from lay-up to finishing techniques. Not one to waste words, he covers the extensive topic in only 125 information-packed pages. One of the extra values in this book is its readability—no need to peruse large quantities of filler common to many writers.

Four appendices include a glossary, a list of composite material suppliers, references, and two programs for IBM-compatible and Macintosh computers. The first, called "Composite," calculates the strains in the composite system. The second, "Spar," is a basic program to calculate the required spar height in a wing.

Lavishly illustrated and with text large enough for the very vain to read without their glasses, this plastic-bound 9" x 11" volume is stuffed with useful information for beginner and expert alike.

It is priced at $20 from Aircraft Designs.

ABCs of Desktop Finite Element Analysis Author Martin Hollman tells me that this book is selling like hot cakes now that this type of stress analysis and design aid is the buzzword amongst engineers. Once again, by being at the forefront of computer aided aircraft design, Hollmann is in an excellent position to advise us which of the many programs will best suit our needs. (You certainly can't listen to the software salesmen if you want an honest evaluation.)

Now, much effort and cost can be avoided by relying on this volume and Hollman's experience in making your selection of a Finite Element Analysis (FEA) program from the approximately 4000 programs available. The following FEA packages are intensively reviewed in the book: NISA, MSC/NASTRAN, MSC/pal, ANSYS, COSMOS/M and SUPERSAP.

Engineers and designers are well advised to add this 151-page softcover reference to their collection, for $32 (second edition). To buy the wrong software program for your stress analysis is not only frustrating but also costly.

Contact the author at Aircraft Designs.

Auto Engines for Experimental Aircraft Now in its second edition, this 188-page abundantly illustrated book (180 photos and illustrations) is very informative for those seeking alternatives to horizontally opposed aircraft engines. Written by Richard Finch, an aerospace engineer and racing car sportsman, its pages are packed with useful information on a myriad of auto and motorcycle engines as well as conversion recommendations, costs, and flight testing.

It also describes various final drives for propeller speed reduction, including gear boxes as well as chain and belt drives. Ignition systems, motor mounts, liquid cooling, turbocharging, and exhaust systems are also covered well enough to serve as a basis for a builder's construction plans.

At $20, this tome is a best buy from Aircraft Designs.

Aircraft Systems/Understanding Your Airplane   Perhaps the best compliment one can give David A. Lombardo's book is, "Wish I were the author."

The book's title is well chosen. This is a major compendium of aircraft systems by an aircraft mechanic with decades of teaching and flying experience. While the 31 chapters could be useful for a student pilot learning what makes an airplane tick, the intensive coverage of various systems, complete with abundant diagrams and photos, would be of greater benefit to homebuilders and pilots proceeding beyond the private license level.

Familiarity with the 290 pages would allow pilots to not only understand the theory of the various systems, but also to troubleshoot and maintain their aircraft (with due consideration to the legalities). Builders would have the additional benefit of being able to study layouts, standard installation procedures, and electrical schematics.

Published in 1988, this up-to-date extremely complete guidebook is written in a clear and concise manner using the precept that a picture is worth a thousand words.

For further information or to order yours, sent $18.95 to TAB Books or $26.95 Canadian to Canadian Manda Group.

Care and Maintenance of Your Rotax Engine   Are you interested in, or operating, Rotax engines? Then you had best invest in this video. Simply put, your bacon could be saved—or at least a significant portion of the contents of your wallet preserved—with this timely maintenance aid.

This high quality two-hour video is marketed by Rotax overhaul experts LEAF INC. (Leading Edge Air Foils).

During the past few years, LEAF has found that 60% of their service calls would have been unnecessary if the Rotax owners and operators had followed the instructions in their operator's manuals. For those of us who hate to sit down and read a dry manual, this entertaining, personalized tape will provide vividly informative images, allowing us to see exactly what can be done at our basic skill level. Believe me, that's a lot!

LEAF's shop foreman shows us how to break-in the engine, set the idle, start the Rotax, check and set the timing, adjust belts, torque heads, and trouble shoot the complete powerplant—essentially, everything you need to know for trouble-free operation. The video covers the five Rotax engines (277, 377, 447, 503 and 532) in depth but with a clarity and simplicity that makes preventive maintenance easy for all.

In discussions I had with the North American distributor of Rotax engines, he told me that the cause of almost all two-stroke powerplant problems was the lack of preventive maintenance by operators. He indicated that few individuals tune or time their engines at the specified intervals. It's no wonder then that some of the engines have proven unreliable for those owners.

Produced in color, this video is an superior training aid. Priced at $45, it is an excellent investment in protecting one's Rotax and prolonging its operational life. Incidentally, that price includes LEAF's 175-page catalog ($6 if ordered separately), with its superb exploded views of the engines, not to mention a very complete offering of products and parts.

Volkswagen Engine Assembly for Experimental Aircraft When I volunteered to sponsor a Sonerai II homebuilt aircraft project for the local boys school, I didn't know the instructor hated engines. Nor did I know that he would wash his hands of everything to do with the powerplant other than cooling—that is, baffle construction. Was I baffled! It didn't appear that there would be any problem with tearing down an air-cooled VW, but rebuilding the hundreds of pieces—and even worse, sitting behind it for the initial test flight—didn't appeal to me at all.

Investing in Rex Taylor's HAPI VW engine rebuilding book was the answer. As they say, a picture is worth a thousand words, and it seems the thousands of pictures in the Hayes and Nolly Production Videos on these horizontally-opposed four-cylinder engines are worth millions of words.

And worth the $45. Available in Beta or VHS, this two-hour tape shows comprehensive assembly from case to completion by Steve Bennett of Great Plains Aircraft Supply Company—a company that's expert in the field by virtue of having built and shipped hundreds of VWs to satisfied customers. With cogent instructions, Steve takes viewers from VW case identifications through the step-by-step buildup of a bored and stroked 2180 cc engine, up to the point where individual accessories would be installed.

Because tolerances and clearances are somewhat close in this hardworking version of the engine, observers are shown how to check that rotating portions of the engine are not meeting catastrophically in dark corners. End play, interference fits, torque values, and clearances are all explained and detailed so that raw amateurs such as myself can rebuild a four-stroke VW with confidence.

The steps are explained in such detail and with such clarity that it was never necessary for me to rewind the tape to fully understand each construction detail. For anyone contemplating having one of these air-cooled VW engines of 36 to 80 hp, this high quality production will pay for itself by helping you avoid construction errors and by rewarding you with peace of mind. (It did so for me.) Then I turned to the next video:

Weekend Mechanic's Guide to Engine Rebuilding   What's an auto engine rebuilding guide doing in an aviation book? Simple. With the homebuilt industry's trend towards auto conversions for low cost, efficiency, and reliability, it's time to look at manuals to aid builders during inspections and overhauls.

Paul Dempsey's book is well written, concise, and penned in a style that allows those of us with little engine rebuilding experience to carry out the instructions with ease. Readers are led from troubleshooting, through work space organization, labeling parts, disassembly, machining, and assembly to factory standards. Tips that can't be found in service manuals, combined with service bulletin updates, provide the first-time rebuilder with extremely useful information to ensure a reliable, powerful reliable rebuild.

This 166-page paperback, available from TAB Books, is priced at approximately $14.95.

Plane Tips   This volume, written by Bob Stevens, has dozens of tips that will be useful to aircraft builders or owners. Tricks from changing your engine oil without a mess, or mountain flying techniques, to removing abrasion marks on your canopy's plexiglass are but a few of the hints on how to reduce the cost and complexities of flying. All of the helpful instructions are written in a pithy manner that, coupled with numerous illustrations, ensures that readers will understand the objective of each lesson.

While there are fewer than 100 pages and no index in this Aviation Book Company softcover book, any one of the tips could save operators more than the $4.95 purchase price.

Fabric Covering with Ray Stits   When my partner and I decided — actually, it was an aviation inspector who decided — that it was time to re-cover our Stinson 108-2 classic (relic would be more apt), we studied all the brochures and talked with numerous fabric aircraft owners.

Our conclusion? The new lightweight Stits fabric HS90X was the clothing to cover this old girl's bones. Visual inspection of the aircraft's interior was possible through the cracks and gaps in the 20-year-old Dacron Ceconite (trade names for this polyester weave). Benefits of the HS90X are the very low weight of 1.7 ounces per yard, full strength of 95 lb per square inch, and no V_{ne} restriction (velocity never exceed speed).

With that decided, materials were ordered and the Stits application manual (very comprehensive and well put together) was studied for a few weeks. Fellow members in our RAAC and EAA chapter, none of whom had any covering experience, were enlisted to share the mistakes. Strangely enough, our efforts were considerably better than those of the local "A&P" aircraft covering "expert." We attribute this success to the ease of using the Stits System.

Unfortunately, the new video tape was not available before we completed our project. However, it was ordered anyway, for future reference. It turned out to be a two-hour long, very high quality production that was crammed with tips. Watching the master and helper cover an aircraft step-by-step taught the viewer many shortcuts and useful tricks. Nine "chapters" cover the materials and methods; wing, control surfaces, plywood and fuselage covering; heat shrinking; poly brushing; rib lacing; finishing tapes; inspection holes; drain grommets; poly spraying and wrap up.

If you are planning to fabric-cover all or some of an aircraft with the Stits or any other process, this video will pay for itself in the first hours of your efforts. It will likely save time and hassle while allowing you to make a first class job of the project. Available for $49.95 U.S. through Stits Aircraft or EAA.

Composite Construction for Homebuilt Aircraft   First printed in May 1984, *Composite Construction* shows builders current "techniques of working with plastics, and the basics of structural and aerodynamic design." A few construction details and brief pilot reports are included for the Quickie Q2/200, Dragonfly, VariEze, Long-EZ, Goldwing ST, Mini-Imp, Bullet, Polliwagon, Glasair, KR-1 & 2 and the Sea Hawk. Multitudinous drawings and charts make the topic easily understood.

Composites considered include foam/fiberglass matrixes, Kevlar, S-glass, graphite and paper cores. Tips for making molds and attaching fittings are followed with a chapter on care and repair of composite structures. Some of the others cover aircraft shapes, exotic composite aircraft, and safety.

Sixty pages of appendices provide additional aid for composite builders. One section details the US locations of a number of materials suppliers. This reduces the hassle of chasing parts and alone justifies the purchase of the book. Also included is a catalog of tools, prices, and materials characteristics.

If you're using or planning to use composites in your project, consider adding this to your library. Softcover, 240 pages, from the Aviation Book Company for $17.95.

Basic Helicopter Maintenance   This is a book I can highly recommend for both pilots and maintenance engineers. While this very complete work was written by Joseph Schafer for educating engineers, I feel it will be of significant value to helicopter builders and pilots as well — from student to high-timer.

The first chapter covers helicopters in use today. The next section, on principles of flight, will inform any pilot or engineer of the aerodynamics and control characteristics affecting flight. The chapter on "Documentation, Publications and Historical Records" is written for operators of factory machines in the US — most of it is applicable in Canada as well.

"Helicopter Fundamentals" is followed by "Main Rotor Systems," the latter giving a very complete coverage of this rather complex topic. As an example of how well this tome is illustrated, this chapter of less than 70 pages has more than 120 drawings and charts.

Mast and flight controls, main rotor transmissions, powerplants, tail rotors, airframes and related systems are covered in turn in a clear, concise manner. The author also provides a very complete glossary of terms to aid those not familiar with "fling wing" nomenclature.

There is no question that this product will be very beneficial to helicopter engineers of all levels. Also, having some knowledge of the systems has allowed this 7500-hour chopper pilot to escape a bush survival situation on at least a couple of occasions. If you're considering a rotary wing career, or building a helicopter yourself, you shouldn't ask whether you can afford this book, but rather, whether you can afford not to have it. With 342 pages and 1000 illustrations, Basic Helicopter Maintenance costs $14.95 from the Aviation Book Company.

EAA Technical Manual 107   Typical of the many high quality — but low price! — offerings from the homebuilder's support group, this powerplant manual is absolutely chock full of useful information. Other books available from EAA cover welding and wood-working tips, to mention only two topics.

Additionally, numerous videos offer invaluable tips to tame the challenges involved in homebuilding. When you send in your check to join EAA, ask for their catalog of books and videos as well.

To join EAA or obtain further information on their products, see their listing in Appendix D.

Sportplane Construction Techniques   This book could be subtitled the Homebuilder's Bible. To sportplane builders, Tony Bingelis is an apostle. His previous writings have included the very popular *The Sportplane Builder* and *Firewall Forward*.

With 366 large pages of up-to-date construction tips and practices, the volume covers getting ready to build, fiberglass components, control systems, cockpit/cabin interior, canopy/windshield, landing gear, instrumentation, electrical systems, painting and finishing. It's a copiously illustrated book with detailed drawings of some of the best ideas to come out of homebuilt aviation.

Bingelis will take you from the inception of your project with an introduction to aircraft hardware and "how to make haste slowly" through numerous steps to perfection. His writing is very readable and his tips and instructions easily followed. There are literally hundreds of fine suggestions in this opus, any one of which will repay the price of the book in time, effort, or materials. In my opinion, a builder can't afford not to have this book. *Sportplane Construction Techniques* is available from the author, Tony Bingelis.

Rotary-Wing Aerodynamics   Take note, students of helicopter aerodynamics and pilots wishing to understand the advanced concepts of rotary wing operation: Your book has arrived.

And it was largely paid for by NASA (National Aeronautics and Space Administration) when they had it written for the U.S. Army Research and Development Laboratory of the Aviation Systems Command.

Authors/Engineers W. Z. Stepniewski and C. N. Keys were commissioned to produce this detailed, concise two-volumes-in-one book of over 600 soft-covered pages. It is almost certainly capable of answering any of your technical questions on helicopters and rotor systems.

Volume one (Basic Theories of Rotor Aerodynamics) includes definitions of rotary-wing aircraft, momentum theory, blade element theory, vortex theory, velocity and acceleration potential theory, and airfoils for rotary-wing aircraft.

Volume two (Performance Prediction of Helicopters) covers description of the hypothetical helicopter configuration, single rotor helicopter and vertical climb performance, forward flight performance, winged helicopter performance, and tandem rotor helicopter performance.

This tome appears to be the definitive book for "fling wing" aerodynamics — certainly not light reading, but an in-depth coverage of the topic. Included are very complete indexes, bibliographic references, 10 black-and-white photos and 537 figures. This handy reference is highly recommended for any serious student of rotary wing aerodynamics. It is available from the Aviation Book Company for $14.50.

Theory of Wing Sections   For those of you who design your own aircraft or simply want to know more about the parameters of various airfoils, this one's for you. This 700-page work is loaded with the juicy data necessary to perfectly match an airframe with the most suitable wing shape to optimize performance.

Originally published in 1949 and recently updated, this engineer's bible is a "concise compilation of the subsonic aerodynamic characteristics of modern NACA wing sections together with a description of their geometry and associated theory." Many advances have been made from recent contributions, necessitating the update. The authors say that, "[While] a knowledge of differential and integral calculus and of elementary mechanics is presupposed...an attempt has been made to keep the mathematics as simple as is consistent with the difficulties of the problems treated."

Further, I would say the charts and graphs speak for themselves, insofar as the characteristics of each airfoil are concerned.

The authors, I. H. Abbott and A. E. Von Doenhoff, with input from other engineers at NACA (NASA), have based all their conclusions on data gathered over the years. In my opinion, even a recent graduate from the private pilot's ground school could derive a lot of benefit and understanding from this book. An improved comprehension of wing function and performance is necessary for superior flying performance. Chapters include the significance of wing-section characteristics, simple two-dimensional flows, theory of wing sections of finite thickness, and theory of thin wing sections. The book costs only $10.95 from the Aviation Book Company.

Gear Design for Light Aircraft; Volume One   Tires, brakes, wheels, and landing gear designs are a few of the topics covered in Ladislao Pazmany's new book. Following his very successful *Light Aircraft*

Design, this book is the definitive reference for everything you need to know to design and understand aircraft landing gear. It's a continuation of the author's dedication to aircraft design, comprising more than ten years of research.

It consists of 245 pages in soft cover including 498 photographs, line drawings, tables, and large fold-out drawings. Now that's well illustrated! The 12 chapters cover an introduction, arrangement of the landing gear, the ground loop, tires, wheels, brakes, wheels and brakes without TSO, brake systems, loads and deflections, main gear, nose gear and tail gear.

Large aviation companies often farm out landing gear work to small specialty companies due to its complexity. Now with this compendium of information they will be able to accomplish landing gear design and construction in house. This volume would be of immense benefit for aircraft designers and serious homebuilders who wish to modify, maintain or build their own landing gear.

It seems so complete it's difficult to believe that Mr. Pazmany is planning a second volume to cover landing gear for sailplanes and motorgliders, floats and skis, retraction systems, steering, shimmy, fairings and doors, testing, trade-offs, stress analysis, weights, shock absorber design, materials, (whew!) and over 500 patents related to landing gear. Volume two may be available by the time you read this. (Incidentally, most of these topics are covered in volume one in considerable depth. One assumes that Pazmany plans a very comprehensive coverage of these topics in the later volume.)

Some of the nice touches and benefits of the book are as follows: Complete specifications of various manufacturers' tires and brakes are given along with addresses enabling one to order the products – no more searching for a supplier. The very comprehensive drawings, complete with AN spec numbers and notes on scale drawings, greatly reduce the effort of designing and building an aircraft landing gear. The use of numerous calculations and equations allows the reader to truly understand the forces and stresses on his airplane's gear.

Ever wonder what happened in the development of spherical, roller or "Tundra" tires? These and other historical perspectives add interest and readability to the book as it takes us from the first landing gear (probably a set of size 8 shoes) through today's trailing arm retractables.

All in all, this is a very useful reference book that is available for $25 plus postage from Pazmany Aircraft Corporation.

Light Airplane Construction   This 92-page softcover reference work by Ladislao Pazmany chronicles the author's design of the PL-2 aluminum monoplane that was a very successful design a decade ago. A recognized and highly qualified designer, Pazmany uses 311 illustrations and photos to allow builders to fully comprehend the considerations involved in a semi-monocoque, lightweight aircraft.

With a current price of $12, this is one of the better books on the market for metal aircraft homebuilders. Order from Pazmany Aircraft Corporation.

Modern Gyroplane Design   This work summarizes author Martin Hollmann's experience in the design, development, building, and flying of his two-place Sportster gyroplane. While the design wasn't successful in a commercial way, Hollmann's purpose is "to explain some deficiencies such that they will not be incorporated into new designs and to help the younger generation develop successful gyroplanes in the future."

He starts by pointing out that the term "gyrocopter" came about due to the popularity of Igor Benson's Gyrocopter. "Gyroplane" is the correct term.

After an introduction that considers the inherent safety of the gyroplane and its unique capabilities, the author guides you, the reader, in an exercise to determine what you want from your aircraft. Then you'll look at design parameters. By comparing the specifications and performance of successful gyroplanes, Martin leads you through the steps necessary to create the performance calculations for your own design.

Based on the stated fact "the gyroplane is a forgiving aircraft and if properly designed it is safer to fly than any other aircraft," Martin explains the techniques of efficient design. He looks at the performance tradeoffs required and discusses the effects of deficiencies of past gyroplanes. His often humorous anecdotes both entertain and educate the reader.

Other chapters include configuration considerations, selecting an engine, selecting a method of construction, making a layout, performance calculations, rotor loads, and structural analysis. There is even a Macintosh computer program for rotor blade analysis.

Starting to think about designing a gyroplane? If so, better add *Modern Gyroplane Design* to your library by sending $20 to Aircraft Designs.

Aircraft Hardware Standards Manual & Engineering Reference   As you might expect, the title says it all. Now into the third printing of the second edition, this reference is a collection of 30 + volumes of condensed information on aircraft fasteners and other hardware. Everything you need to know about these devices is well covered in this work. In its 142 soft-covered pages are hundreds of illustrations, pictures, and specification charts for any fixtures you've thought of, and then some.

Facts about corrosion, the torque law, types of screws, and "nut and bolt talk" are just a few of the topics that are well covered by prolific author Stanley J. Dzik. It surprised and impressed me to find a chapter that allows fastener identification in German, Spanish, French, and of course English (perhaps I should say American).

A very worthwhile book to add to your collection, from the Aviation Book Company, for $14.95.

The Loran, GPS & Nav/Comm Guide Greatly expanded in its fourth printing, this offering remains the definitive guide to these avionics packages. With 72% more text than the first edition, including a well researched section on the Global Positioning System, Keith Connes' book advises purchasers not only how to buy and use these aircraft electronics, but also how the systems work and what their respective futures offer pilots. An easy-to-read style ensures that pilots will be able to understand these complex systems, and the buyers guides ensure that the price of the book will be saved by readers during their purchases—many times over.

I strongly recommend sending $16.95 plus $2 for shipping and handling to Butterfield Press.

Magazines

At fly-ins and other aviation events, keen individuals often surprise me by disclosing they are unaware of the aviation magazines that support their building interests. The following periodicals list is provided so readers can subscribe. If you can't afford at least some of these recommended periodicals, you probably can't afford to build or operate an aircraft. Tips, warnings, and money-saving suggestions in each issue can be so beneficial they will pay the subscription back many times over. For builders and shoppers alike, these publications can be worth their weight in gold—or at least in aircraft silver wiring. Here are the major supporters of homebuilt aviation:

Sport Aviation This monthly magazine of the Experimental Aircraft Association is likely the most-read sport aviation publication in the world, with over 100,000 readers worldwide. A mixture of experimentals, ultralights, and warbirds, coupled with a large advertising, calendar and classified section, has provided copious amounts of information for decades. To join EAA, send $30 for your first year's dues to P.O. Box 3086, Oshkosh, WI 54903-3086, or phone 800-322-2412. For an extra $18, the EAA Experimenter magazine is also available to members.

Canadian Homebuilt Aviation News   Complimentary with the $25 (Canadian dollars) membership in the Canadian Owners and Pilots Association (COPA) at PO Box 734, Ottawa, Ontario, this monthly magazine has industry advertisements, editorials, and columns by individuals associated with the homebuilt movement. Both EAA and RAAC are represented, as well as the Ultralight Pilot's Association of Canada (UPAC) The subscription also includes the Canadian General Aviation News.

Kitplanes   This monthly covers a broad spectrum of homebuilts and a few ultralight aircraft as well. In the last year, it has become increasingly technical in format thus providing increasing detail for designers and advanced builders. Editor Dave Martin seeks to paint an honest, no-hype picture on the pros and cons of aircraft and aviation products through product and aircraft evaluations. The rapid growth of the readership is a good indication of its popularity. The classified ad section is chock full of projects, parts, and custom aircraft for sale. At $25.97 yearly, this excellent value can be ordered from Kitplanes at PO Box 487, Mt. Morris, IL 61054-0487.

Recreational Flyer   This bi-monthly magazine, produced by the Recreational Aircraft Association of Canada, is sent to RAAC members along with complimentary bi-weekly copies of Canadian Aviation News. The yearly $35 (Canadian dollars) membership in this organization includes the magazine. The fact-filled pages keep readers up to date on Canadian regulations and unique happenings in the Canadian recreational flying scene. Homebuilts, warbirds, and ultralights and their owners are featured in a format whereby builders submit their experiences in lieu of professional writers. The complimentary copies of Canadian Aviation News include messages and updates from the RAAC president as well as broad-based information on Canadian general and business aviation. To subscribe to both of these offerings write RAAC at 152 Harwood Ave S., Ajax, Ontario, L1S 2H6 Canada. Phone 416-683-3517.

If That's not Enough...

Browse through your favorite newsstand for those publications that cover the entire general aviation spectrum. The emphasis is usually on production aircraft, but some attention is given to the experimental world. Included are *Flying, Plane & Pilot, Private Pilot, General Aviation News & Flyer,* and *Canadian Aerospace* (previously *Canadian Aviation*). Another fine magazine is *AOPA Pilot,* available with membership in the AOPA.

– Appendix D –

Organizations and Events

For Fun, Help, Motivation, and Whatever

In this appendix, we describe associations that will help you, as a would-be builder, to locate local groups that can give you guidance in the selection and completion of a homebuilding project. We've also included aviation events that should stimulate your interest, provide contacts, and help you locate aircraft parts. For dates, see the calendars of the various recommended magazines listed in Appendix D.

These are only a sampling of happenings that might interest the aficionado; there are literally hundreds of fly-ins every month during the summer. Ask locals about the events in your area.

While attendance at events and membership in the organizations is in no way mandatory, as a builder you will derive so much benefit from these affiliations that you would be foolish not to join in. And you'll be missing a lot of the fun—and the knowledge infusion—of the various fly-ins.

Besides, when you finish your project, you will need somewhere to show it off!

Experimental Aircraft Association   The largest fraternity of builders, restorers, war birders, etc. in the world, EAA has it all: political clout, a wide selection of publications, builders tips and forums and, of course, "the world's premier aviation event" – OSHKOSH.

The EAA Fly-In Convention   It's known informally as "Oshkosh," because that's where the EAA is headquartered and where the convention takes place. This yearly week-long extravaganza is like a religious experience. When 13,000 planes and 850,000 or so believers descend on the Wisconsin city at the end of July and beginning of August—well, it certainly has to be experienced to be believed. If you want to see the prototypes and homebuilt projects of hundreds of experimentals, be there.

Sun 'n Fun   The next largest exposition occurs at Sun 'n Fun held in April at Lakeland Florida. This EAA show has grown by leaps and bounds each year as thousands of builders just can't wait for summer and their Oshkosh "fix."

Arlington Air Show and Fly-In   In mid-July, this EAA- sponsored event attracts aviation worshipers to the Pacific Northwest — Arlington, Washington, to be specific. Like Oshkosh and Sun 'n Fun, tents with informative seminars abound, while peddlers sell aviation parts at vastly discounted prices in the flea markets. Afternoon flying displays have attracted more and more of the general public to the joys of aviation.

To join the EAA or obtain further information on the events, write EAA Aviation Center, Oshkosh, WI 54903-3086 or phone 414-426-4800 or toll-free 800-322-2412. Yearly membership is $30. Canadian members of the EAA can seek support from the Experimental Aircraft Association Canadian Council at 2348 Garnet Street, Regina, Saskatchewan, S4T 3A2, Canada. This organization specializes in educational programs for homebuilders.

Recreational Aircraft Association of Canada   This organization grew out of the EAA when the different rules and requirements of Canada needed local representation with government. The RAAC produces a bi-monthly magazine and publishes news bi-weekly in *Canadian Aviation News*. Fly-ins occur throughout the summer in the various regions at airports on a rotating basis.

For further information, contact the RAAC at 152 Harwood Avenue South, Ajax, Ontario, L1S 2H6, Canada. Phone 416-683-3517, FAX 416-428-2415. Yearly membership is $30 Canadian (approximately $24 US at this writing).

– Appendix E –

Aircraft Construction Guide

Here is a list of the aircraft models we've reported on, categorized by their availability as kits only, plans only, or as both kits and plans.

Projects Available as Kits Only

Manufacturer/Model	Construction Method	No. of Seats
Aces High Cuby II	Steel tubes, fabric	2 side by side
Air Cmd Dual Commander	Chromoly tube, f-glass	2 side by side
Air Cmd Commander Elite	Chromoly tube, f-glass	1, 2 side by side
Avid Hauler	Tubes, plywd, f-glass	2 side by side
Avid Speedwing	Tubes, plywd, f-glass	2 side by side
Earthstar Laughing Gull	Steel, f-glass, fabric	1
Earthstar Ultra Gull	Steel, f-glass, fabric	1
Kestrel Kit Hawk	Aluminum	2 tandem
Kestrel Sport/Float Hawk	Aluminum	2 tandem
Loehle 5151 Mustang	Wood, fabric	1
Macair Merlin	Tubes, alum, fabric	2 side by side
Neico Lancair	Composite	2 side by side
Prowler	Aluminum	2 tandem
Questair Venture	Aluminum	2 side by side
RotorWay Exec 90	Chromoly, f-glass,alum	2 side by side
St-HamiltonGlasair II FT	Composite	2 side by side
St-HamiltonGlasair TD	Composite	2 side by side
Van's RV-6	Aluminum	2 side by side

Projects Available as Plans Only

Manufacturer/Model	Construction Method	No. of Seats
Buethe Barracuda*	Wood	2 side by side
Elmwood Christavia MK1*	Steel tubes, wood	2 tandem
Elmwood Christavia MK4*	Steel tubes, wood	4
Marquart MA-5 Charger*	Steel tubes, wood	2 tandem
Osprey GP-4*	Wood, fiberglass	2 side by side
Tr. Super Emeraude	Wood	2 side by side

Projects Available as Kits or Plans

Manufacturer/Model	Construction Method	No. of Seats
Mirage Celerity	Wood, foam, f-glass	2 side by side
Murphy Renegade Spirit	Tubes, alum, fabric	2 tandem
P-B Mini Master	Tubes, f-glass, alum	2 side by side
Van's RV-3	Aluminum	1
Van's RV-4	Aluminum	2 tandem
Zenair CH300	Aluminum	3 to 4
Zenair STOL CH701	Aluminum	2 side by side
Zenair Zodiac CH600	Aluminum	2 side by side

*Materials package available

Index

About the Author

The Royal Canadian Air Force introduced Ken Armstrong to piloting, where he first served as a multi-engine instructor and then flew operationally with 10 Tactical Air Group. Pioneering helicopter operations and carrying VIPs such as Premier Kosygin of the USSR and Princess Anne of the UK's Royal Family have been opposite ends of a broad based aviation spectrum.

With more than 6500 hours of rotary wing experience, he pioneered crop spraying with an experimental helicopter in Canada by spraying hundreds of acres of crops in Victoria with an amateurbuilt RotorWay Exec.

Armstrong is a director of the Recreational Aircraft Association of Canada and primary regional inspector of amateur-built aircraft for Canada's western area. He also serves as an observer for the Aviation Safety Board, working with the CASB during accident investigations involving experimental aircraft in the Pacific Region.

He has also been a Cessna sales manager and chief pilot of various aviation organizations.

Armstrong's amateur-built aircraft have included two BD-4's, a Baby Great Lakes, a Volksplane, a Jodel D 11 and the sponsoring of a Schoolflight Project Sonerai II LTS.

He has been published in *Kitplanes, Plane & Pilot, Canadian Aviation, In Flight, Sport Pilot Hot Kits & Homebuilts, Canadian General Aviation News, and Canadian Homebuilt Aviation News.*

His flying credentials include Single/Multi-Engine Land and Sea, Instructor, Instrument, and over 150 types flown during 11,000 flight hours on three international licenses.

Which Radios Are Best for Your Plane?

Today there's a huge choice of nav and comm radios out there. Which ones are best for *your* needs? *The Loran, GPS & Nav/Comm Guide* by aviation writer Keith Connes has the answers. Here's what you get in this up-to-date 192-page book, complete with many photos and illustrations:

- Explanations of the VOR system, the loran system, and the high tech satellite based Global Positioning System that uses radio signals from space to give you super accurate 3-D navigation. Chapters include "GPS — The Wave of the Future," "Will GPS Make Loran Obsolete?" and "The GPS and Multi-Sensor Models."
- Features, specs, and prices of the latest avionics. The current loran offerings by Morrow, ARNAV, Bendix/King, Northstar, and all the rest — including the portables with self-contained power. Plus the GPS panel-mounted and portable receivers, and the multi-sensor systems that combine loran with GPS or VOR-DME signals. Also, all the panel mounted VHF nav/comms and RNAV sets, as well as the handheld transceivers.
- Flight Evaluations of leading loran sets, including their good points, as well as the *not-so-good* points. No holds barred!
- Reports on the moving map systems that *show* you where you are!

Plus such important topics as "Should You Buy an IFR Loran?" "The HSI Explained," and "How to Choose a Radio Shop." The section on "Loran Antenna Installations" will be worth the price of the book for many homebuilders. And there's lots more.

The Loran, GPS & Nav/Comm Guide is in stock and available for immediate shipment. To get your copy, fill in the form below and send it with your check or money order for $16.95 plus $2.00 shipping. California residents add $1.02 sales tax. VISA and Master Card accepted, and you can phone in your credit card order toll-free, any hour of the day or night. The Guide comes with a coupon good for a free issue of our Avionics Update newsletter to keep you current. 30-day money-back guarantee.

NAME _____

ADDRESS _____

CITY, STATE & ZIP _____

VISA/MC_____Exp _____

Butterfield Press, 990 Winery Canyon Rd, Templeton, CA 93465

VISA/MC Orders, phone toll free: 1-800-648-6601—24 hours a day!

About Butterfield Press

We are a small but growing publishing company with a love for aviation that dates back to the '50s, when we learned to fly in Aeronca Champs. We've seen general aviation grow in sophistication and complexity, and we've also observed, happily, that grass roots flying is still alive and well.

We are operating this enterprise because we take great joy in communicating — interestingly, we hope — with our fellow pilots. We'd like it to be a two-way communication. Other books, on a variety of subjects, are being readied for production. Please let us know what topics interest you the most by returning this form. You'll be casting your vote for the kind of books you'd like to read, and you'll receive mailings about our books as we publish them.

SUBJECTS OF INTEREST TO ME

- ☐ Budget priced used production aircraft
- ☐ Sophisticated singles and light twins
- ☐ Avionics and instrumentation
- ☐ How to buy and sell aircraft
- ☐ How to avoid FAA violations
- ☐ Aviation humor
- ☐ Others _____

_____

Your comments, please, on *Choosing Your Homebuilt:*

_____
_____
_____
_____

To receive our mailings, please include your name and address:

NAME _____

ADDRESS _____

CITY, STATE, ZIP _____

MAIL TO

 Butterfield Press, 990 Winery Canyon Rd., Templeton, CA 93465